(101 things to know when you go)
ON SAFARI IN AFRICA

(101 things to know when you go)
ON SAFARI IN AFRICA

Paperback Edition

Patrick Brakspear

Published by Tablo

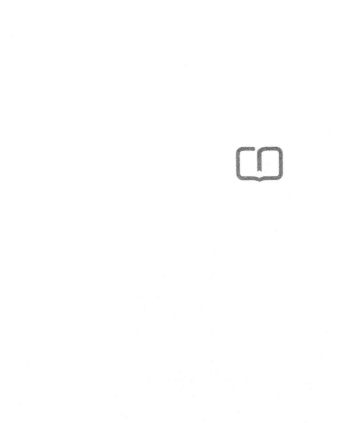

Table of Contents

CALL OF AFRICA

When you've acquired a taste for dust,
The scent of our first rain,
You're hooked for life on Africa
And you'll not be right again
Till you can watch the setting moon
And hear the jackals bark
And know that they're around you,
Waiting in the dark.
When you long to see the elephants
Or to hear the coucal's song,
When the moonrise sets your blood on fire,
You've been away too long
It's time to cut the traces loose
And let your heart go free
Beyond that far horizon,
Where your spirit yearns to be.
Africa is waiting - come!
Since you've touched the open sky
And learned to love the rustling grass,
The wild fish-eagle's cry.
You'll always hunger for the bush,
For the lion's rasping roar,
To camp at last beneath the stars
And to be at peace once more.

Emily C. Dibb (*The Conundrum Trees*)

Map of Africa

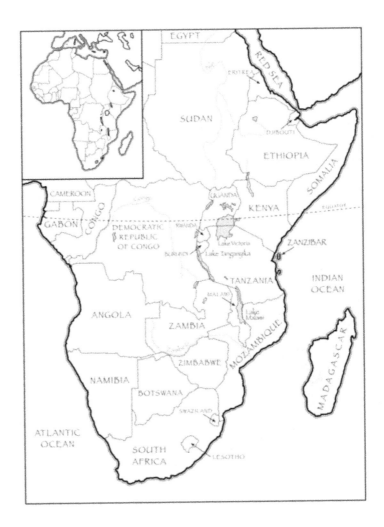

Introduction

On Safari in Africa has but a single purpose - to enhance your safari experience. There is so much for you to see and experience on safari, so much to take in, that it would be all too easy to get only a superficial glimpse of what a safari is all about. By introducing you to the many facets of an African safari, to which you might not otherwise be exposed, it is hoped that you will become more fully immersed in the bounty it offers. In the following chapters you will be presented with many interesting and poignant facts and theories, an A to Z of the safari world if you like, designed to help you observe more keenly and question more often. If you hold to the belief that through knowledge comes understanding, and through understanding comes true appreciation - then you will gain much from these pages.

Although I have not always been successful, this narrative attempts to be simple and uncomplicated - intended to be light reading and an easy reference. The dialogue is intentionally 'light' and tries not to get bogged down in tedious 'technical' details. Sometimes this has been done 'tongue in cheek' - I mean only to pique your interest and feed your curiosity, not provide a scientific reference work. I am not an accredited Zoologist, nor a noted expert on Africa's wildlife or its peoples, but I am passionate about Africa and what it has to offer the safari-goer. I must apologise that certain aspects are sometimes repeated – it is just that some things are worth repeating!

Your first encounter with an African elephant will certainly leave quite an impression. But if you were to return home with only the memory of having seen an elephant in the wild, that would be a shame. The experience should be far more than that. After all, this is a living thing, one of a vast array of animals that make up our amazing world. How does this, the world's largest surviving land animal, live its life, raise its young, communicate with others, and live out each day -

what is its future? The answers to these questions will go a long way to
enhance your safari experience and help you to fully appreciate the
privilege of being in the company of a truly wild animal. It is these
answers that *On Safari in Africa* hopes to share with you.

Having grown up in Africa, and later sharing the thrill of being on
safari with people from around the world, it is my hope that *On Safari
in Africa* will enable you to share the insights and passion that I have
been privileged to enjoy for so long. I trust that I have done justice to
the flora, fauna and people of this amazing continent and that this book
may in some small way fulfill your dreams of an African safari.

Through *On Safari in Africa* I hope to encourage you to get more
out of your safari experience: from tips on your preparations before
you leave home, including what to expect and what to look out for,
through to insights into the wildlife, landscapes and people you will
encounter. For many, a safari to Africa is a once-in-a-lifetime
adventure, but even for 'repeat-offenders' it is always a fascinating
journey, one that you will undoubtedly remember for many years to
come.

Finally, *On Safari in Africa* serves as an unashamed celebration of
our natural world and all it contains – at least that one corner of it,
known to us as Africa.

"Africa…it grabs hold of your heart, and never quite lets go."- Robert Ruark,
author.

Acknowledgements

Although I have made every effort to acknowledge, by way of quotations or notation, the many books written on Africa, I am aware that many of the 'opinions', 'observations' and 'arguments' expressed in this book have had their source in the many magazine articles, books and related texts written about Africa that I have read over the years. Each of these texts have inspired me with their insights and have added to my knowledge, or helped to reinforce my own observations. In part, I present this book as a précis of those works and trust that I have done so in accordance with their individual thinking. If I have misrepresented them in any way I apologise, and I would welcome any corrections to any stated 'facts' by anyone prepared to share their expertise.

I should also add that although I have expressed a number of opinions on a range of topics, none of these should be taken as the opinions of the safari profession at large, although some may be shared by others within the industry.

Author's note

This book restricts itself predominantly to safaris conducted in east, southern and central Africa, with little reference to West Africa and virtually none to North Africa. Countries north of the Sahara, including Morocco, Tunisia and Egypt, are not considered 'safari' destinations per se. West Africa, including Cameroon, Benin, Ghana, the Central African Republic, the DRC, and Mali specifically, although welcoming visitors, suffer from a lack of infrastructure and are generally not considered to be part of the mainstream safari circuit. Other countries, like Ethiopia, Gabon, Chad and the Republic of Congo have begun receiving the more adventurous tourists, and like other parts of West Africa, will surely be adding their unique attractions to the list of safari destinations in the years to come. I certainly look forward to visiting these countries myself, discovering new landscapes and unique habitats, and searching out those forest-dwelling species found nowhere else in the world.

DEDICATION

If any person, or group of people, deserves recognition for their tireless efforts it must surely be the many rangers (and their families) across the length and breadth of the continent. They are the unsung heroes, protectors and caretakers of Africa's wildlife and wild places. So I dedicate this book to them; past and present, young and old; who, through their dedication and conviction, stand guardian over many of the world's last wildlife sanctuaries at a time when we seem powerless to halt the progress of our own destruction.

What is a safari?

The word 'safari' originates in East Africa from the Arabic verb *safara* meaning 'to make a journey', with implicit connotations of discovery. The derived noun *safariya* – a voyage or expedition, becomes the Swahili synonym *safari*.

Once long and arduous, fraught with danger and requiring both stamina and a significant amount of time and money, today's safari is now within the reach of many, is safe, and is considerably more luxurious.

The modern safari has evolved to offer a vast array of possible styles; from the more basic participatory camping safaris through to privately guided fly-in safaris where your every comfort is catered for. Yet the modern safari still incorporates many of the features from its long and exciting history...for a safari is at its heart an adventure.

This will not be like any holiday you have had before – and it is certainly not your sleep-in, lie-about-at-the-beach style holiday. It is more akin to the adventures of an intrepid explorer - prodded awake at 5am, made to walk, paddle or suffer countless miles of bumpy tracks in order to look for what? No one can say exactly! Each day brings its own rewards and excitement – and learning too.

A safari is about getting close to nature ...and simplicity. You will either be enthralled by its simple comforts - or you may just be appalled. This depends on how adventurous you are! If you cannot bear the thought of not being able to get your favourite caffeine hit, or you miss the closeness of your mobile phone...then perhaps a safari is not for you.

A safari, especially the more rustic mobile tented or bush camp variety, can teach you much about how to reduce life to its more simple components...a hot shower, comfortable bed, hearty food, a cold beer and some good conversation around the camp fire. Revel in the clean, crisp morning air, the heat and the dust, the clear night skies, the cooling comfort of a shady tree at midday, the stark beauty of a panoramic sunset, the silence of the nights, and the sense of wilderness all around you. Then there are the sights, sounds and smells...all around you.

"What is a safari but the recreation of a dream, an intangible journey into the past and into the mind where this uncluttered world still exists, alive, harsh, vital, as it should be, and perhaps we all understand that deep down because we are all, each one of us. Children of Africa." - Dereck Joubert (National Geographic film maker)

'Going on safari' is the backbone of the tourism industry in many parts of Africa. In recent years, wildlife tourism has become an increasingly important industry in several African countries. This has brought with it an increasing awareness of the economic benefits from tourism, which in turn is driving a resurgence in conservation, employment and community involvement. Tourists bring much needed funding to wildlife areas and the people who live there. In this way, each safari goes some way to providing the economic justification for maintaining vast tracts of land in its original state, and for protecting animal and plant species for future generations - both Africans and visitors alike.

The essence of a safari is not just about seeing the bountiful wildlife – it should also be about the dramatic landscapes unique to this continent, its people and its cultures. For those who value getting closer to nature and being in the great outdoors, Africa is something special, something quite unique.

Africa combines the richness of its wildlife, its peerless landscapes and distinctive cultures with the added spice of adventure!

"All I wanted to do now was get back to Africa. We had not left it, yet, but when I would wake in the night I would lie, listening, homesick for it already." - Ernest Hemingway, Green Hills of Africa

To Do List (before you go)

Some of this advice is general travel advice, somewhat pedantic, but run your eye down the list - I'm willing to bet there will be more than one suggestion that you will find useful:

- **Travel Insurance**
  Essential. You really must take out travel insurance. This is doubly important if you are travelling with children. I cannot begin to tell you how important this is. Things do go wrong – baggage gets lost, flights are delayed, stuff gets stolen and on occasion, you might fall ill and need to go to hospital. Worse still, you might somehow be prevented, by unforeseen circumstances, from even leaving home. Get yourself covered. It really is well worth the added cost – I promise.

- **Passport**
  Check that your passport is current. Important: Your passport must be valid for a minimum of 6 months from the date of entry into your destination country AND should have at least one blank page for each country you will be visiting (for visas and entry stamps), including a page for your home country. These are actual requirements and not merely precautions.

- **Tourist Visas (and Tourism levies)**
  Ask your Africa travel specialist which tourist visas you will need, and decide whether you would prefer to get these before you leave home, or on arrival. Most African countries will grant you a tourist visa on entry, either at the airport or border post. A number of countries including Uganda, Rwanda & Mozambique now prefer or require you to pre-register or obtain an eVisa on-line *prior* to your arrival. You should be sure to check and confirm

these requirements with your travel agent. Obtaining a visa on
arrival does mean joining the visa queue first, before going through
customs and immigration and this does add to the process – but it is
usually just a revenue collecting exercise and not especially
onerous. If you are short of time, have a tight connection, you
might want to consider pre-completing the visa application forms
prior to arriving in that country (you can get PDF visa forms for
most countries from your travel agent). If doing so online, do start
the process early – it can take a week or more to be approved. DO
NOT LEAVE THIS UNTIL THE LAST MINUTE.

- **Dietary requirements & any medical issues**
  If you have not already done so, be sure to make your travel agent
  aware of any specific dietary preferences or requirements you may
  have (and any medical issues that you may have that would be
  helpful for your hosts to know about, e.g. diabetic, sleep apnea or
  any walking difficulty re stairs or climbing in and out of safari
  vehicles). Most safari lodges and camps can cater for most dietary
  requirements or allergies if given prior notice, and will gladly
  reserve the closest room should you need it.

- **Communications & Recharging (phones, cameras, laptops)**
  Try to check which of the camps/lodges on your safari itinerary
  will actually have mobile (cell) phone reception before you leave
  home, and do not forget to contact your telephone service provider
  to be sure that your phone is registered for international
  roaming (and to find out about any idiosyncrasies or
  incompatibilities that may apply in the countries you will be
  visiting). Remember too that voice and data roaming are two
  separate beasts – speak to your service provider about your options
  before you leave home. Wi-Fi is becoming more available in
  camps/lodges and this can be a real boon (and reduces your
  dependence on mobile coverage). Ask your travel agent for more
  information on the phone and Wi-Fi coverage throughout your
  itinerary.

Be sure to purchase the necessary converter plugs/adaptors for recharging your mobile phone, video, digital camera or tablet/laptop. Each African country has its own plug type (more details below under *Safari travel tips*) and so a converter/adaptor plug will be necessary (possibly more than one type if you are travelling to multiple countries). If you only remember this at the last minute, you can generally get these at the airport – do not wait till you get to Africa – this is likely to be too late!

- **Immunisations & Prescription drugs**
  Make arrangements to visit a travel clinic, tropical health centre or your family doctor (GP) for advice on which inoculations you might need, and get them done in good time. This may take a couple of weeks to complete, and some, like yellow fever, should be done up to 10 days prior to travel. Don't forget malaria prophylactics if appropriate. But do not be alarmed, getting your immunisations up to date is a good thing all round, and especially if you plan to travel (a tetanus booster, Hep A & B, cholera, typhoid are all worth keeping up to date irrespective).

  If you take regular prescription drugs you will need to work out how much you should have on hand whilst on safari and get your doctor to prescribe the required amounts. Be sure to do this well in advance of your departure, and at the same time, you can discuss your immunization requirements (see above).

  If your prescription, either by its nature or quantity, is likely to attract the attention of the authorities (i.e. they might suspect you are drug trafficking – I'm serious), it is advisable to get a letter from your physician stating the reason for the medication, the dosage and clearly state that it is for your personal use *. It is advisable for such medication to be kept in their original containers displaying your name and the dosage, and should be carried in your hand luggage rather than your check-in luggage to reduce the risk of loss.

* Carrying prescription medication not for your own personal use, or for someone not travelling with you, is illegal (you don't want the authorities to mistake you for a drug mule).

NB: Anti-malarial: Be sure to read the instructions for your anti-malarial tablets to check when you need to start taking them – generally this will be at least a few days, or up to a week, prior to entering a malaria area (and for some days after leaving the area).

- **Flights:** When you receive your airline etickets, take a moment to double check all is correct – specifically the spelling of your name (must match your passport) and your travel dates. You will be surprised how often this is not done and complications then arise as a result. It is also a good idea to double check with your travel agent that they have recorded a contact telephone number on your booking and confirm that all seating and meal requests have been noted together with your frequent flyer number (if applicable)…and be sure to note the luggage allowance as this can vary between airlines and fare classes.

These days most airlines will allow **online check-in** which is advisable, saving you time at the airport (with shorter bag-drop queues) and the possibility of making your seat selection.

- **Cash & Credit Cards**
Purchase any cash that you will need before you leave home, and check that the credit cards you are planning to take with you are not due to expire whilst you are away! It is also advisable to notify your credit card company (or bank) that you will be travelling overseas (make that a must!). By making a note on your account they are better able to monitor and detect any fraudulent use of your credit card whilst you are away (and not embarrass you by declining a payment when checking out of your hotel in a foreign land).

The introduction of 'cash cards' or 'travel cards', which can be preloaded with the desired currencies, are generally not suitable for Africa – in the main because the destination currencies, even the South African Rand, are not commonly traded (and hence are not offered by travel card companies). Hopefully this will change in time.

- **Plugs**
  Purchase any necessary converter plugs for your video, camera and mobile phone. See the *Safari travel tips* section for more details on plugs types for each of the African countries. If you forget this until the last minute you can generally get these at your local airport – do not wait till you get to Africa – this is likely to be too late!

- **Duplicate your documents**
  Make copies of your itinerary, passport, visas and details of your travel insurance policy, travel vouchers and etickets. Carry one copy in your suitcase (separate from the originals) and leave a copy with your next of kin, business partner, colleague or friend at home, together with any emergency contact details so that you (or your travel agent) can be contacted in the event of a tragedy or other emergency at home (and vice versa). Or you could scan these same documents and email them to yourself (or upload them to your phone or tablet) so that if you were to lose your etickets, vouchers or itinerary details while away you can access an electronic copy. A couple of passport photos would not be a bad idea either – to go with the photocopies of your passport should it get lost. Make sure your travel agent has these details too (including your travel insurance policy details). In the event of an emergency, the safari operator will most likely contact the booking agent first.

  Not everyone can be bothered to do this – but it is a sensible safety precaution.

- **Alert the authorities**
  If you are at all apprehensive about being away from home then you might be advised, for your own peace of mind, to register your

details and travel plans online with your foreign affairs department and/or, when overseas, register in-person at your embassy, high commission or consulate.

It is always a good idea to check the latest travel advisory notices issued by your own government about the countries to which you will be travelling. In some cases you can also subscribe to receive free email and/or text notification each time the travel advice for your destination is updated. Be aware that it is their role to provide conservative and cautious travel advice from which you can make your own decisions about your travels.

Last, but not least, don't forget to pack in good time. Do not leave this to the last minute. Going on an African safari presents somewhat more of a challenge than your average holiday with regard to packing!

"There is something about safari life that makes you forget all the sorrows and feel as you have drunk half a bottle of champagne – bubbling over with heartfelt gratitude and being alive" – Karen Blixen, Out of Africa

Safari travel tips

There are a number of important steps in getting ready to go on safari, and it is probably fair to say that there are perhaps a lot more 'unknowns' when travelling to Africa than most other destinations around the world. Your Africa Travel Specialist (or travel agent) will already have worked with you on selecting a suitable safari itinerary and secured your airline tickets, and have possibly even been able to assist with advice regarding travel insurance, entry requirements and other aspects of going on safari, but I strongly recommend that you read the Travel Tips, and make use of the To Do List and Final Check List offered below.

Dietary requirements

More and more people are requested specific dietary needs, whether it be vegetarian, gluten free, vegan or a host of food allergies. It is important to provide adequate notice to the camps and lodges on your safari itinerary. In general, most luxury camps and lodges in Africa can accommodate even the strictest of dietary needs. However, this may not always be the case in some of the more remote or less sophisticated styles of safari camp - specifically mobile safaris and fly-camping where cooking and refrigeration facilities are limited. You should be careful to distinguish between food groups that may bring on an allergic reaction (seafood, nuts, gluten) and those you merely do not eat (eggs, red meat, milk products by way of examples).

Cash & Credit Cards

I would recommend that you carry a combination of cash (preferably US$ for most countries...and Rand for South Africa) and at least one credit card (preferably more than one).

You may find little use for local currency on safari, although it can be handy for road-side purchases and possibly tipping (with US dollars, or South African Rand in southern African countries, accepted keenly by staff as a gratuity). Nearly all bills can be settled using your credit card (be sure to ask if there is a surcharge) and most items in camp/lodge gift shops are priced in US$ and can be purchased using cash. In the major towns, ATMs will allow you to draw additional funds (in local currency only – please note).

Travellers cheques (checks) have become less acceptable in Africa in recent times (Tanzania is no longer accepting them) and they may be refused outside of the banking system (or not accepted at all).

Cash

Whilst most major western currencies (USD, Euros, and Sterling) are welcome throughout Africa, United States dollars remains the most widely accepted.

Whilst it is difficult to set a figure, I would recommend taking at least US$150 to $250 per person per week in cash from home (excluding what you might need for entry visas and airport departure taxes). This cash is specifically for paying for small incidentals (including taxis, tips and souvenir purchases). Visas secured on arrival must be paid in cash and often the exact amount i.e. officials will 'claim' not to have change - so carry an assortment of US$5, US$10 and US$20's (plus the required US$50 notes).

Be warned – some countries are not accepting US$ bills dated before the year 2000 due to suspicions of counterfeiting. Don't be surprised if your US$ notes are run through a 'counterfeit-checking' device. Generally, large bills (US$50 and US$100) obtain better exchange rates than smaller denominations (US$5, 10 and US$20) if you need to exchange for local currency.

Be wary of street money-changers! They may offer a better rate but are not averse to using any number of underhand techniques to short change you. If you do use one, be sure to count each note separately to satisfy yourself that the whole amount is there BEFORE handing across any of your own cash. Once counted, be sure not to let the pile out of your sight – it is an old trick to switch bundles and for you to later discover that the new bundle is mostly newspaper. If the money traders are legitimate they will not be offended!

Credit & debit cards

Most establishments will accept international credit cards and I recommend using credit cards as a method of payment wherever possible - as much for the convenience as the efficiency. It makes sense to carry more than one brand of credit card as not all types are accepted by all outlets/hotels. On the downside, credit card companies do not offer the best exchange rates going around and will often add a foreign transaction fee for good measure!

BE WARNED: credit cards in Africa will often attract a surcharge - up to 5% in some cases, and possibly more! Be sure to ask about any surcharges before you hand over your credit card.

IMPORTANT: Most banks and credit card companies advocate that you advise them before you travel overseas so that their credit card monitoring systems do not suspend your card when they detect any unusual purchase sequences (paying for hotels, flights and rental cars in a foreign country) that occur on a holiday. Such purchases can sometimes trigger the suspension of your card and leave you with the embarrassing consequences. Secondly, be cautious of providing your credit card details when travelling. It is an unfortunate feature of credit cards that your card number can be obtained without your knowledge (at hotels desks, shops or rental companies).

BE CAUTIOUS AND VIGILANT.
Do not let your card out of your sight when paying your bill.

ATM machines

ATM machines in Africa are becoming more commonplace but are certainly not as ubiquitous as elsewhere in the world. They supply only LOCAL CURRENCY and you may need an international PIN code – be sure to check with your bank/credit card facility at home about how this should work. Not all ATM's in Africa will accept all credit card types. In my experience, VISA appears to have the best coverage in Africa. Try also to use an ATM at a bank – this way, if your card is retained for any reason, you can go in and get it back! Keep in mind that you may not even get the opportunity to locate an ATM as your itinerary will likely be designed to get you to your next destination – not to the next ATM. My advice – don't rely on using ATMs as your main source of cash on safari!

Electric current

Electricity in Africa is all 220 -240V/50Hz AC as is much of Europe, the UK, Australia and New Zealand and virtually all the Asian countries and India. Those of you from North America, where 110V/60Hz is the standard, will need both an adapter for the proper plug configuration and converter to step down to the lower current required by your electrical equipment.

Type C (European) - Two-prong round (unearthed)
Type F (Schuko plug) - Two-prong round (with 2 x earth contacts)
Type G (UK plug) - Three-prong rectangular
Type M (South African plug) - Three-prong round (large)

Type D, G and M plug sockets are the dominant plug types in Africa although some countries do offer the two prong round (Type C & F) plug socket types (see Table below). A number of hotels have international wall sockets which will take an array of both two-prong and three-prong plugs. North America and Japan use Type A & B plugs, and Australia a Type I plug - all will require an adaptor plug!

Country Plug type:

Botswana - G
Kenya - G
Namibia - M
Malawi - G
Mozambique - C, F & M
Uganda - G
Rwanda - C
South Africa - M
Swaziland - M
Tanzania - G
Zambia - G
Zimbabwe - G & M

Please note:

- Not all safari camps and lodges will have an electrical outlet in the tents/rooms but they will always have a central location where you can recharge your camera / video and phone / iPod batteries.

- Some camps will only run a generator at certain times of the day – so be sure to check with the manager when you arrive.

- A number of mobile safari operators have inverters in their vehicles (an inverter changes 12 volt DC from a vehicle battery to 220/240 volt AC) and in this way you can charge your camera/video batteries on the move.

Mobile (cell) phone & WiFi access

Generally speaking, communications in Africa are not what you are accustomed to at home, but mobile (cell) phone coverage, and even WiFi, is certainly becoming more widespread throughout Africa –

although not in some of the more remote safari destinations (thankfully).

A tip before you leave home: check with your service provider that your phone is registered for international roaming (and check that the phone you have is compatible with the networks in Africa - almost all of which operate GSM digital networks running at a frequency of 900 MHz (and some 3G/4G networks too)). If your phone is a dual or tri-band GSM phone it is likely this will work just fine.

More and more we are seeing WiFi being offered at safari camps/lodges * – some as an extension of that countries communications grid, and some connected via satellite. Check with your travel agent before you leave home about which camps/lodges have WiFi as this can be a real boon for sending/receiving email whilst on safari (and accessing the internet if speeds allow), including Skype, rather than using your mobile phone to text and call at exorbitant international roaming charges!

Please note: Not all conventional communication options (phone, fax, internet and email) are available at the more remote safari camps (and mobile camps particularly). Communications may sometimes be via HF radio only.

* The provision of WiFi in the safari industry is still a contentious issue, with some more traditionally-minded operators refusing to offer WiFi on the grounds of not wanting to 'interrupt' their guests appreciation of the 'wilderness' experience. Some camps/lodges provide WiFi only in the common areas (lounge/dining), whilst others have chosen to make WiFi available only in the rooms or have settled on providing a WiFi 'hub' at a suitable (low impact) location within the camp grounds.

"There is no wi-fi in the forest, but I promise you will find a better connection" – author unknown.

Check-in luggage

There is such a great selection of luggage styles to choose from these days that I hesitate to make any strong recommendations other than to say that it is IMPORTANT that you use only soft-sided bags if you are making use of light aircraft charters for your inter-camp transfers. This means no hard suitcases or cases with frames (this includes soft bags with wheels if they have a frame for the retractable handle). In this situation you will also be restricted to as little as 15kgs (35lbs) – including your hand luggage and camera equipment *. Check with your travel agent to confirm the actual allowance as this will vary from country to country and from one air charter company to another. The pilot needs to squeeze your luggage into compartments only 25cms high. There is of course the safety issue (overall weight) and it is important that he/she gets it right. Such weight restrictions will present quite a challenge. Start packing well in advance of your departure date and use your bathroom scales to be sure to keep within the limit. Having to repack on arrival only causes embarrassment, is unfair on the pilot and results in delays. When you see your pilot trying to stuff the luggage into every available nook and cranny you will see why the need for restrictions!? Do try to work with them on this.

Please keep in mind that most safari camps/lodges provide basic toilet amenities - shampoo, conditioner, bug spray and even suntan lotion; that laundry can generally be done on a daily basis (and many camps provide this service free of charge); and finally, that only casual clothing is required.

One other thing to mention as regards inter-camp charter flights: if you weigh more than 100kgs you must advise your travel agent in advance as this may affect the overall carrying capacity of the aircraft, and its safety, and require that an additional seat be assigned.

If you are not making use of light aircraft on safari then I would strongly recommend that your luggage choice has wheels! Not that you will be required to lug your bags on safari, but more because the international airports seem to be getting bigger and the distances you need to walk longer and longer!

With regard to securing your luggage, I would strongly suggest using one or more combination locks to secure zips together if your suitcase does not have its own locking mechanism. I also swear by luggage ties! These are invaluable for those small outside pouches. Luggage tampering in airports does occur, unfortunately. Luggage straps that wrap around your suitcase can also deter, whilst shrink-wrapping facilities are available at some airports.

* Please note that should you NOT strictly adhere to the luggage restrictions on air charters you can incur additional charges arising out of the transportation of any excess luggage. One possibility is to leave any extra bags at the airport with the charter company and collect these on the way back through. This assumes that your itinerary routing is such that you return to the same airport – if in doubt, check with your travel agent.

Hand luggage

Firstly, try to restrict your hand luggage to one item only - for no other reason than more than one item makes travel that much harder (and yes, a handbag qualifies as a second item!). Secondly, that one item should be of a size acceptable as carry-on luggage by the airlines.

If you are a photographer then this will mean having sufficient space in your camera bag for travel documents, your prescription medication and/or glasses, binoculars and (possibly) even a change of clothes.

For overnight flights (and long flights - over 8 hours) I highly recommend a neck pillow, ear plugs and eye mask, and something comfy to change into - along with warm socks. Noise cancelling headphones are brilliant too (be sure you take the adaptor to allow you to plug into the inflight entertainment system).

Bear in mind that restrictions on what can and cannot be taken on board an aircraft are still in place – including liquids, flammables and sharp objects. The rules change frequently – so please double check and take heed.

Jewellery

Do not take any expensive personal jewellery on safari – be minimalist or take only those everyday items that you normally wear, like your wedding band, inexpensive earrings (or perhaps consider leaving these at home too). You will be on the go most of the time and there will likely be little opportunity to 'dress up'. On the other hand, you might like to wear some jewellery at dinner when staying at some of the more up-market safari camps and lodges. Of course I am referring mostly to the women folk - for the guys, less is more!

Drinking water

Drink bottled water. You are always safe drinking the bottled water that is readily available at all the camps and lodges. Carry a bottle of water with you at all times – including on transfers between camps. Make it a practice to always have a bottle of water with you - period. If you are at all apprehensive about the quality of water where you are staying, check with the staff, and if the water is not treated or bottled then avoid ice in your drinks or cleaning your teeth with the tap water (use the bottled variety). Take water purification tablets for emergency use if you think bottled water will not be available (unlikely).

THE SAFARI INDUSTRY IS MAKING A CONCERTED EFFORT TO REDUCE THE USE OF PLASTIC WATER BOTTLES - TRY TO WORK WITH THEM.

A number of safari operators are making sterilized water bottles (mostly stainless steel) available for you to fill with purified water at their camps and lodges. This is an initiative that you should adopt wherever possible as this will have a significant and positive environmental impact. By doing away with the factory-filled (sealed) plastic water bottles you will not only save fuel in transporting these bottles to remote regions (by their thousands) but also solve the problem of the enormous pollution to roadsides and towns that these plastic bottles foster. Do your bit (please).

CAUTION: Dehydration is a real danger on safari and you should be careful to drink at regular intervals and have water at hand at all times.

Heat

At certain times of the year, especially late October / November before the rains arrive in southern Africa, the heat can build through the days (and nights too). It is not uncommon for temperatures to reach over 40 degrees Celsius (over 100°F) during the early afternoon in Botswana, Kruger and the Zambezi Valley at this time of year. For visitors from Europe and elsewhere, who are not accustomed to such extreme temperatures, being on safari can be tough in such conditions. This will generally be when you are back in camp and can lie under the fan or go for a swim (if the lodge has a pool). Some camps/lodges do have air conditioning but this should not be expected. If you have a sarong (or kikoi), wet it and lie underneath it - it really helps. Be sure to keep the flaps of your tent open and ensure a through draft by opening any doors/flaps/windows in the en suite bathroom. If your tent is just too hot, take your book and go through to the central area which is often more elevated and sited under good shade (and drink lots of water to avoid getting dehydrated).

Dust

In the winter months (June to October), the game reserves can be extremely dusty. Contact lens wearers should be sure to bring eye drops, or you may want to consider taking a pair of standard prescription glasses in case your eyes become extremely irritated and scratchy. Cameras and videos should be cleaned regularly and stored in a camera bag throughout.

Personal safety

Your personal safety and security is mostly a matter of common sense. So take the same precautions while travelling in Africa that you would in any major city at home:

- Do not carry large sums of cash (see below for more information on Cash, Credit Cards & ATM's).

- Any cash money (together with your passport and other travel documents) is best carried in a money pouch under your shirt (not in a bum-bag or fanny-pack on your hip in plain view – all too visible and easily cut away) or stowed in your camera bag or day pack (which should remain in sight at all times).

- Keep a close watch on your personal bags (camera bag, day pack etc.) when walking in crowded areas (airports, markets, restaurants and on the street).

- Avoid walking alone at night. In some of the major African cities it is not advisable to walk the streets at night (Nairobi and Johannesburg among others).

- Consider leaving your passport, airline tickets and cash in a safe place (the hotel/lodge safe) when venturing out.

- Keep tempting valuables (including phones, cameras, wallet pouches, handbags) out of sight, and certainly not on the back seat, in your hire car or tour bus/4x4 and especially not in your room at safari camps/lodges – lock them up in the room safe or hand them in to management (rather than as temptation for staff).

- Consider leaving your jewellery at home.

Tipping

Should we tip, and if so - how much?? This is a common dilemma for most visitors to any foreign country!

In Africa, tipping is not expected but has become customary. The traditional gratuity to safari guides or camp staff is not included in the price of your tour and is completely discretionary.

Bear in mind that what may seem like an inconsequential amount to you may be significant to local African staff and will certainly be received with a display of gratitude that is genuinely humbling.

Most safari lodges will have a 'tip box' at reception for the staff – this covers all the 'unseen' services you have enjoyed during your stay, including the person who cleans your room and the many staff who work in the kitchen. However, you may wish to reward your guide or perhaps a particularly attentive waiter individually.

Guidelines: Tip moderately and in accordance with the level and quality of service provided – and only if you are satisfied with that service. The following can be used as a guide and is generally accepted practice, based on a per person basis (i.e. a couple travelling together should consider doubling these figures):

Driver/guide - US$10 and upwards per day.

Private safari guide - US$25 and upwards per day;

Camp staff - US$10 to $20 per day, as a pooled tip to be shared among the housekeepers, waiters, bartender, etc.

If you spend a great deal of time with a single guide, as is the case on a number of mobile safaris or private vehicle + driver/guide itineraries, you may want to increase the above amounts in accordance with the enthusiasm and effort displayed (or your overall satisfaction level)…and you might even consider leaving behind your binoculars or books on mammals/birds to show your appreciation i.e. something other than money that you have noticed the guide does not have (or could use in his job) – just a thought.

Tips can generally be paid in US dollars or local currency.

Tipping for gorilla trekking: trackers, guides + porters

I thought some additional information on tipping when gorilla trekking might be useful, as you can find yourself caught out if you are not 'in the know'. Whilst all treks are conducted by a National Parks guide, they are assisted by a team of trackers and armed guards whom you may not see until part way through the trek. Whilst a tip for the guide is welcome (at your discretion) there is an expectation that a tip be arranged between the trekking group to offer the trackers and armed guards once your time with the gorillas is completed. I mention this because you will not necessarily know who will be in your trekking group until the morning of the trek, and your group could be made up of different nationalities from around the world. Once your group has been formed it might be an idea to raise this with them before you set off on your trek. As a suggestion, I would say that US$10+ per person from each member of the trekking group would be fair. I would strongly recommend a porter too, which will be arranged by your guide (a set fee + tip), as this not only allows you to trek unencumbered, but also provides local employment. The porters are also often incredibly helpful in 'giving you a hand' when the physical demands call for a little assistance!

Charity on safari

Many visitors to Africa feel a strong urge to help the less fortunate whom they encounter on safari, or when visiting a local village or school. People often ask what they can take, especially for the children – pens? books?

By and large it is probably better to keep a look out for an appropriate opportunity while you are traveling rather than carry along gifts from home. My suggestion would be to talk with your guide or with the management of the camps/lodges where you are staying. Many of the safari camps and lodges are actively involved in working with their local communities to sustain schools, clinics and other projects. Ask about this when you are there and visit the school, clinic or project if you can – making a donation to something you have seen on the ground will bring you more satisfaction (and directly help the neediest). Try to contribute in a way that helps a person (or community) help themselves - a donation towards a project that will enhance their way of life.

What I would ask is that you resist the temptation to offer 'hand outs' to kids on the side of the road. This only encourages dependency on such generosity and teaches these children that begging brings reward. There is no dignity in begging and the harassment it fosters will not endear you to the next group of tourists either!

A rather fun idea is to gift a football (soccer ball) – all of Africa loves soccer yet not all the children have a ball with which to play – for more information go to Footballs For Fun or merely buy a couple of balls before you leave home. Or take a look at Pack For A Purpose for more ideas.

Keeping a travel journal

I can strongly recommend that you keep a travel journal whilst on safari. But don't take my word for it - here are some thoughts on the subject from some notable travel writers (and they should know right?):

"Photos show you what scenes looked like, but they won't remind you of interesting details like sounds, smells, tastes, or how you felt. Most travel experiences are transformative, so it's good to keep a written record of what changed you each day." - Sarah Duff, freelance travel writer

"A journal is a great place to convey the spirit of the place you're visiting, not just the facts, which you can easily get from a guidebook. When you go back and read a journal years later, it's those esoteric, private details that will transport you back to the moment." – Justin Fox, former Getaway magazine

"It doesn't matter what you write, or doodle, or draw. Take time to record your surroundings and indulge in the moment – something people are forgetting how to do. Instead of chasing the ultimate photograph, sit quietly with your notebook and create memories that way instead." – Narina Exelby, freelance travel writer

Tips for self-drivers

If you are planning to pick up a hire car and self-drive, a possibility in countries like South Africa, Namibia and Zimbabwe, be aware of the following:

- All these countries drive on the left-hand side of the road and display distances and speed limits in kilometres (kms).

- In South Africa there is a prevalence of four-way-stop intersections – these require you to come to a complete stop and give way to all other vehicles that have arrived at the 4-way stop before you – only then can you go proceed. Simple, but a little disconcerting initially.

- Vehicles in traffic circles (often referred to as roundabouts) travel clockwise. Drivers wishing to enter traffic circles should give way to the right i.e. to those already on , or entering the roundabout from your right.

- If you're driving behind another car and that car pulls to the shoulder but continues driving, it means they are letting you pass. If it's safe to pass you may do so (only if there is a dotted line and no cars coming from the other direction). When you pass someone, be sure to turn on your hazard lights as a way of saying "thank you" – it's what they all do. And then, if someone is tailgating you or wants to get past you, the polite thing to do is cautiously pull into the shoulder and slow down slightly to let the driver pass (only do this if you can clearly see that the shoulder is clear) – do NOT do this when going around a bend.

- Fuel – whilst fuel is generally readily available not all petrol/fuel stations are open 24 hours. You should always fill up when passing through major towns and plan your journey with fuel stops in mind (and carry extra fuel if deemed necessary in more remote areas).

- Fuel stations are generally not self-help but manned by attendants who can also check oil, water and tyre pressure if required. Gratuities for this service are at your own discretion.

- Be sure to have not only your driver's license to hand but also the car's papers – registration, car insurance and any required reflectors/chevron or triangles (in case of breakdown). Wearing seat belts when driving a car in the region is mandatory. The use of a mobile phone while driving is prohibited, with the exception of a hands-free system.

- Be conscious of your own security and that of the vehicle – be sure to lock the vehicle when unattended and do not leave any valuables in plain sight.

- In the cities and towns you may notice that there is a system of "unofficial" parking attendants who will tell you where to park, guide you into the appropriate bay, and will then watch your car whilst you go into the shops. Get their name, and when you return back to your car, pay the attendant a 'tip' as a thank you for watching your car. It is all about peace-of-mind.

- If possible, avoid travelling at night (abandoned/unlit vehicles, pedestrians and stray animals could present a danger).

- Large antelope or other wild animals (even hippo and elephant) crossing the road can also be a hazard in certain areas.

- Drive safely and take heed of speed limits.

"To adventure is to live. To break the shackles of habit and custom, to shake free from the ordinary and the mundane is to make life a never ending journey of discovery and reward." - Clive Walker

Some dangers..

Africa has a number of diseases that have been eradicated, or do not occur, in most parts of the developed world – diseases such as yellow fever, Hep A & B, typhoid and polio are still prevalent in some African countries and you should be wary. Malaria is certainly a threat, while bilharzia, and African sleeping sickness are uncommon. Ebola continues to occur in some remote regions but so far has been restricted to a limited number of countries mostly in West Africa).

Whilst the list of diseases is long, the risk to you as a safari goer should not be over-played. Please read the recommendations offered below, and be sure to consult your local doctor or health professional before you leave home.

The African sun

Always take precautions against the persistent overhead sun. Proximity to the equator makes the African sun particularly strong and dangerous so ensure you use the highest level of protection. A sun hat, sunblock, lip balm / chap stick, moisturising creams and insect repellents are essential when travelling in Africa. Be especially wary during water-based activities like canoeing or rafting, as the reflection off the water adds to your exposure. Most open 4x4 game drive vehicle will have a protective canvas roof – but not all.

Malaria

Malaria is a common and potentially deadly infection in hot, tropical areas of the world. The disease is caused by a parasite introduced into the bloodstream from the bite of the female Anopheles mosquito. When properly treated, a patient with malaria can expect a complete recovery.

Firstly, check with your Africa travel specialist whether you will be travelling through any malaria areas on your itinerary. Not all, but many of the safari lodges and camps are likely to be in such areas. If you are travelling with young children then you may already have discussed this with your travel agent and chosen areas which are malaria-free.

There are several preventative medications to combat malaria but it is important to check with your local GP or travel clinic as to the correct one for where you are going. Be sure to start taking your malarial prophylactics well before you leave home. A small percentage of people can have adverse reactions to certain brands – it is best to find out before you leave and not while on safari! And don't forget that you need to continue to take the prescribed dosage for at least 4 weeks after returning home (check the instructions).

Just as important as preventative prophylactics is to take active measures to protect yourself from being bitten at all. This is definitely the most effective means of avoiding malaria – if they don't bite you then you can't get malaria! Generally mosquitoes start feeding at dusk – so, from just before dusk, clothing should be worn that covers the arms and legs. In addition, a mosquito repellent should be applied on exposed areas. It is a good practice to spray inside your tent before you zip up on the way to dinner – by the time you return the smell would have dissipated and all the mosquitoes that were lurking inside will be dead.

Pregnant women (and children) are especially vulnerable to malarial infection. In fact, pregnant women are twice as attractive to malaria-carrying mosquitoes as non-pregnant women. This is mostly due to a warmer skin surface and the fact that pregnant women exhale a greater volume of air. Be more cautious.

Bilharzia (schistosomiasis)

Bilharzia is common in the tropics where lakes, streams and dams (still water) harbour bilharzia-transmitting snails. Parasite larvae develop in snails from which they infect humans, their definitive host, in which they mature and reproduce. There is no prophylactic available against bilharzia but treatment is now readily available in pill or injection form (a drug called praziquantel). The condition can be unpleasant so it is better not to swim in rivers, streams or dams, particularly where the water is stagnant or used by local villagers as a laundry or bathing area.

African sleeping sickness (Nagana)

Sleeping sickness or African trypanosomiasis is a parasitic disease which affects people and domestic animals. The disease is transmitted by the tsetse fly which is endemic to many parts of Africa. Although a serious threat to local populations, the incidence amongst visitors is extremely low. Symptoms include severe headaches, irritability, extreme fatigue and malaise.

Tsetse flies are relatively resistant to standard insect repellents and can bite through light clothing. They are attracted to bright and also very dark colours and to clouds of dust such as that kicked up by a herd of buffalo – and moving vehicles! Their bite can cause severe discomfort (itching and swelling) and they are extremely difficult to kill (you can squash them between two fingers and they just get up and fly away!). My advice is, when travelling through a tsetse area (generally a woodland), to remain vigilant and use your hat to brush them out of the vehicle (and keep an eye out on the necks and exposed skin of others in your vehicle). In my experience, the more you try to kill them, the more replacements fill the void – spend the energy keeping them away from you and only kill those trapped inside (if you are in an enclosed safari vehicle).

Vaccinations

It is important to check with your local health professional / physician / GP for information on recommended vaccinations or other precautions relating to travel in Africa.

A POINT OF DIFFERENCE: There is a subtle difference between a vaccine that is recommended and one that is required. A number of vaccinations (Hepatitis A and B, typhoid, polio, tetanus, measles) are recommended. This does not mean that you must have them – only that they are recommended. On the other hand, if you are told that a yellow fever inoculation is required for example, then you stand the risk of not being allowed into that country should you not have the appropriate vaccination certificate.

Staying at a luxury safari camp or lodge does to some extent set you apart from everyday exposure to many of these diseases. Whilst it is always a possibility, it is fairly unlikely that you will be exposed to any of the infectious diseases on the recommended list while on safari. The kitchens are generally well schooled on hygiene and food preparation and all aspects of staff health are actively monitored. However, if you are planning to spend extended periods of time living in close contact with the local people, perhaps as an aid worker or volunteer, or you will be in known areas of infection, you should certainly have the inoculations. If you are in any doubt, or at all concerned about the possibility of contracting any of these diseases, then the vaccinations are the safe and sensible choice.

Please also keep in mind that a number of tropical diseases can remain dormant for some time, only making an appearance many months later. If you become ill after your safari - even up to a year later – be sure to mention your visit to Africa to your doctor so that he / she can take this into consideration and order the appropriate tests (if warranted).

Vaccination certificates

If you are required to have a vaccination be sure that you have the certificate on you (in your hand luggage with your passport and airline tickets) – **do not pack this in your suitcase.** Please note that Yellow Fever vaccines are often only available from designated clinics and may not be readily available at your GP.

IMPORTANT

The Centre for Disease Control (CDC) recommends the following vaccines – no matter where you are visiting in Africa:

- Hepatitis A or immune globulin (IG)
- Hepatitis B (a disease transmitted via blood)
- Typhoid
- Booster doses for tetanus-diphtheria, measles, and a one-time dose of polio vaccine.

Yellow Fever

This infection is caused by a virus carried by monkeys and then transmitted by mosquitoes to humans. The symptoms are a short, mild fever often leading to jaundice, failure of the liver and kidneys and eventually death. The yellow fever vaccine is effective and is valid for life (the WHO recently amended this from being valid for 10 years). The vaccination is generally only available in specialist clinics or hospitals and children, people over 65 years, and auto-immune sufferers should discuss the potential side-effects with their doctor.

Yellow Fever is the one immunization that is required when travelling to most West African countries as well as Uganda and Rwanda (and is still listed by the WHO as occurring in Kenya).

Following advice by the World Health Organisation (WHO) South Africa has become especially vigilant, and if you travel from any of the countries above they will request to see your Yellow Fever Certificate and refuse entry should you not be able to supply it (or insist you have the inoculation then and there!).

It is therefore advisable to have a valid yellow fever certificate if arriving at your destination from or via ANY of the following countries in Africa:

The Yellow Fever Endemic Zone in Africa includes Senegal,

Gambia, Guinea Bissau, Sierra Leone, Liberia, Cote D'Ivoire, Burkina Faso, Ghana, Nigeria, Mali, Niger, Chad, Central African Republic, Togo, Benin, Sao Tome and Principe, Cameroon, Gabon, Congo, Democratic Republic of Congo, Angola, Uganda, Kenya, Rwanda, Burundi, Ethiopia, Somali, Sudan and Equatorial Guinea.

Medical reasons not to receive the vaccine:

- Infants under 9 months must not get immunized without consulting a doctor.

- Adults over 65 years of age should not get immunized without consulting a doctor.

- Persons severely allergic to eggs should not be given the vaccine. Generally, persons able to eat eggs or egg products can safely receive the vaccine.

- It is prudent on theoretical grounds to avoid vaccinating pregnant women, and for non-immunized pregnant women to postpone travel to epidemic areas until after delivery. Pregnant women who must travel to HIGH RISK areas should consult their doctor to discuss their specific situation.

- Persons, whose immune systems are suppressed due to HIV infection, or those travellers undergoing treatments for cancers (leukemia, lymphoma, etc.), or receiving corticosteroids, alkylating drugs, antimetabolites or radiation, in general, should not be vaccinated unless travelling to an area of known yellow fever transmission. Patients with suppressed immune systems have a theoretical risk of encephalitis due to the yellow fever vaccine virus. Consult your doctor.

If you have a medical reason not to receive the yellow fever vaccine you should obtain a written medical waiver from the respective consulate or embassy before leaving home.

HIV/AIDS (and Hep B.)

The HIV virus and AIDS (and Hepatitis B to a lesser extent) are serious health issues in many African countries. However, the risk to travellers is negligible assuming proper precautions are taken. HIV (and Hep B.) are largely transmitted through exposure to bodily fluids containing the virus. Use the same precautions while in Africa as at home.

Hepatitis A

Hepatitis A, also called 'infectious hepatitis', is generally contracted from contaminated food and water. The infection causes an inflammation of the liver and presents as nausea, fever, aches and pains (usually beginning 3 to 6 weeks after coming in contact with the virus). Most people recover completely but it can put adults off work for about a month. Obtain your immunization before you travel. Vaccination against Hepatitis A (or immune globulin), together with Hepatitis B (and typhoid) is recommended.

Typhoid

Typhoid or 'enteric fever' is a common life-threatening illness prevalent in developing countries, including parts of Africa. It is contracted by consuming food or drink handled by an infected person shedding *Salmonella typhi* bacteria (found in human faeces). It is also found in sewage contaminated with the bacteria, which can get into the water used for drinking or washing food. Symptoms are a rapidly fluctuating temperature, drowsiness, diarrhea, abdominal rash, delirium and coma. Immunization is effective and the disease is treatable with antibiotics. Being careful with your personal, food and water hygiene on safari is therefore paramount.

Tetanus

Tetanus (also known as lockjaw) is a disease caused by infection with 'clostridium tetani' which is present in soil and in the intestines of humans and animals. Infection can enter the body via cuts after which bacteria produce a toxin affecting the motor nerve cells in the spinal cord. This is followed by convulsions and muscle spasms. The vaccine is effective and the disease can also be treated by an antitoxin and penicillin. It is advisable that EVERYONE be vaccinated irrespective of their travel plans - check with your family physician as to whether you should have a tetanus-diphtheria booster shot.

Polio

Poliomyelitis (polio) is an acute infection caused by a virus which attacks the nervous system and can lead to paralysis. Transmission is by fecal contamination of food, usually by unhygienic food handlers or flies, or directly from infected nasal secretions. Polio is a serious disease which attacks the central nervous system causing muscle paralysis. It is however preventable with a vaccine that is very safe & effective.

Although most countries have immunization programs in childhood it is important that travellers be aware that the efficacy wanes after ten years & a booster dose is advisable prior to travel especially if visiting a country where the disease is still found.

Polio continues to occur (endemic) in four countries: India, Pakistan, Afghanistan and Nigeria. In 2011, in addition to the 4 endemic countries there were cases reported in Angola, Burkina Faso, Chad, Congo, Côte d'Ivoire, Democratic Republic of the Congo, Gabon, Guinea, Mali, Niger (all countries in Africa). All travellers need to get vaccinated if they are going to polio endemic countries, neighboring countries, or those countries where recent cases of polio have been reported.

Travellers' diarrhoea (& probiotics)

According to the World Health Organisation, over 50% of people travelling to developing countries will experience travellers' diarrhoea. Whilst Africa certainly qualifies as 'developing' I would not classify the safari camps and lodges in that third world category. However, diarrhoea is not unheard of on safari and if it is something that you know you are prone to, it may be worth considering taking along a suitable preventative medication. The most common cause of travellers' diarrhoea is infection by the bacterium *Enterotoxigenic E. coli.* To negate this it is advisable to seek out a medication that contains a rich source of antibodies (what are commonly referred to as probiotics). Such antibodies, such as found in Bovine Colostrum Powder, bind to the E. coli in the gastrointestinal tract, preventing it from attaching to the intestinal wall and thereby neutralising its ability to cause fever, belly cramps and diarrhoea. Speak to your GP or pharmacist.

It's important to distinguish between travellers' diarrhoea and food poisoning. The latter is the result of eating toxins that have already formed in the food, and while it may cause both vomiting and diarrhoea, it's usually over within 12 hours. Beyond avoiding uncooked or poorly cooked food, the best advise I can offer is to wash your hands regularly with an alcohol based hand santizer (or soap if sanitizer is not available).

"Everything in Africa bites, but the safari bug is worst of all." - Brian Jackman (travel writer).

Considerations for families (& solo travellers)

It is a common (and perplexing) question - should you take your (young) family on safari? Will they get enough out of it (to warrant the expense)? Won't they get bored (and annoying) and spoil the experience for their parents? Is it safe?

Only you, as the parent, can answer that question (or questions). All kids are different. Some are just born to outdoor pursuits and being 'on safari' will clearly be the 'experience of their lives'. Others are not so taken! But on balance I would have to say that, from my own experience, it will be all they will want to talk about to their friends when they get home. After all, they have been to Africa, seen an elephant up-close, heard a lion roar - wow! Beat that.

And don't forget - it is all about shared experiences.

That's not to say that being on safari with the kids will be all plain sailing! When going on safari as a family there are a number of challenges worth keeping in mind – here are few things you need to know when travelling with children...shall we say 'considerations worth noting' when planning for a family safari:

- **Mix it up**
  Make sure there is enough variety in their day and don't be shy to include some 'obvious' teasers - meerkats, quad bikes, bows and arrows...you know what I mean. Don't just drive them around for hours on end.

- **Be flexible**
  Kids are renowned for their (limited) attention span...so try to be flexible in terms of the safari activities. If possible, arrange a private vehicle and guide - that way, when the kids have had enough, you

can go back to camp and throw them in then pool.

- **See the world through 'young' eyes**
  A child's excitement at seeing an impala for the first time is
  infectious enough to rub off on even the most seasoned of safari
  goers. When you start seeing the bush from a child's point of view,
  the priority of ticking off the big 5 quickly fades – replaced by the
  excitement of watching dung beetles at work and imagining the
  inner-workings of termite mounds. Go with the flow.

Lastly, please try to keep in mind that most safari lodges and camps
place a strong emphasis on peace, tranquility and getting back to
nature! This may not be your children's style! An 'adults' safari is really
not suitable for many young children who often become bored and act
up! Please keep in mind that it is the responsibility of the parents to
ensure that their children do not infringe upon the enjoyment of other
guests.

Anti child-trafficking

New rules on anti child-trafficking have come into force in South
Africa and Namibia and may soon be required elsewhere in Africa.
These rules require parents to provide airlines and immigration
officials with the birth certificates for any accompanying children
under the age of 18 years. This will apply even when both parents are
travelling together with their children. When children are travelling
with guardians, these adults will be required to produce affidavits from
the parents proving permission for the children to travel. Airlines will
be been given instructions not to allow clients to board without the
necessary documents. Check with your Africa Travel Specialist before
you leave home as these rules change regularly.

General precautions

Some general precautions on safari for children (and parents) include
taking extra care with regard to the hot African sun – hats and

sunblock are a must on drives and walks. Mosquito repellent and 'covering up' areas of exposed skin in the early evenings is a warning that should also be heeded in malaria areas. And be sure to explain to your children about drinking only filtered or bottled water.

Swimming pools

Many safari camps and lodges have swimming pools, so if your child is not a confident swimmer, do take the time to check that you are comfortable with the access to the swimming pool (pool fence) and accompany them if they want to swim (swimming is at your own risk).

Safety

Most importantly, you should take heed of issues of safety as prescribed by the lodge/camp regarding walking/running in camp and the need to be escorted to/from the room if required. You need to ensure that your children are aware of, and fully understand, these restrictions (and that you keep an eye on their movements). Many camps are unfenced and you may need to take special care to keep a closer watch on your younger ones.

Meals and meal times

Another aspect worth clarifying, when you arrive at a new lodge or camp, is the question of meals and meal times (for younger children particularly). Advise the manager of your child's dietary requirements and try to work out suitable meal times that fit with your child's, and the camp's routines. Some camps, although able to arrange earlier meal times for your children, may then require a parent to be with the children when they go to bed (for safety reasons).

Sleeping arrangements

Depending on the ages of your children, the safari camp/lodge where you are staying may require one adult to sleep in the same room/tent with the under age child (or children) - usually under 12yrs. This is a safety measure to avoid the possibility of young children wandering from their tent or reacting badly to an animal that might approach their tent. Many camps now offer family tents/rooms to prevent parents having to split sleeping arrangements, or can provide a babysitter allow parents to take a few hours out to enjoy an evening meal together without the kids.

Children's activity programs

Many safari camps have now developed children's activity programs and some even have a dedicated guide for families.

For the ages of 4 to 8 years these programs mostly consist of a guide who takes the children under their wing, entertaining them with a range of activities around camp (including story-telling, painting/drawing animals, birding and bug collecting amongst others) – keeping an eye on them while the parents go on a game drives or other activity. This can then develop into short bush walks (or "poo walks" during which they help the children collect pods, feathers, insects and leaves, and teach them to identify different animal spoor and droppings) and game drives.

Most parents would like to share the many wildlife experiences with their children – especially when the children are a little older (8 to 12 years) and able to fully appreciate going on a game drive or walk. To this end it may be an idea to request a private vehicle if it appears that the camp, or your travel agent, has not already considered this. This way you are not infringing upon other guests and can return to camp when the children have 'had enough'.

Age restrictions on activities

You will certainly encounter age restrictions on some safari activities. As you might expect, not all safari activities are open to children of all ages, for example, gorilla trekking and white-water rafting have a minimum age of 15 years (essentially an issue of safety). Walking is another that can vary according to the camp/lodge's discretion (and may relate to the prevalence, or otherwise, of dangerous game). You may need to exercise your parental discretion when it comes to activities like walking, and canoeing or mokoros for that matter – this is an area of personal preference (and apprehension tolerance). Some camps/lodges may allow child participation, that does not automatically mean it is OK (or safe) - that decision is yours (as a parent).

If you have teenagers, a few planned adrenalin-inducing safari activities may be just what is needed to keep them focused (and enjoying themselves).

Pregnant Women (flying in small planes)

First of all, let me just say that the medical profession 'recommends that pregnant women do not to fly in an unpressurized small plane. There are concerns that women and their babies may not receive enough oxygen during non-pressurized flights'.

That said , many charter companies in Africa that use small, unpressurised aircraft have introduced some simple guidelines as follows:

* From 0-22 weeks: pregnant women will be allowed to fly as long as they have not experienced any complications during this phase of their pregnancy.

* From 22-32 weeks: pregnant women allowed to fly only with a doctor's note (and this assumes that they have had no complications to date).

If you are pregnant when going on safari, it is important that you

advise your travel agent of this so that they can advise the various camps/lodges and charter companies and get clarification on how they view this.

Tips for solo travellers

Travelling alone in Africa can present some challenges but should by no means be allowed to discourage you. Here are some tips to help with your planning:

- Be aware that most hotels, lodges and safari camps charge an additional single supplement fee on top of their standard rate. This is to compensate for the effective loss of the other bed in the room that you will occupy. When a property has only a dozen rooms/tents or less, this is understandable (and common practice in the industry). There a couple of strategies for avoiding the single supplements mentioned above - firstly, look to join small touring groups where there is the opportunity to share with a like-minded traveller or those tours that do not charge a single supplement at all. Alternatively, look to travel in the green or shoulder seasons where many camps and lodges waive the single supplement to encourage bookings. Speak to your Africa Travel Specialist about the options.

- You should note that although most inter-camp flights/transfers are sold on a seat-in-plane basis and so are just like booking a normal A to B flight anywhere, but do be aware that in some instances there is a 'minimum of '2 pax' stipulation - just be aware.

- Travelling alone does not mean being alone on safari! Although many of the lodges are small, personal and intimate all meals and afternoon tea are generally a communal affair, ensuring that you will interact with other guests and seldom left at a table alone. At the end of the day most guests will gravitate to the camp fire and this is also a good place to interact with others.

- Activities are also shared with other guests, and it is here where you are most likely to strike up some friendships. Most game drive vehicles will take from 6 to 9 guests, a small enough number so that you don't feel swamped by other people, but big enough to have plenty of socialising.

- Don't forget too, that you will be with like-minded people from around the world - interesting people, with an adventurous spirit - just like you. My bet is you will make lifelong friends on safari.

"The only man I envy is the man who has not yet been to Africa...for he has so much to look forward to." - Richard Mullin

What to pack for your safari

You've waited months for your safari to finally come around...now you have to decide what you should take, what clothes to pack...and how to fit it all in. Here are a few tips:

Clothes and toiletries

Hello! Of course you're not going to forget clothes – duh! But are you taking the right clothes...and are you within those weight restrictions your travel agent told you about for those light aircraft flights?

Most international airlines will restrict your check-in luggage to around 20 to 30kgs (44 to 66lbs), but if your safari itinerary includes any light aircraft flights then this can mean as little as 12 to 15 kgs (sometimes including your hand luggage!).

Don't panic! Remember, a same-day laundry service is usually available in most safari camps and lodges. This means you do NOT need a change of clothes for each day you are on safari! The exception will be for mobile tented safaris where it is often difficult, due the mobile nature, to offer a laundry service. It may also be possible to leave a bag with the charter company, or person meeting you, for the duration of the safari portion – ask your travel agent.

Generally speaking, casual, comfortable clothing is suitable throughout the year when on safari. Whilst you may elect to start a completely new safari 'wardrobe' it is really not necessary to look like an extra on the set of Out of Africa! Apart from selecting reasonably neutral or 'non-bright' coloured clothing, safari-wear is generally casual and practical. Be sure you take clothes that you feel comfortable in – especially when it comes to your walking/hiking boots. The newer quick-drying fabrics, shirts with ventilation and trousers that convert into shorts are all worth considering.

Wearing clothes in layers is the most practical way to cope with fluctuating day/night temperatures and cool evenings whilst on safari. As the day warms up you can peel off another layer, then as it begins to cool toward evening, so they can go back on. A T-shirt, shirt or blouse (long sleeves help to protect from the sun and mosquitoes), plus a fleece or warm jacket along with a pair of safari trousers (those that zip off at the knees are very handy too), shoes (or boots) and socks should about complete the ensemble. Don't forget that shirts with collars are far better for protecting the back of your neck from the sun. Always be careful to 'cover up' around the camp fire in the evenings to avoid mosquitoes (trousers and long sleeves).

Ask your travel agent (or get onto the internet) and find out what the weather will be like where you are going – you may not need any serious cold weather gear at all (and that will really help with the luggage limit!). Alternatively, if you are going anywhere in winter where the temperature drops dramatically when the sun goes down you may need gloves, a scarf, a thick jacket and a beanie! I mean it! Places like Hwange, Okavango, Linyanti and even Kruger are freezing in the early morning and late evening during the winter months (June through August), and this is magnified by a significant wind-chill factor once on the back of an open game-drive vehicle. Most camps will provide blankets and/or a warm poncho-style covering - but don't count on it.

Some suggestions:

- A wide brimmed hat. Yes, a cap is OK, but for proper protection from the sun you need something that will protect the back of your neck too!

- Don't forget a pair of comfortable walking shoes which you have 'worn in' before you leave home.

- You might also like to consider a pair of open sports sandals (Tevas or similar) for general daytime use in the warmer months (my choice of footwear – comfortable and cool).

- Take a swimming costume too - a number of lodges and camps have swimming pools.

- Dull and/or neutral colours are more suitable for safari, white and/or bright colours are not practical as they tend to stand out – definitely not advisable on a walking safari.

- Cotton clothing is recommended although the newer synthetic safari clothing lines are quick drying and extremely comfortable.

- Ladies – despite being loathe to offer advice in this area, I should mention that game drives can be VERY bumpy and a good (sports) bra would probably not go amiss!

- Think about packing a bandanna or cotton scarf and a sarong (kanga, pareo, kikoi). They might just be the most useful and versatile items you take on safari.

- Bring an elegantly casual outfit for dinner at the smarter hotels.

- Consider a light, compact raincoat if it is likely you will encounter rain (gorilla and chimp trekking). Fantastic lightweight raincoats are available these days.

- Pith helmets and zebra-striped pyjamas are no longer mandatory!

Camera, video and binoculars

Whilst most people will remember to take their camera and/or video (or will use their mobile phone) not everyone thinks they need to take binoculars! In my opinion, binoculars are ESSENTIAL for optimum wildlife viewing on safari (and a GOOD pair of binoculars will make a BIG difference to your safari). I strongly recommend a pair of binoculars on safari – get the most expensive you can afford, at least 8x or better still 10x magnification*. You WILL thank me.

Africa is a photographer's dream. Not only does the boundless wildlife come in all shapes and sizes but the continent is also blessed with stunning landscapes, colourful people and fabulous light! Don't miss out – buy a camera if you don't already have one.

For more insights on what camera equipment to take on safari, or if you are considering taking a 'drone' (UAV) for aerial photography, please refer to the section below on *Digital photography*.

* If you wear prescription glasses, look for binoculars that have dioptric compensation (allowing you to set each side independently to match your prescription for left and right eyes) and twist-in eye cups for a more comfortable fit. Size (and weight) should also be a consideration - too heavy a pair of binoculars will come to be somewhat uncomfortable over time (if worn around your neck).

Phone, music, tablet or laptop

Again, I doubt you will leave these behind but don't forget their respective chargers and the correct adaptor plugs for the countries you are visiting (and perhaps even a double-adaptor if you have multiple devices plus a camera or video which will also require charging).

Passport, itinerary, travel insurance docs and etickets

I know, I know. Not rocket science...but we do need to have these on the list.

Prescription glasses (sunglasses, hat, sunblock et al)

If you wear prescription glasses be sure to pack more than one set (in case you lose one or they get broken). You will be outdoors for much of the time, so be prepared – hat, sunblock, long sleeves, and lip balm.

Prescription meds

Do not forget to put your prescription medications in your hand luggage (in case your check-in bag goes astray – it happens!)...and make sure you have enough of each type to last your entire safari.

Preventative pharmaceuticals

Here I am talking about 'meds' that you might need if the worst happens: diarrhoea, headaches, heartburn, insect repellent, hand sanitizer, bites (antihistamine), indigestion, sore throat (lozenges), eye drops, and most important – anti-malarial tablets.

A ban on ALL plastic bags

Plastic bags are now banned in Rwanda, Kenya and Botswana (including duty free bags) and all visitors to these countries need to be aware of this. I suspect that this prohibition may soon spread to other countries in the region. Please respect these initiatives.

Odds & ends

A good torch (flashlight) is a must - it can be pitch black in the bush or in your tent in the middle of the night. A rechargeable torch is ideal but a small battery-powered torch is sufficient. The new LED miner's lights that fit on your head (and leaves your hands free) are also a good option. A smaller (pencil) torch for your camera bag or looking at star maps is also worth considering. Most camps will provide a torch, or will walk you back to your tent as required, but being self-sufficient is always a good idea.

A good book. It never hurts to have an interesting book when travelling – you never know when you are going to be delayed at the airport or fall victim to Africa time!

A travel diary or journal is something I do recommend. You will see and experience so much in such a short period of time on safari that the only way to maintain a good record, and the correct chronology, will be to write it down. It does require discipline, but will serve as an invaluable record of your safari adventure.

Finally, don't forget your **sense of humour, patience and some common sense**!

A word of warning:

It is not advisable to wear any form of clothing that may be construed as "camouflage". By this I mean any form of brown/green "combat" style colouring. Even if it is the latest fashion statement - and even if it is only your 12 year old wearing it - and even if it is just a cap. Many African authorities have a disproportionate phobia about such garments and this could conceivably result in you being questioned or harassed by the police. It has the potential to cause you grief – don't do it.

What to expect on safari

Try to read this chapter before your safari starts – it aims to get you thinking the right thoughts about what it means to be on safari, what you can expect and how you can get the most out of your safari experience.

There is a saying that everyone who lives in Africa gets to understand over time – *"Africa is not for sissies"* (the fainthearted) – but perhaps that is what makes it so alive, so unpredictable and even fascinating. That's not to say that life on safari is overly harrowing. On the contrary. But, as I have already alluded to, a safari is not like any other holiday. Let's take a look at what lies ahead…

Be prepared for/to:

- **Early starts**. Most camps will wake you at first light (sparrows!). Be warned.

- **Up to 4 hour game drives** in the hot African sun, hard seats (sometimes), and a lot of bumping and bouncing around (safari massage – no extra charge!). But it is exciting and the time will fly past. A good hat and sunblock a must.

- **HOT and dusty conditions**. Hot in summer and dusty through the dry winter months. Just so you know…expect it.

- **COLD (near freezing) game drives** in winter (June to August inclusive) in southern Africa, especially in the region termed the 'Kalahari Sands'; stretching from the Kgalagadi in South Africa, up through Central Kalahari and Okavango Delta in Botswana, all the way north to Hwange NP in Zimbabwe. Even in lowveld areas like Kruger NP, and other private reserves in South Africa, winters can get very chilly. Gloves, scarf, heavy jacket and a beanie are not an over-reaction! The wind-chill factor in an open 4x4 just adds to the misery unless you are wrapped up warmly – so be (mentally and physically) prepared.

- **Taking your 'comfort break' in the bush** when out on game drives. That's right – no flushing toilet, no toilet seat and no toilet paper! You will be 'going to the loo' behind the nearest bush. Ladies, it is a good idea to carry tissues and a small bag to deposit them in until you can dispose of them back at camp (and a hand sanitizer too). Do NOT leave toilet tissues lying in the bush. A hand sanitizer is a good option too. Guides are predominantly male, and seemingly under the

impression that everyone gets to do this at home! If you haven't
had to 'go' outdoors before – start getting your mind around it
now!

Keep in mind that it is worth ensuring that you go to the bathroom
last thing before getting on the vehicle for your drive - and don't
consume too much tea or coffee beforehand either – there's
nothing worse than having to 'hang on'!

Although darting behind a bush in the middle of Africa to drop
your pants doesn't sound especially dignified, you will get used to it
(and will have little choice in the matter…nature calls us all).

Your guide will plan to stop for regular 'comfort' breaks but if you
need to 'go' at any other time you only need let your guide know
and he/she will find a suitable location where you will be afforded
some privacy (most likely bushes) and will be safe (no lions hiding
behind them!).

- **Resting through the heat of the day**. Most safari camps and lodges
  will co-ordinate their activities so that you spend the heat of the day
  in camp – snoozing, reading, relaxing and dining. Get into the
  rhythm of an afternoon nap – you will be up at first light, so you
  have probably had a full day already!

- **Small 4-seater, single-engine charter flights** into short dirt
  airstrips. Perfectly safe mind you – but not a bad idea to be mentally
  prepared. Flights through the middle of the day can get bumpy. No
  on-board toilets on these flights either!

- **Biting tsetse flies** and bothersome mopane flies (actually a stingless
  bee). There will quite possibly be times when you will be
  incessantly harassed by one (or both) of these little devils. Tsetse
  flies are particularly unsettling as they can really bite and are
  devious little buggers. They have the unnerving ability of landing
  so lightly on your skin that you do not feel a thing until they bite,
  and then ZING! They can get you through your clothes too – and
  are fond of getting into your hair too! On top of all that, they are
  truly tricky to kill as you can virtually squash them flat between
  thumb and forefinger and they will merely get up and fly off!

Trying to kill them is a waste of effort and I recommend being vigilant and merely using your hat/cap to brush them away and out of the vehicle as you drive. Unfortunately they are actually attracted to the moving vehicle (and dark places - like the foot-well).

Of course mosquitoes are prevalent in many safari areas (although less so through the winter months) – be sure to cover up in the early evenings to avoid being bitten.

Whilst we are talking creepy crawlies...don't worry too much if you find the odd spider, frog, grasshopper or other insect/reptile inside your tent/chalet. You have come to spend time in the great outdoors - so it shouldn't come as any surprise. Even so, if it bothers you, it is quite OK to ask a staff member to remove them!

- **Over-eat**. There is an ever present danger of over-eating on safari! Most safari lodges serve three full meals a day. Now that might be OK if you were also exercising correspondingly – but as you will likely spend most of the day in the back of a game-drive vehicle, this is not going to be the case. Although most safari camps and lodges stick to a regimen of three cooked meals every day, interspersed with teas, coffees and cake, some have acknowledged that guests are quite comfortable with an early light breakfast to precede the morning activity, a respectable brunch closer to midday after returning to camp and tea, coffee and cakes served after an afternoon nap and prior to the afternoon drive. The main meal of the day, dinner, is then served on your return to camp after the afternoon/evening activity and following a hot shower and a drink by the fire.

  Oh yes...and to be waited on hand-and-foot. You really will not have to lift a finger! Enjoy...

- **Quiet.** Initially, especially if you are from a big city, you may be overwhelmed by how quiet a safari camp can be - no traffic, sirens, people chattering...but after a few days it will become the new 'normal' and you will begin to really appreciate its soothing effect. Of course it is seldom completely quiet, but it may take you a while to 'notice' the many sounds of bird and animal activity that is happening all around you!

- **No cell (mobile) phone coverage** in the more remote camps. Turn it off – what were you thinking? Many camps nowadays, even some remote ones, have WiFi (via satellite in some cases), so you can often get on-line and get down your emails (in case you are suffering from communication deficit disorder!).

Don't expect:

- **To be driving off-road**
  In most National Parks and Game Reserves your guide is not allowed to leave the road. This varies between countries – in parts of Zambia and Kenya for example, limited off-road driving is permitted. Your guide will know where and when. It is only in the private game reserves and concessions areas that driving off-road is allowed (and is common practice at important sightings).

- **To go out at night**
  As per off-road driving above, night drives are generally not sanctioned in most National Parks – Zambia being the notable exception. Again, it is in the private concession areas and private reserves that your guide may take you out at night. This may be one of the reasons why your Africa Travel Specialist would have suggested certain camps/lodges.

- **To get out of the game-drive vehicle**
  You must stay in your game drive vehicle at all times unless specifically sanctioned by your guide, who will carefully select an appropriate location to do so (to stretch your legs, have a picnic or sundowner).

- **That all game-drive vehicles will be open (or closed) 4x4's**
  Vehicle layouts and styles can vary from country to country and Park to Park. In East Africa, where you might be using a private

vehicle and guide to visit the various parks and reserves, and where
you will travel between the different reserves in that vehicle, it is
normal for your vehicle to be enclosed with side windows and a
pop-up hatch – this is to accommodate travelling at higher speeds
on sealed roads. In southern Africa (and a number of private camps
in East Africa), where you tend to fly between camps in light
aircraft, the game-drive vehicles will likely be more open – perhaps
with a canvas roof covering but certainly open on the sides. Not all
open 4x4 vehicles have the roof covering either – so be sure to have
a hat.

- **Elaborate airport terminals**
  In Africa the airports are fairly rudimentary. The big shopping
  arcade style airports have not arrived in this part of the world (with
  the possible exception of South Africa) and luggage, check-in and
  security checks are conducted at a relaxed pace. When taking
  private air charters you are also likely to land on deserted airstrips
  that look very similar to a wide gravel road – no outbuildings,
  customs officials, bureau de change or drinks dispenser!

- **That animal sightings can be guaranteed**
  Whilst some game reserves or national parks may be considered
  excellent for seeing a particular species, leopard for example, no
  sighting is ever guaranteed. Seasons vary, animal habits change and
  nature is unpredictable.

- **Things to go according to plan**
  More than occasionally it may appear that nothing seems to be
  happening –even when you are pretty certain that something
  should have already happened (and no one is bothering to explain
  why it is not). Africans have an unnerving view of time! It has been
  said that "Westerners have watches, but Africans have time!"
  Maybe it is just that we have grown more impatient in the
  West…but do not despair, they usually get there in the end. Africa,
  and its bureaucracy, can be frustrating but there is usually a reason
  for the hold-up even if no one is bothering to explain it to you.

- **To pet a wild animal**

  I know, I know…it sounds cool to 'walk with lions' or 'stroke a cheetah' but honestly, this is not why you have come to Africa (I hope). Going on a safari is about immersing yourself in the natural world…petting wild animals is more akin to entertainment. If you would really like to get closer to your favourite wild animal consider visiting a wildlife orphanage or rehabilitation centre – you will be helping a good cause and may very well be able to get the close-up experience you are after.

- **Mobile (cell) phone reception or WiFi**

  Whilst mobile phone coverage in Africa is fairly good considering, and getting better each year, the fact is that a number of the safari destinations you are going to will be remote with limited infrastructure and services. Chill. Being on safari means getting away from it all. Enjoy the break. WiFi however is getting more ubiquitous but is still not everywhere!

- **Elaborate meals**

  The world has gone mad. Foodies now rule! What with Master Chef and all the other 'Foodie' TV shows going round it is hard to keep up with all the new ingredients and combinations (jus, quinoa, a sprig of thyme)! Whilst I must admit that many of the fancier lodges are getting much more elaborate with their meal offerings, most safari camps still offer what is commonly referred to as 'comfort food'. Nothing wrong with that (if you ask me). In some of the more remote camps I am constantly amazed by not only the high standard of the food, but by how it is cooked – over an open fire in many cases. Amazing really.

Do not be surprised/alarmed:

- That a man has more than one wife. Polygamy is permitted in a number of African cultures, although this is less common today. Many Africans will also talk about multiple 'mothers' and of seemingly endless brothers, sisters, aunts and uncles – these are not necessarily all blood relatives but more a reflection on the closeness and bond between families of the same village.

- That Africans talk loudly – it is considered rude (bad manners) to talk softly or to whisper. Talking openly assures others that you are not gossiping or spreading innuendo.

- To find most Africans extremely friendly and willing to stop and chat, even when meeting for the first time. Africans set great store on the formality of greetings and the exchange of pleasantries. This courtesy is extended to all, including visitors.

- To see men holding hands in public – this is a sign of friendship in Africa. Conversely, men and women seldom hold hands or show signs of affection in public.

- That when shaking hands Africans will place the left hand along the underside of the outstretched arm – this is to signal that no malice is intended (by clearly showing both hands).

- Africans generally do not point with a single finger either. To indicate the location of an animal they will more often extend their arm with the palm open and all fingers extended in the direction intended.

- By poorly dressed (and barefoot) children. This is the third world. In the main, children in Africa may not be well attired but they are happy and carefree, and Africans by nature dote on their children.

- To hear Africans burst into song – they are very rhythmic and love to chant and sing while working or at social gatherings.

- That nothing seems to be happening (and no one is bothering to explain) - Africans have an unnerving view of time! It has been said that "Westerners have watches, but Africans have time!" Maybe it is just that we have grown more impatient in the west…but do not despair, they usually get there in the end. Africa, and its bureaucracy, can be frustrating but there is usually a reason for the hold-up even if no one is bothering to explain it to you.

- That you may sometimes get the sense that you are not being told everything. In wanting to please, Africans will more often and not tell you want they think you want to hear - or they will hedge their bets: how far is so-and-so may be asked by 'a little bit long way, but no so much'!

- By a range of somewhat unusual names - Innocent, Goodluck, Godsent, Gladness, Beauty, Honest, Kissmore and others are a reflection of the free-wheeling nature of westernisation in Africa.

- To see both men and women wearing beaded jewellry. For the Maasai people, beads incorporates the whole of their culture; representing strength, tradition, beauty, marriage, warrior hood, marital status and their deep devotion to their cattle. Both Maasai men and women wear the beaded jewellery and every piece has a meaning. Introduced by foreign traders, and originally made of glass, coloured beads took the place of seeds, sticks, shells and dry grasses traditionally used for adornment. These glass beads have since been replaced by cheaper plastic beads which come in all colours, shapes and sizes.

Be sure to:

- **Slow down**. Try to pick up on the tempo of Africa – slow but deliberate. Take the time to reflect on what is around you, and all that you are seeing and experiencing – take it all in.

- **Be enthusiastic** and make the most of being 'on safari'. Your enthusiasm is what your guide feeds off and will bring out the best in him / her. Ask questions, be enquiring and give your guide feedback on how the safari is working out for you. Participate in whatever's going on – walking, canoeing, night drives or just sitting in a hide!

- **Try always to be ready** at the agreed time to go on your morning or afternoon activity (having already made a last minute visit to the

bathroom, gathered up ALL the 'bits' that you need for the day –
camera, binoculars, hat, sunblock, sunglasses, jumper (sweater)
etc).

- **Take the opportunity to walk** with an experienced and
  knowledgeable guide. Walking offers a new perspective and an
  added dimension to your African safari. No longer confined to your
  safari vehicle you are free to see, hear and smell all that surrounds
  you (away from the engine noise). The added excitement of
  becoming part of the food chain will heighten your appreciation of
  being on safari! Highly recommended and always informative.

- **Be patient**. Sometimes, just being in one place brings its own
  rewards. It is very tempting to race from one sighting to the next,
  or to whiz around in the forlorn hope of bumping into something.
  Have a strategy to stop and listen – take out those binoculars and
  look around, you'll be surprised what's been there all along.

- **Speak up!** If you want to continue watching a particular scene
  unfold and your guide starts to make signs that you should return
  for breakfast – tell him, no! Breakfast can always wait – a lion hunt
  or an elephant taking a bath may not come around again – sit tight.

- **Appreciate the intimacy of the smaller camps**. Your hosts may in
  fact be the owners who have put their life into providing
  unforgettable experiences to their visitors. Enjoy the many
  wonderful characters that are part and parcel of this exciting
  industry, for although it might appear idyllic it is hard work and not
  without its sacrifices.

- **Take in the aerial views**, and photo opportunities, that come with
  those inter-camp charter flights. Flying across the Okavango Delta
  or down the Zambezi Valley will give you a completely new
  perspective that you just don't get from a vehicle.

- **Take the opportunity to meet other travellers** from around the
  world – enjoy shared experiences and learn from each other's
  observations and viewpoints. Part of the fun of travel is the people
  you meet – being on safari is no different.

Listen out for the sounds of Africa. When you find yourself relaxing on your bed in your safari camp, with just a piece of canvas between you and what's out there, start to identify the sounds that you hear. Make a mental note and get your guide to help you to label some of these fabulous sounds of Africa – they *will* live with you for a long time as a soundtrack in your mind.

Sounds to listen out for on safari:
- The distinctive (five bob, two and six) duet of the ground hornbill
- The snorts and grunts of hippo
- The distinct double-click of crickets
- Bell frogs that clink like ice cubes in a glass
- The whoop of a hyena
- The eerie sound of a nightjar calling after dark
- The rasping (sawing) cough of a leopard
- The call of the fish eagle
- The trill of a scops owl or the mutter of a giant eagle owl
- The gurgling sound of a coucal
- The roar of a lion with its unmistakable dying grunts that fade into the night air - almost felt rather than heard.

- **Keep your tent zipped up** at night and don't wander around camp after dark unescorted.

- **Learn the art of listening, seeing and observing** (and being still and quiet). Our basic senses of sight, sound and smell have become somewhat dulled with city living. But with a little perseverance you will find that even your ability to discern a soft sound, recognise a shape or outline, or pick up on a movement in the grass will improve the more time you spend on safari – so keep working on it!

- **Always listen to the instructions of your guide.** This is especially pertinent when on a walking, canoeing or other adventure activity where the element of danger is heightened, and the need for composure is paramount.

- **Be aware of your responsibility** to the social, economic and

environmental fabric of the places you visit by respecting the
people and the environment, and by being aware of the impact that
your behavior can have on a community. Remember, travelling
responsibly means conserving natural resources, supporting local
cultures, and making a positive impact on the places we visit.

- **Be polite** (and try not to show your impatience). A smile combined
  with a please or thank you can go a long way – especially when
  things may not be happening as you might expect.

Try to avoid:

- **Arguing with customs officials, money changers, mosquitoes,
  and birders** (twitchers)!

- **Becoming dehydrated**. Drink filtered/bottled water whenever and
  wherever possible.

- **Photographing anything relating to the government or military**,
  including personnel (soldiers and police) and buildings (post offices,
  banks, airports, border posts, railway stations and bridges). Most
  African countries have disproportionate security paranoia.

- **Missing a single game-drive, walk or excursion into the bush** –
  the day you decide to sleep in will be the day that your group finds
  that elusive leopard that you have been dying to see. Remember,
  like everything else in life, the more you put in – the more you are
  likely to get out. That means early mornings, long drives, sitting in
  a hide, walking with your guide, taking that evening game drive
  and keeping your binoculars and camera at the ready at all times –
  even when in camp. You can rest when you get home!

- **Stepping out of your tent, chalet or lodge at night** without either
  a good torch (flashlight), an escort or at the very least - good
  walkway lighting. If you do 'bump' into something – don't panic!
  Try to remember that whatever is there is likely to be more scared
  of you than you are of it (well perhaps!). If it hasn't seen you, back

off slowly and return to your room. Don't throw something at it to get it to move, and don't do anything to startle it – like scream!? If it has seen you, and hasn't already bolted into the bushes, do not scream, bolt for the bar or run in any direction – stand still and begin to move back very slowly until you can put some distance between you – then bolt for your room! This is going to be fun...yes?

- **Rushing about from one sighting to the next**. Take the time to savour each animal interaction, unfolding scene or wildlife sighting. I guarantee that if you spend just that little extra time at a sighting (after you're ready to move on) that something will happen to make you glad that you stuck it out. Trust me on this.

- **Picking up or attempting to 'collect' anything you might come across on safari** including skulls, ivory, horns, bird's eggs and the like. This is strictly against National Parks rules and is extremely frowned upon. If in doubt, check with your guide. Remember, your guide is responsible for your actions and can get into hot water with the authorities if you are found with anything untoward.

- **The temptation to feed the animals**. Do not EVER feed ANY animal or bird on safari. I don't mean the elephants and lions – I think most people understand that this would be foolish. I'm talking about the monkeys or baboons that you may come across at various designated picnic spots or camp sites, or even the birds that appear when you take out your sandwiches. Over time this dependence on people for food will invariably result in an unprovoked attack from an animal that does not understand why the next visitor hasn't got something edible at the ready.

- **Boldly taking endless photographs of the locals**. Not all African cultures are accepting of cameras or having their photograph taken. Many rural Africans will shy away from having their picture taken. Please be sensitive. However, many may merely want a fee for having their photograph taken, while others will gladly pose for you if you ask courteously. It is always advisable to strike up a conversation, exchange greetings and ask about their lives and families before you start to snap off pictures – and if you have a digital camera they will always enjoy seeing their image on the small screen.

- **Purchasing goods made from endangered resources**, including ivory, coral, or skins.

Think about...

- Taking off your watch, turning off the mobile (cell) phone, stashing the iPod, losing the make-up, tossing the high heels…(it's time to go COLD TURKEY – no half measures – you can do it - go ahead I know you want to!)

- Pick up an Animal / Bird / Tree check list when you start your safari. These are available at most lodges (and will cover the region you are visiting). Mark off what you see each day. At the end of your safari you will be staggered to see how your list has grown. This is not to say that a safari is all about ticking off all the animals on the lists – absolutely not. But after a while it is very interesting to go back through your list to see just how many animals and birds you have seen – just in pure numbers. The diversity of wildlife in Africa is astonishing. There is also an *Animal Check List* further below in this book - just in case.

- Keeping a diary or journal. A record of the day to day events, camps, sightings and people you meet will be invaluable when you get home and have forgotten the exact sequence of events on a particular day, the name of that little animal that you were lucky enough to see – or the name of the guide with whom you spent the day. When you get home you will be able to look back with fondness at the experiences you shared on safari.

- And if the prospect of sitting down each evening to write it all down doesn't appeal, think about using a voice-recording device –

some MP3 players and tablets (using an app.) have this capability these days!

- Experiencing the romance of a true bush camp, whether that is a fly-camp or mobile tented camp. If your travel agent has included a bush camp in your itinerary, take a moment to really appreciate what taking a hot bucket shower under the stars really means. Savour the feeling of going to sleep with just a layer of canvas between you and the African bush.

- Waking up to the sounds of the African night (and the early mornings too).

- Not expecting too much! National Geographic documentaries are chock-full of exciting chases, kills and confrontations but you need to be realistic, after all, these one hour documentaries can take up to a year to film. Going on safari is not necessarily going to be like that. Any lion, leopard and cheetah sighting should be cherished and truly appreciated, along with the myriad of other things to see on safari – including the scenery itself. A big herd of buffalo or an interaction with an elephant group can be just as rewarding, as can the discovery of a 'special' bird or the small details and explanations given by your guide about a particular tree or shrub. Life and death scenes are not around every corner – and that's part of what is so exciting about a safari – you never know quite what is going to be around the next corner!

- Taking the opportunity to appreciate the night sky (on clear evenings). Away from the bright city lights you will be amazed at the beauty of a moonless sky festooned with clusters of stars, constellations and planets. Most safari guides are adept at pointing out the more interesting constellations – see more under the chapter titled: The night sky.

- Taking that half-empty bottle of water out of the vehicle after a game drive and finishing it through the day (or night). Otherwise, that half empty (or half full) bottle will have to be thrown away!

Safari Jargon

Every industry has its own jargon – made up of ingenious (and some disingenuous) metaphors and anagrams aplenty. You will hear safari guides expounding at length using terms that are unlikely to be familiar to you. Apart from their fondness for scientific classifications of all animals and plants, you will undoubtedly hear terms like crepuscular and arboreal, ungulates and ruminants, predators and scavengers, solitary and territorial, browsers and grazers. We will discuss all of these terms, and their meanings, throughout the various chapters of this book – all will be revealed. But if you just need a quick definition or explanation, you should be able to find it in the Glossary toward the back of the book.

I can reveal one rather ubiquitous term right now though:

You will hear the word 'game' in a raft of disguises – there will be talk about big game, going on game drives, finding good game in that area , references to various game reserves…and so on. The term 'game' is actually an old English word that was originally used to refer to 'animals of the chase' and by inference – sport and amusement. Game laws (stewardship) were instigated to protect, or reserve, specified areas for the amusement and sporting pastimes of royalty and the 'well to do'.

Today the word 'game' refers to the abundance (or lack of) wild animals in a particular location. The term 'big game' is a reference to the Big5 (lion, leopard, elephant, buffalo and rhino) and 'plains game' describes the less dangerous (in hunting terms) trophy antelope such as sable, eland and kudu.

We talk more on this topic in the chapters that follow.

Vehicle Etiquette

Most of your time on safari will be spent in the back of a safari vehicle which you will likely be sharing with a number of other keen 'safari goers' – it is worth keeping a few basic rules of etiquette in mind:

- **Be ready on time**
  Always try to be ready to board your vehicle at the agreed time, having been to the toilet and with everything you will need for the day (cameras, binoculars, sunblock etc).

- **Be considerate (and courteous)**
  Be prepared to indulge the interests of others in your group – they will hopefully do likewise for you. And don't always rush for the 'best' seat. Be considerate of others.

- **Talk in moderation**
  Try to avoid talking incessantly during game drives – this can be very disruptive to the other guests and even off-putting for the guide!

- **No sudden movements**
  Avoid standing up or making any sudden movements when close to animals – this will likely startle them and they will either run off or take offence! You should also be careful not to 'rock' the vehicle (shuffling in your seat or unnecessary movements) when the other occupants are attempting to get that perfect photograph.

- **Be patient**
  There is no script on safari and it may be that you need to wait by a waterhole or stop to scan the horizon to find something of interest. Be patient (and vigilant) – the next great sighting is likely just around the corner.

- **Do not hog the guide**
  By all means take the opportunity to learn from your guide by asking questions…but be careful not to hog his/her attention at the expense of the other guests.

- **Be prepared**
  Do try to be self-sufficient in terms of binoculars, storage cards, warm clothing, sunblock, bottled water etc.

- **Talk quietly** (rather than whisper) – as much so that the other participants can enjoy the outdoor experience as not to disturb the wildlife. Do not whistle or bang on the vehicle to attract an animal's attention – this is very poor form!

- **Advice for smokers**
  Don't automatically assume that because you are in the great outdoors that your smoking habit will not bother the other passengers. Try to be considerate and request a 'smoke' break/stop – perhaps while the others are taking their 'comfort' break. And please DO NOT leave your cigarette ends stomped into the dirt – put them in your pocket and dispose of them when you get back to camp.

- **Advice for families**
  If you are a family with small children, be aware that others in the vehicle may not think that little Johnny's antics are very conducive to an enjoyable safari! Where possible it is always advisable to arrange, or at least request, the sole use of a safari vehicle if you have a family with young children.

Safety on safari

Safety concerns in Africa tend to take multiple forms – from inherent caution and fear of the wildlife (both big and small) to your own physical safety from thieves, thugs and the unscrupulous - and on to diseases, plagues and parasites!

The Read This Before You Go chapter deals with issues of personal safety and infectious diseases, but perhaps some discussion on whether it is safe to be out there with all those wild animals might just help to put your mind at ease…

The first thing to remember is that everything out there is actually scared of you! The likelihood of being 'attacked' is extremely small. More to the point, animals don't 'lie in wait' to attack any unsuspecting human that passes by – I promise! Incidents do happen though, and most of these can be attributed to an animal having been 'surprised' or perhaps aggravated by the victim's actions. If you surprise any animal at close quarters you leave them with just two choices – flee or attack (fight or flight). Most often they will flee, but on occasion they will attack, and sometimes they are just fleeing in your direction! Buffalo bulls and black rhino require little provocation – and are seldom just putting on a show (mock charging). Luckily, their eyesight is not all that good and they will generally need to scent you first - which means you need to keep an eye (or damp finger) on which way the wind is blowing! Lion and elephant on the other hand, will almost always 'mock' charge a standing threat - the rules change if you start to run! You noticed the use of the words – almost always, didn't you? Well, you see, female elephants (and lions for that matter) with little ones tend to be more irritable and protective by nature – so with elephants it is always a good idea to keep your distance around family groups with females and small calves. Lionesses too will protect small cubs with real commitment. Feeling better? Probably not. I only mean to caution you when it comes to wildlife – these are wild animals and should be treated with respect (and from a respectable distance!).

Secondly - given the opportunity, most animals will offer clear signals that they are feeling threatened or uncomfortable – try to read the signs. Your guide will recognize these signs and act appropriately. But should you see that an animal is obviously agitated and acting aggressively, be sure to draw your guide's attention to the fact. Wild animals are extremely wary of a physical encounter, both with other animals and especially with humans (defense of their offspring being the exception). They cannot afford the risk of injuring themselves and will avoid a confrontation if at all possible. That should give you some reassurance at least...

Do not be scared if an animal moves toward you – they can be inquisitive at times too! Lions are insatiably curious and will often come through a newly established camp to see what is going on. Buffalo, when part of a herd, will sometimes move toward your vehicle out of sheer curiosity. Elephants, used to getting their own way, regularly advance toward the vehicle (often in a threatening manner) – only to register a very 'put out' expression when the object of its annoyance (the vehicle) fails to yield!

A quote from an 'old Africa hand' about the Cape buffalo, considered the most dangerous of the Big5, is worth noting: *"Buffalo rank among the most dangerous of all wild game when wounded (or threatened) and can rarely be halted except by a fatal or disabling bullet. Unmolested, however, the buffalo is not an unduly aggressive animal, and is by nature placid and peacefully disposed."* - Charles Maberley – The Game Animals of Southern Africa 1963.

Lastly, let me just say that if you hear alarming sounds in the night – stay in your tent. You are safest there. If you feel you are in immediate danger yourself use the whistle/horn provided to alert your guide or camp staff (and wait until they come to check on you).

A Warning:

All wild animals are unpredictable, and should always be shown the appropriate respect. Many animals, including elephant, are temperamental despite their apparently tranquil and peaceful demeanour. Listen to the instructions of your guide at all times and resist the impulse to flee at the first opportunity - unless advised to do so by your guide.

Your safari guide

Your guide is probably *the* most important single factor in ensuring that your safari is an enjoyable and interesting experience. A good guide will without doubt make all the difference in ensuring that you get the most out of your safari. A good guide needs to be many things: your host, your teacher, your driver, your mechanic, your encyclopedia of knowledge, your first aid nurse, and your friend in a foreign land.

Being a guide might look to be 'The Life' but it is far more demanding than it would at first appear. Added to the intense pressure of dealing with people ALL day, the hours are also long - up before dawn and to bed after the last guest. A great deal of time is spent away from family and friends with little opportunity to exercise (going for a run is generally discouraged!) or to de-stress. Time off is infrequent and irregular, especially in the high season. That said - most guides wouldn't even consider doing anything else!

So what makes an exceptional guide?

"They have an in-depth knowledge of mammals, rock art, plants, African history and culture, conservation issues, geology, reptiles, fish, insects and astronomy, apart from human skills. They make life-long friends with most of the clients through this common bond of nature's uncomplicated and diverse beauty, enhanced by unorchestrated experiences." Garth Thompson, A Guide's Guide to Guiding

Guide styles

The standard and style of guiding throughout Africa can differ from camp to camp and from country to country. Each country has its own training and licensing requirements to qualify to become a guide. This can lead to differing standards and levels of qualification. In some countries guides trained to walk with guests are a feature whilst in others the guiding is limited to game drive vehicles. Canoeing, rafting and climbing guides are localized and separate again. You may have a single guide throughout or a series of guides as you move from location to location. As a generalization, in East Africa it is most likely that you will have a driver/guide who stays with you throughout your safari. This is also the case on a mobile safari or a special interest (e.g. photographic or birding) tour too. In southern Africa (and at certain camps/lodges in East Africa) each lodge or safari camp will have their own complement of guides, and so you will encounter a number of individual guides throughout your safari.

There is also a wide range of personal guiding styles, from brash and macho to quiet and reflective. Although good guide training attempts to temper such extremes, these traits are just part of each individual's personality. They are trained to deal with your idiosyncrasies – do your best to work with theirs, after all, we all have good and bad days!

Individual guides will also have their own areas of expertise or special interest – birds, reptiles or trees perhaps. Some may even have studied a single species – elephant or giraffe for example, and be the recognized expert on the subject. Others are expert trackers and are a wealth of knowledge about animal spore (tracks and signs). I know of one guide who conducts "sound safaris" with the help of a directional microphone and headset! Listen and learn.

The tourism industry is also welcoming more and more female guides too (admittedly not that many so far). Not having to be a 'macho' guy, female guides are often more attentive and in tune with guest's needs.

In the main, and as a consequence of the inherent friendliness of the African people, nearly all the safari guides you will encounter are fantastic – eager to show you their small patch of Africa and willing and able to hunt down the birds, animals and landscapes that you have read so much about. They have both a passion for the wilds of Africa and the knowledge borne of experience.

How to help your guide:

- When you arrive, let your guide know whether you have been to Africa before, where you have been on your safari so far, what you have seen to date, what your specific interests might be, what type of activities you prefer - walking, game drives, canoe/mokoro etc. This will give your guide some essential background information and allow him/her to take these facts into account when introducing you to their particular piece of wilderness.

- Ask questions – this helps the guide to get a feel for where your interests lie and alleviates the need for him/her to 'fill in the silence'.

- Try to get to know your guide as a person – ask about their family, home town, training and background. Take the opportunity to engage with them on a more personal level. Whilst they might love what they do, like us all, they have a whole different side to their lives that you might find equally as fascinating.

- Perhaps the most important thing of all - be enthusiastic. Your enthusiasm is what brings out the best in your guide!

- Listen to the instructions of your guide at those crucial times when the situation requires judgement and experience – they are in the best position to make a decision for your group. Not following instructions may well put everyone in danger.

- If on a walking safari (or other adventure-orientated activity including canoeing, mokoro trails or horse riding), be sure to stay in single file behind your guide, keep together as a group, pay attention to your guide's instructions, try to keep quiet and do not distract the guide unless he/she has stopped to address the group.

An old safari joke: *If you see your guide run, try to keep up!*

How to help yourself:

- Ask in advance about what you might need before going out on a drive, walk or other activity (a warm jacket, walking shoes or water-proofs by way of example).

- Try to be READY to go out at the agreed time so that you are not rushing or holding up your group, and so that you get the most time 'on safari' as you possibly can.

- If your guide gets too close to an animal – make him/her aware that you are uncomfortable with the situation and ask him to back-up (either on foot or in a vehicle).

- If you are apprehensive about an activity you are about to embark on – let your guide know so that he/she can keep your concerns in mind and 'guide' you through the early stages.

- Do not be afraid to ask about matters of safety – can you walk around camp at night? What should you do if an elephant is standing outside your tent? Ask away…

- Refrain from encouraging your guide to disturb an animal or manipulate a situation to allow you a better photo opportunity. This not only places the guide in an awkward position, but more often than not, such 'forced' animal behaviour does not pay dividends in the viewfinder.

- Be prepared to be out longer than anticipated - you might get a sighting of particular interest toward the end of your drive which might mean staying out for that extra hour or two. Enjoy it (and don't feel bound by meal times).

- If your guide is driving too fast or the (inter-camp) radio is too loud – politely let your feelings be known. The radio can be especially annoying if used too frequently or left on too loud. You are the guest and if you find it is spoiling your enjoyment you are –perfectly entitled to bring it up with the guide (or the camp manager). No use being shy.

- When you have seen enough lions (and it may happen!); suggest to your guide that you set out with a different objective in mind – hyena, serval or buffalo perhaps. The reason I say this is that most guides will at some point fall into the habit of focusing almost exclusively on the one thing that everyone coming to Africa wants to see – LION. This can develop into a never-ending cycle of 'lion lust'. This is not good – not for your safari - nor for your guide's job satisfaction or guiding skills.

So as you go from camp to camp on safari, and meet different guides, be sure to keep these suggestions in mind and you will definitely get more out of your safari.

The difference between a safari guide and a driver/guide

I do not want to make too much of this distinction as I would not want to be thought disparaging toward one or the other of these professionals, but I do think that it might be helpful to understand the essential difference between a trained/licensed *safari guide*, and what is often termed a '*driver/guide*'.

The driver/guide is more common in East Africa than other parts of Africa, and is employed to transport visitors on their safari itinerary - to be their driver. But they are also the guide when they get to their destination - the desired National Park for example. The aptitude required of a driver/guide is based more on experience than qualifications. He/she needs to know how to get from A to B to C and how to get around that area when they get there. The required level of knowledge of the animals and birds needs to be thorough without being exceptional. Good eyesight is a bonus, and being a people person essential. They are generally not required to perform the role of host in the evenings or at meal times.

A licensed professional safari guide seeks to be not only licensed by an official body, but to strive to advance his/her knowledge by obtaining higher qualification levels throughout his/her career. Depth of knowledge becomes a hallmark, often together with a specialisation - birds, trees or elephant for example. Safari guides will either travel with their guests (as a private guide) or be based at a safari camp/lodge where they can become experts on that particular area. They guide their guests but will often additionally take on the role of host (especially in the case of mobile tented safari guides).

I often think that the essential difference between a driver and a guide as the amount of time that that person spends with their guests - in other words, how much social skills and people skills (and knowledge) they need to have to be with a group of people 24/7, for up to two weeks at a stretch. Yes, guiding is about knowledge, but it is also about people management - management of their expectations, having the required patience, confidence and congeniality.

Safari activity options

The tourism industry has developed a range of activities for you to choose from while on your African safari. If you are not already aware of the different options it might be useful for you to know something about them at the start. I have placed them into three broad categories - thrill seeking, active and passive.

Thrill seeking

If thrills are what you are after then you have the choice of bungi-jumping, a gorge swing, flying-fox and the high-wire (all available at Victoria Falls and other adventure locations), along with jet boating on the Zambezi River, abseiling on Table Mountain in Cape Town or diving with Great White Sharks.

For those who would like to ride an elephant, walk with lions or stroke a cheetah these options are available too at some destinations, but generally outside of the main reserves.

Active

For the active or adventure orientated you can canoe down the Zambezi (either above the Victoria Falls or on the Lower Zambezi), pole a mokoro in the Okavango Delta, get wet white-water-rafting or river-boarding below the Victoria Falls or on the Nile, go horse-riding (offered in most countries) or experience a guided walking safari. Please note that all of these activities are only recommended when under the tutelage of an experienced and licensed professional guide, who may need to carry a weapon for your protection.

Passive

For the more sedate there is the standard game drive (by day and by night) together with Hot Air Balloon rides (Serengeti/Masai Mara, Loisaba, Namib or Pilanesberg, South Africa), sunset cruises (Lake Kariba, Chobe, Okavango, Lake Malawi and Victoria Falls), scenic flights (over the Victoria Falls, Okavango Delta or Namib desert and elsewhere), time spent viewing animals in specially constructed hides or perhaps historical lectures on the Battlefields of Natal. There is also a range of fishing opportunities in a selection of locations along the Zambezi River, the Okavango Delta, Lake Victoria and along the east and west coasts from Cape Point to Malindi in Kenya. Not to be forgotten are village and school visits within the nearby communities – always fascinating and a great way to meet the people.

There is one other opportunity that I believe you should not miss, and that is a visit to a wildlife orphanage or sanctuary. There are a number of extremely well run orphanages where wild animals, who have been found deserted or injured, are taken in and cared for. These sanctuaries save many animals from human cruelty and serve as both a research facility and a centre for education. In some cases, unfortunately not all, these rescued animals are later returned to the wild after a period of convalescence. Both these lucky few, and those that remain, provide invaluable research data that offers us a better understanding each of these animal's feeding habits, life cycle and idiosyncrasies. Many orphanages also involve themselves with endangered species breeding programs and are good places to see, among others, cheetah, rhino and even wild dog along with seldom seen nocturnal species like porcupines, honey badgers and civets. Here you will not only see a range of Africa's wildlife, which you might otherwise not have the opportunity to encounter, but also to learn about them from the dedicated staff who run these much needed institutions.

So what types of activities are available 'on safari'?

Each of the activities listed below should go a long way to enhancing your safari experience – grab the opportunity with both hands.

- **Game drives and guided walks**
  Nothing new here....but I couldn't leave out either of these now could I? After all, this is how most of you will experience your safari – either from the back of a game drive vehicle or, where available, on a walk with a qualified guide.

Game drives, in either open or closed (with pop-top) 4x4 vehicles are pretty much standard fare on all safaris – either as a shared experience with other camp guests or with your own driver/guide in a private vehicle.

Guided walks are generally also available from most camps and lodges where walking is allowed. Here I am specifically excluding walking trails which I will deal with in a separate post – *10 top walking destinations in Africa.*

They say that going on a game drive is like going to see the movie, but that taking a guided walk is like reading the book. Actually, I don't know if anyone ever said that, but I think you get the idea. Walking is more about the smaller things (and the big things look even bigger on foot!).

Most walking on safari is done in the mornings with an armed (and licensed) guide, and generally for only a couple of hours as an activity option. Be warned: some walks offered are really only nature walks and are conducted in close proximity to camp or within its. There are also walking trails and trails camps. In recent times the true walking trail, where you walk from camp to camp, has been dumbed-down somewhat and now mostly consists of a walking camp, from where the main focus of the safari is on walking (although game drives are also offered). Very few true walking trails remain. A slight variation is the fabulously down-to-earth walking safaris in Laikipia and Loita Hills in Kenya, where all your overnight camping gear is transported by a string of camels (or mules) and local Maasai guides escort you across the open savannah – very cool.

Speak with an Africa travel specialist about the type of walking safari you are looking for.

- **Canoeing / kayaking / rafting / mokoro**

Any of these options should be definitely be considered by the more adventurous among you – each offers a totally unique wildlife experience; gliding silently downstream, navigating the channels and open water in search of wildlife, great birding, open skies and stunning sunsets. What's not to like?

Although canoe safaris are offered on the Zambezi River above the Victoria Falls, it is the Lower Zambezi (below Kariba dam) that is the home of the most exhilarating multi-day canoe safaris – from participatory (putting up your own tent, helping with food preparation) through to luxury camping (large tents and serviced – waiter/cook and camp staff). This is an exciting adventure activity that I highly recommend although you will need to overcome any apprehension about crocodiles and hippos beforehand! All canoe safaris are guided by experienced river guides and incidents are few and far between.

Kayaking and rafting are not your standard safari activity it must be said…but you can kayak down the Orange River in South Africa or raft the Kunene River in Namibia, so I felt it warranted a mention…and if you are visiting the Victoria Falls, the white-water rafting there is some of the best in the world – compulsory! (also available on the Nile near Jinja).

If it's a mokoro (dugout canoe) we must be talking the Okavango Delta, the only place that uses these traditional dugout canoes (although you might see something similar in Chobe and possibly in parts of Zambia or along the Zambezi). The mokoro is usually 'poled' along by an experienced 'poler' who needs to know his way around the maze of channels…don't miss out.

- **Boating (including houseboats)**
  Wherever you find water you will find motor boats and boating activities on offer. Whilst boats are sometimes only used to transport guests to/from camp, many safari operators offer game

viewing by boat (Okavango Delta, Selous GR, Lake Kariba, and the
Zambezi River to name a few). It offers a whole new perspective
and will often allow you to get a lot closer to the wildlife than in a
vehicle or on foot.

I will also include houseboats here too – a fabulous alternative
accommodation option that allows you to live on the water and
find overnight locations well tucked away – a couple of the best
locations being Lake Kariba in Zimbabwe and on the Chobe River
in the far north of Botswana (& Namibia).

- **Balloon Safaris**
  In my humble opinion, some of the VERY best locations to enjoy a
  balloon ride are on safari; whether it be over the vast open grass
  plains of the Masai Mara and Serengeti, or above the sand dunes of
  the Namib desert in Namibia, or the remote wilderness of the
  Busanga Plains in the far north of Kafue National Park in Zambia,
  or over the lush waters of the Okavango Delta in Botswana! Don't
  miss out.

- **Horse Riding**
  If you are an avid horse rider, or even a competent weekender, to
  be able to get up close to some of Africa's wildlife (elephant, lion,
  giraffe, buffalo, zebra etc) on horseback is possibly the ultimate
  thrill. If this is your fancy, you will need to seek out an established
  horseback safari operator with well-schooled horses and
  experienced guides. Good locations include the Okavango Delta in
  Botswana, Laikipia, Chyulu Hills & Masai Mara in Kenya, Kwa-
  Zulu Natal, Kruger and the Cape region in South Africa, and at a
  number of lodges in Tanzania & Mozambique.

- **Microlight and Helicopter Flights**
  Whilst on safari you may transfer between camps by small charter
  planes (e.g. Okavango Delta) or between game reserves (Samburu
  to Masai Mara in Kenya for example). These flights offer a
  wonderful view of these regions from the air and you should
  always have your camera at the ready (fast shutter speed, min

1/500, and a polarising filter if you have one). But if the opportunity arises, I can strongly recommend a microlight flight (from the Zambian side at Victoria Falls) or a flip in a helicopter (available by prior arrangement throughout the Okavango Delta in Botswana)…or you can arrange a complete helicopter itinerary along the Great Rift valley in Kenya. Going aerial will certainly offer some truly stunning photographic opportunities and an exhilarating experience.

- **Quad bikes & Mountain biking**
  You might think there would not be place for either of these on safari – but you would be wrong! In certain locations quad bikes come into their own and are a wonderful experience – for example: on the Makgadikgadi Pans in Botswana quad bikes are the best way to get right out onto the pans and experience the remoteness and isolation of this region. Some of the Kalahari game reserves in Namibia also offer quad bike trails as a game drive, and in Swakopmund and Walvis Bay you can arrange for quad biking adventures in the nearby dunes, whilst in Laikapia quad bikes are an activity option at some lodges.

  Only a few game reserves offer mountain biking, usually with an armed ranger/guide: these include South Luangwa in Zambia, Mashatu in Botswana, Mihingo Lodge at Lake Mburo in Uganda, and on a number of private reserves in the Eastern Cape in South Africa.

- **Field Guide & Wildlife Courses**
  If you are passionate about Africa's wilderness & wildlife you may want to consider undertaking a field guide's course. A number of training organisations in South Africa have started courses of various lengths – for both trainee guides and overseas visitors. Learn about the vast biodiversity to be found in the African bush, the elements that make up the ecology and varying ecosystems, and how they affect and interrelate with each other. Through a series of daily lectures and practical activities in the field you will built up

your knowledge and experience…and you can even work towards an industry qualification (FGSA accredited courses). Courses range from 2 to 6 months for field guide courses and 7 to 14 days for a general bush skills course.

In addition, some safari operators have encouraged their regular clients to join their own annual 'guide training exercises' conducted at their respective camp/lodge e.g. Chiawa Camp in Zambia and Alex Walker in Kenya & Tanzania. Ask your Africa travel specialist.

- **Sound Safaris**
  I'm just going to put this out there. This is something rather unique…but I only know one person who has ever offered this (take note safari operators!) - an old Africa-hand by the name of Derek Solomon.

  It is what it sounds like (pun intended): everyone in the vehicle gets to put on a set of headphones and Derek uses a parabolic microphone to capture, and explain, the different sounds of the bush around you. Can you imagine…your guide picks up a call, swings the microphone in that direction - it's a leopard's rasping cough; you listen through your headphones to the amplified sound as clear as if it were sitting next to you! Wow. Or picture yourself, sitting quietly after dark, listening to the eerie night sounds all around you - trying to work out which nightjar it might be, which are crickets and which frogs…and then, wait, what was that? Brilliant.

- **Photo Workshops**
  We all love to take photos on safari, whether it be with our phones or using the latest high tech DSLR….and we could all do with a bit of help if truth be told (not you of course!). So if getting better wildlife photos on safari is something you want to focus on, then a photo workshop is the answer. Generally ranging from 4 days to 2 weeks (photographic tour), and accompanied by a professional photographer, these workshops offer practical photographic advice

and an opportunity to review and improve your skills whilst enjoying all the attractions of being on safari.

You will notice that I have not included activities such as elephant-back riding or walking-with-lions. There are good reasons for this – simply: it is wrong (on so many levels). Whilst I do understand that people have a strong urge to get up close and personal (touch and feel) with large, dangerous animals it is, in my opinion, disrespectful, demeaning and misguided. The animals may appear well cared for, in good health and treated well but you have to ask yourself – should they be in captivity at all? Where do they come from? Where are they sent once they get too big or too difficult to handle? Wouldn't they be better off in the wild? Don't forget, that it is your dollars that are creating this 'tourist attraction' and once such attractions are created, and patrons pay a fee to experience them, the whole thing becomes a money making enterprise and ethics often take a back seat. It is also interesting that more recently Botswana has banned outright the practice of elephant back rides and that TripAdvisor will no longer showcase any suppliers who run unsustainable animal activities, including elephant rides and lion petting.

This is a pet issue of mine…but I will leave it there for now! Sorry.

I should also mention that, whilst there are a good many activity options possible on safari, not all safari camps/lodges can offer more than a small selection – mostly due to location, nature of the activity, or Park regulations. If you like the idea of any of these you need to raise this with your Africa travel specialist in the planning stages.

I have only talked about activities that are offered when 'on safari' and thus I have not included scenic flights over the Victoria Falls or dhow cruises off the islands in Mozambique or Zanzibar. Nor have I included 'birding' which should be on everyone's activity list on safari…and can usually be done whether walking, on game drive or ANY of the other activities listed. And yes, I am unrepentant in encouraging all of you going to Africa to take up birding – and the pursuit of our amazing feathered friends.

Safari camps vs. lodges vs. bush camps & fly-camps

"We act as though comfort and luxury were the chief requirements of life, when all that we need to make us happy is something to be enthusiastic about." – Charles Kingsley, priest, university professor, historian and novelist.

Although I realise that your itinerary has already been set, it may be helpful for you to know what to expect from the different accommodation styles.

One of the great things about going on safari is the camps and lodges in which you will stay. There is nothing quite like a traditional safari camp in the wilds of Africa for that feeling of remoteness, exclusivity and excitement. In fact, the safari camps and lodges are a big part of what it means to be on safari – that raw excitement and feeling of being in Africa. I guarantee you will love them.

So what different accommodation styles can you expect?

Putting aside the hotels and guest houses found in the main tourist hubs and cities, the types of accommodation on safari tend to fall into five broad categories:

- **Luxury Safari Camp/Lodge** - this is a category that has evolved more recently with many of the new safari camps/lodges being built, and those undergoing extensive re-design. These newer properties, at the higher end of the market, are moving away from traditional safari 'styles' and more reflect the influence of city architects and interior designers. These lodges will more likely have glass sliding doors, bath tubs, twin basins, indoor and outdoor showers, 5 star fittings, elaborate fabrics and decor, air conditioning and possibly design 'features' or 'themes' - a distinct shift away traditional canvas, reeds, grass and other natural materials. These properties are clearly aimed to provide an ever higher specification of luxury than previously existed (with appropriate pricing). I am not necessarily a big fan, but the wealthier guest appears to want this (so I'm told)#.

- **Safari lodge** – generally built of brick and mortar (or stone), with thatched or tiled roofs, luxuriously fitted bedrooms with en suite bathrooms (perhaps even an outside shower), plus a main dining/lounge area including a bar and deck (and possibly a library and air conditioning).

- **Safari camp** – these tend to have large walk-in, walk-around tents either under thatch or canvas fly-sheet and shade-cloth, comfortable beds and en suite bathrooms (including flush toilets and hot and cold running water) with a central lounge/dining area as above (but usually have fewer rooms than a lodge).

- **Bush camp (or mobile tented camp)** – either erected for a particular safari or as seasonal camp (dry season only) such camps are generally made of local materials (timber, grass and reeds) or are tented (mobile). They can be very elaborate in the form of 'silver-service' with large East African luxury tents and en suite bathroom, or more modest with comfortable beds, linen and a bedside table with toilets and showers often shared. Most mobile safaris now offer at least a chemical toilet attached to the tent so that guests do not have to venture out at night. Some bush camps will have a central dining tent but many merely have the dining table under a shady tree and a set of chairs around the camp fire.
  Zambia has in the past had a reputation for its rustic bush camps which, in my opinion, are some of the most appealing safari camps to be found anywhere (but are unfortunately starting to disappear or be 'upgraded').
  Ditto mobile tented camps erected for the few days of your stay (and totally removed once you are gone…to leave not a trace of your having being there at all).

- **Fly camp** – a much simpler, bare basics tented camp setup - camp beds, bedroll or sleeping bag, no en suite and without the luxury of being able to stand up in your tent, washstand and hot water bucket shower.

All of the above, with the exception of the fly camp, would provide crisp linen, blankets or duvets, bedside lighting, hanging and shelf space, shower, wash basin and toilet. Many have a writing desk/dressing table, towel rail and luggage rack.

I confess to liking my creature comforts as much as the next person, but I am saddened that the experience of being on safari is being compromised by ever more luxurious accommodation offerings. There seems more of a disconnect in the need of ever more luxurious safari camps, thereby losing the simplicity intrinsic to being outdoors and close to nature! To a safari purist, this trend detracts from what I believe it actually means to 'go on safari' - the pleasure in immersing yourself in the natural world - all in the name of luxury (and presumably, to justify charging ever larger sums of money for the pleasure).

On the upside, there is definite move toward more sustainable practices within the safari industry in general - from entirely solar-powered camps (for both lighting, hot water and back-of-house) to more environmentally-friendly waste disposal systems and the use of recycled materials. Some camps/lodges have even installed cooling systems, run on solar power, that offer a cool breeze over your bed to help you sleep at night at those times of year when the heat can be stifling - far more environmentally friendly than air conditioning!

"We act as though comfort and luxury were the chief requirements of life, when all that we need to make us really happy is something to be enthusiastic about" Charles Kingsley (writer 1811–1875)

Wellness & Health Spas

In recent years the concept of health spas and wellness centres has begun to spring up throughout the safari industry. The traditional African safari has been redefined (or refined!). No more the heat, sweat and dust of an untamed wilderness. Now you can succumb to the ultimate temptation of a health spa after a particular gruelling day on safari, or get those taut muscles massaged after a long flight – sheer heaven. Don't miss out.

What else you can expect on safari..

Food & Wine

Although you will certainly be well fed on safari you should be careful to be realistic in your expectations. Many of the camps and lodges that you will stay in are remote, with the nearest shops many miles away. Electricity, if there is any at all, is usually supplied via a generator which operates only a certain number of hours each day. Refrigeration is a constant battle and ice is a prized commodity. Camp and lodge staff are kept on their toes by baboons, hyena and mice (amongst others) who raid the pantry whenever possible, and cannot be 'disciplined' because this is a National Park and we are the intruders! The chefs generally do not have any insight into the latest food styles or the more fashionable culinary techniques you have back home. You are unlikely to see Japanese sushi, a good hearty Tom Ka Gai or Singapore noodles on your safari (although many of the more established lodges are really stepping up to the plate – pun intended!). Having said that – you will be surprised with what comes out of a true bush kitchen – with only a cold box and a naked fire to cook on!

Most hotels in the main centres offer bed and breakfast rates, whilst safari lodges, camps and country hotels generally offer full-board rates with full English breakfast, a buffet lunch and three/four course dinner, with teas and coffee served between main meals. It is quite unlikely that you will go hungry while on safari!

Africa (outside of the Cape Province in South Africa) is not renowned for its wine! If you are on the lookout for an aged Semillon or a delicate Pinot Noir, you have come to the wrong place! But do not despair – the excellent wines from South Africa are generally available in most tourist hotels and safari lodges throughout Africa. And if you are going to Cape Town, do not miss out on a tour through the winelands – the wine is fabulous, the scenery stunning and the restaurants – some of the best on the continent.

Then of course there is the humble G&T (gin and tonic), a throwback to colonial days and now a tradition at the end of a long day on safari!

Beer is another story altogether...

If you are anything like me you will surely crave a cold lusty lager at the end of a dry and dusty day on safari! No soapy Bitter here I'm afraid – although, surprisingly enough, Guinness is the favoured beer in Nigeria of all places!

Most African countries are quite parochial about their local brew, and since you are away from home you really should kick-start an appreciation for the local beverage yourself. Here are some to look out for:

- Mozambique – 2M, Manica & Laurentina

- Kenya – Tusker & Summit lager

- Tanzania – Safari Lager & Kilimanjaro

- Uganda – Nile Special Lager & Bell lager

- Botswana – St Louis

- Zambia – Mosi

- Zimbabwe – Zambezi Lager, Bolinger & Castle Pilsener

- South Africa – Castle, Lion Lager, Hansa Pilsner, Amstel, Heineken, Millers and Windhoek Draught

- Nigeria – Star Lager, Heiniken & Guinness

- Cameroon – '33' Export & King Beer

- Ghana – Star Beer & Club Beer

- Ethiopia – Harar Beer & Bati Beer

- Egypt – Stella Export Lager

- Namibia – Windhoek (pronounced "vinthook") & Tafel (pronounced "Tah Phil")

Always remember: *"Beer is proof that God loves us and wants us to be happy"* – Benjamin Franklin

Tea & Coffee

Another beverage you should definitely keep your eye out for is the local tea and coffee – it can be superb. Kenya, Tanzania, Uganda, Ethiopia* and Zimbabwe all boast quality products, with their reputations now growing internationally. The coffee has been described as "robust and long on after-taste. Just like Africa, really".

Rooibos tea (literally 'red bush' in Afrikaans), is a native bush of South Africa with many, much celebrated, health benefits and growing worldwide acclaim.

That said – the local safari industry itself has not (as yet) caught on to the vast array of specialty coffee alternatives you will have become used to in Europe, North America or Australia. You might find your request for a 'flat white' or mocha light frapuccino gets you a somewhat bemused look in most safari camps and lodges!

* Ethiopia is of course where *Coffea arabica*, the coffee plant, originates. According to legend, a 9th-century goat herder discovered the coffee plant after noticing the energizing effect the plant had on his flock. Today, Ethiopia itself accounts for around 3% of the global coffee market and it is an important commodity to the economy of Ethiopia.

Meat & Veg

Venison (game meat) is also something you should try if the opportunity arises - leaner and richer-tasting than farmed meat and naturally low in cholesterol although it can be tough unless properly prepared (the tenderising is done by marinating the meat for anything from 24 hours to 3 days!). In the right hands, venison has been described as sublime, and both tender and distinctly flavoured. Beef, pork and fish are commonplace. Lamb and mutton less so. Green salads and cooked and raw vegetables are also a feature.

Vegetarians should not despair either – most camps/lodges are quite used to, and capable of, offering vegetarian meals.

Likewise, most dietary requirements where allergies and other preferences are an issue, can all be catered for if notified in advance.

Shopping & Buying tips

Africa is not your duty free destination of choice, but apart from the obvious curio-type goods, keep a look out for some of these great African products (in no particular order):

- **Amarula** – a delicious (and intoxicating) creamy liqueur made from the fruit of the Marula tree (an African version of Bailey's Irish Cream). The Marula tree, a member of the same family as the mango, grows widely in the wild in southern Africa. Its sweet, yellow fruit is used for making jam, wine, beer, and this liqueur.

- **Wines of the Cape**, South Africa.

- Kenyan, Tanzanian, Zimbabwean or Ugandan **tea and coffee**.

- **Kikoi** – originating from the east coast of Africa (specifically Kenya) these colourful rectangular 'wraps' are made from the finest 100% cotton grown in the region. With a stunning array of vibrant (coastal) colours, a Kikoi is a fashion statement of its own.

- **Kanga** – a piece of colourful cloth generally worn by women in East Africa from chest to knees. Kanga's were originally created in the late 19th Century by sewing together six printed handkerchiefs, or lenco's, which were traded from the Portuguese. The word Kanga is the Kiswahili word for guinea fowl, the spotted plumage of which were reminiscent of the early cloths.

- In Mozambique, the **lenco** (here a head scarf) is worn with the **quimau**, a tailored blouse, and a **capulana**, a wrap around dress (or sarong).

- **Maasai shuka** - worn by most Maasai & Samburu men, with striped/check patterns and colours (mainly red, black and blue) – Kenya & Tanzania.

- West African fabrics including **Kente cloth.**

- **Wire art** – mostly of animals (but I have a unique wire saxophone!).

- **Wildlife and landscape paintings** – available in many curio shops and on the side of the road.

- **Carvings & sculptures** (both wooden and stone) – vary greatly in quality and design and are a unique African memento. The wooden giraffe is a favourite but you can purchase masks, salad servers, collapsible tables, book ends, bowls and a vast range of sculptures. The Shona stone carvings from Zimbabwe are especially sought after with their ethnic styles and use of native stone including verdite, rapocco and soapstone.

- Spears, shields, walking sticks and African drums (be sure to check import regulations when returning home).

- **Tanzanite** – a rare gem from the foothills of Mt. Kilimanjaro (violet blue in colour).

- **Music** from west and North Africa particularly.

- **African bead work, pottery, basketry and batiks.** Both art and craft, they combine technical skill, knowledge of materials and creativity to produce forms that are simultaneously practical and graceful, utilitarian and beautiful - a genuine piece of African culture. If travelling through Botswana be sure to look out for woven mohair rugs and wall hangings with designs depicting African tribal life – my favourite.

- SAY NO TO IVORY (and other animal products).

Entertainment on safari

Entertainment (as you know it) is a little light on safari – there certainly will be no TV or internet beamed into your tent! In its place you will have the privilege of experiencing some of Africa's more unique (tongue-in-cheek) entertainment options:

On the Breakfast Show

Lying awake at first light you can tune in to the early breakfast show featuring the melodious sounds of a nearby coucal or the distant drumming of a ground hornbill. Listen for the grunts and splashes that greet the Hippo's return to the nearby river - or perhaps pick up the roar of a lion calling or the rasping cough of a leopard near camp or the alarm bark of an impala or baboon. Yes, you will hear all of these, but for the discerning I venture you will take home a selection of 'not so expected' sounds – like the approach of feet in the pre-dawn as your hot water arrives at your tent, or the sound of "knock knock" outside your tent indicating the arrival of tea, or even the distinctive sound of tent zippers being opened – and if you are really lucky, the frantic shouts of "come quickly...look...over there, over there – lion/shumba/simba!"...

African Idol

Africa has many fine song birds and boasts an array of wonderful duets. For sheer showmanship you can't beat the dramatic twists and turns of the Lilac Breasted Roller as it performs its aerobatic rolls over the savannah or the 'strut your stuff' showiness of the luxuriant Crowned Crane. Watch for the desperate efforts of the disorientated firefly as it flits along trying desperately to attract a mate, glowing intermittently in the darkness! The Fish Eagle is in a separate category entirely with its iconic call - possibly one of the most recognized calls throughout Africa and one which has become symbolic of the African wilderness. And then there is the humble Marabou Stork – now there's a bird with a make-up malfunction!

On the Catwalk

Take one look at a flock of flamingos (all dressed in 'hot pink') as they strut their stuff and you will know what's hot and what's not!

Flower Power

Africa is shy when it comes to putting on a flower show but at certain times of the year stunning sprays of flowers bedeck the bush – from the deep maroon of the Sausage Tree (*Kigelia Africana*) with its bell-shaped, velvety-textured flowers that hang down in sprays to the spring flower extravaganza of Namaqualand and the Karoo in South Africa.

The All Africa Games

If there is one game that is universal throughout Africa, it is the board game known as either bao, zoro, or wari (part of the mancala family of games). Bao is the Swahili for wood, referring to the board on which it is played and which are available in markets throughout Africa (and make a wonderful souvenier). The board has four rows of eight round 'cups'. Each player owns half of the board – two rows each and receives 32 'counters' (these can be stones, shells or whatever comes to hand).The game involves moving the counters around the board until your opponent can no longer move. It is a relatively simple game to learn and play – ask a local to show you how.

African Opera

When night falls and you are sitting out in the African wilderness – stop for a moment and you will be treated to the sounds of an African opera. Alongside the percussion of the scops owlet comes the bass sound of a distant lion roar followed by the high pitched tempo of the hyena, and joined by the sharp resonant cries of the jackal...

accompanied by the constant peal of frogs and crickets. Stop for a moment and listen.

Ballet

There is no other way to describe the exuberance of the dance-like 'pronking' of the springbok...or the leaping kick of an impala - the ballerinas of the bush.

Art Galleries

Part of being on safari is just about the thrill of being outdoors, away from the skyscrapers that blot out the sun and into a living tapestry of panoramic colour. Not much can better an African sunset, or the distinctive shape of a baobab tree silhouetted against the horizon, or the outline of a giraffe as it walks gracefully in front of the setting sun.

Find out more about Africa's intriguing Rock Art in a later section...here depictions of animals and hunters etched on cave walls for generations to enjoy.

Circus Acts

The bird life too, will thrill you with a variety of avian aerobatics...including the daunting skill demonstrated by the endangered African Skimmer as it swims just centimetres above the surface of the river, with its lower mandible slicing through the water just beneath the surface, only to close shut as it scoops up an unsuspecting fish as it rises to the surface to feed. Or you may be lucky to be treated to the sudden and alarming appearance of a Bat Hawk, in the wee hours of dawn or last light of day, as it scythes through the air panicking the bats that in turn have come out to feed on flying insects...

The Night Life

If you think it is hectic out there during the day – boy, you should see what goes on at night. Africa after dark can get busy! Out of every tree and hole in the ground comes some form of bird or animal – there are over 20 Owls in Africa, more than 15 species of mongoose - nearly all of which are nocturnal. Add to that most of the cat family, a raft of termite feeders and so the list goes on.

Some of the more interesting nocturnal species include:

Civet, genet, polecat and porcupine
Mongoose (White-tailed, Marsh & Selous)
Side-striped jackal
Aardwolf and aardvark (anteater)
Leopard, lion and serval
Caracal and African wild cat
Hyena (Spotted, Striped & Brown)
Honey badger, pangolin and springhare
Galagos (Bushbabies or Night Apes)
Owls, nightjars and night heron

As you can see, with so many nocturnal species out there, a lot of activity takes place at night. So if you get the opportunity to go on a night drive – don't miss out!

Around the camp fire

In the early morning, and again after you return to camp from the afternoon activity, you will gather around the camp fire to mix and mingle with people from around the world – to share and astound one another with tales of your adventures, or hear the spell-binding stories of your hosts as they relate the many wondrous experiences they have had in choosing this amazing way of life.

The Sundowner

A sundowner, in colloquial British English, is an alcoholic drink taken after completing the day's work, usually at sundown. On safari it has become somewhat of an institution. On the afternoon game drive your guide will take along a selection of 'beverages' including beers, wine, and spirits (with mixers). As the sun starts to set on the horizon he/she will find a suitable spot in which to see out the day and drinks will be served alongside a selection of snacks (crisps, nuts, or cooked nibbles). A ritual not to be missed!

"Nothing is wanting, nothing is superfluous, the smallest weed or insect is indispensably necessary to the general good. Nothing more bespeaks a littleness of mind, than to regard as useless all that does not visibly benefit man." - William John Burchell, English explorer, naturalist, artist and author (1822)

Final Check-List

You've read the section on *Safari travel tips*, run your eye down the list of *What to pack for your safari* , done your best to fathom the section on *What to expect of safari,* and completed your *To Do List* - yes?

But that was all months ago!

Here is a final check-list to make sure you have everything you'll need:

Passport (+ photocopy to be left with friends, relatives or colleague) - should be valid for at least 6 months and with ample spare pages (for visas and entry/exit stamps).

Airline (e)tickets - check that all names match those on your passports. Check that all the stopovers that you require are listed on your ticket (for the correct dates). Note down your airline reservation number somewhere safe – just in case.

Itinerary – print a copy of your itinerary including a list of contact details for the places where you will be staying (+ photocopy to leave with a friend, relative or colleague).

Travel Insurance documentation (+ photocopy to be left with friends, relatives or colleague).

Vaccination certificates if required.

Money – see *Cash & credit cards* under *Safari travel tips* above.

Prescription medication- sufficient for your entire safari.

Prescription glasses – and a spare pair if possible (both for 'reading' and sunglasses for outdoors).

Mobile (cell) phone – pre-registered for international roaming.

Sunglasses, sun hat, sun block, lip balm, moisturizer and eye drops.

Camera & Video equipment - plus batteries and storage media, power adaptor etc.

Binoculars – an IMPORTANT piece of equipment on safari.

Clothing & Luggage – see *What to pack for your safari* for recommendations.

Entertainment options – if you are travelling with children it is not a bad idea to take along a favourite book, Gameboy or comfort toy.

Toiletries
• Toothpaste, toothbrush
• Antibacterial soap
• Razor and razor blades
• Brush, comb
• Creams, lotions etc.

Travel diary/journal and a pen.

In flight necessities - neck pillow, ear plugs, eye mask, and noise cancelling headphones!

Medical Kit including:
• Throat lozenges, eye and ear drops
• Indigestion tablets

- Diarrhea (Imodium) tablets &/or preventative (pro-biotic).

- Aspirin/Paracetamol

- Antihistamine (for bites)

- Multipurpose antiseptic / hand sanitizer / wet wipes

- Painkillers

- Cold prevention (Vitamin C/Echinacea/garlic)

- Insect repellant (DEET)

- Anti-malarial tablets

Common sense (v. important)

Patience and a sense of humour!

"Even today, to visit Africa is a feast for the senses. The bush literally brings one's faculties to life, as you learn to see better, to smell for the first time, to be silent and to listen....the wildlife, the landscape and the people of Africa remain an exhilarating contrast to the world we seek to escape." - Bartle Bull, Safari – A Chronicle of Adventure

Getting the most out of your safari

Observing (& Questioning)

Throughout your safari you will hear much talk of animal behaviour, physiology, survival strategies, medicinal uses of plants etcetera. It can all be a bit overwhelming! How is anyone supposed to remember it all? The answer is that you probably won't. But perhaps the best way to get your mind around some of it, and to help you to get the most from your safari, is to learn the art of observing (and questioning).

"To acquire knowledge one must study, to acquire wisdom one must observe" Garth Thompson, The Guides Guide to Guiding

Now observing presumes that you notice things! We can all see the kudu that the guide is pointing at, but do you notice how well it blends into the trees, that only the male has horns, that they have huge bell-shaped ears and vertical white stripes down their bodies? Take another look – notice how still they stand, how wary they are and how directly they stare at you. And what do all these observations mean? These signs all point to a browser – an animal that feeds on leaves, rather than grass (grazer), and so lives in thick bush, relies on scent and hearing to detect predators and on its camouflage, and standing still, to remain unseen.

On safari there is so much to take notice of, and from these things you can learn. This is the simple art of observation – knowing what to look for and relating what you see to what you already know, have read, or have been told by your guide.

We need to question too (that's why a good guide is so important – he/she has the answers!). Have you ever asked yourself the simple question - why the sky is blue? Never thought about it? All the same, the answer is quite interesting. You see, as light from the Sun enters the Earth's atmosphere (white light – being a mixture of all the colours of the rainbow) it strikes molecules of gases in the air, deflecting each colour differently. This is because each colour has its own wavelength – red and yellow are the longest, blue and violet the shortest. The sky looks blue because the gas molecules 'scatter' the short wavelengths more than the longer ones. The short blue wavelengths are scattered at random, changing direction again and again as they pass through the atmosphere. While the long wavelengths reach our eyes in almost a direct line from the Sun, the blue waves reach us from all parts of the sky, and so it appears blue!

So let us try to develop those powers of observation and look for answers to the questions such observations lead us to:

Physical attributes

You can start enhancing your powers of observation by taking particular notice of some of the following physical attributes of the animals you see:

Standing, walking and running

Most animals walk in a bipedal manner (two legs on the ground at any one time, one from each side). But take a look at a buffalo – it has 3 legs on the ground at all times! Giraffe on the other hand, move both legs together on the same side – alternatively one side then the other. What is the significance? Not much, but would you have noticed if I hadn't pointed it out? Interesting though, don't you think? But when giraffe start to run then this individual style translates into a distinctive lurching motion. Mountain gorillas, with the knuckles of their forearms firmly planted on the ground, can swing their entire body between their arms as they walk. Elephants cannot actually run – it is more an ambling gait that just gets busier. Take a look. Wildebeest, with their hindquarters being lower than their forelegs, have a rocking gait when they run. The gerenuk can stand virtually upright on its hind legs to browse (bull elephant in some areas have learnt to do this too – amazing balance). But why do hippo and white rhino always seem to stand with their chins nearly on the ground? Yes, they are grazers and so this is how they feed, but it is also due to the fact that their skulls are solid bone and extremely heavy to hold up. An elephant's skull on the other hand is not solid but has a honeycomb construction which makes it much lighter (and so easier to hold up). But if a hippo or rhino raise their heads, you can be sure they are either alarmed or feel threatened – look out!

Tails

The tails of lion and leopard will often give them away. A lion's mood can often be interpreted by the 'flicking' of its tail. Generally this means that it is becoming increasingly annoyed at your presence – time to take a step back. A leopard's tail is often what can draw your attention to a particular tree; as it hangs down or twitches in the breeze, and is sometimes the 'give-away' you need to locate this elusive feline. You will notice that its tail is conspicuously white towards the tip. This is used as a 'follow me' signal to its young when they need to follow their mother through thick grass. On the other hand, the cheetah's long, thick tail is used like a rudder when chasing down its prey at up to 100km an hour.

The tails of browsers like the kudu, nyala and bushbuck, who live in thick under-growth and riverine bush, are short with a distinct white underside. When panicked they raise their tail as a 'follow me' sign that helps them to stay together when fleeing through thick bush. The tails of oryx (gemsbok) and wildebeest, which inhabit the open grassy plains and desert areas, are long and bushy and are used to swat away flies. Both the elephant and giraffe have long tails with stringy tufts at the end – another good fly swatter! Smaller antelope, like impala, springbok and Thompson's gazelle, all have a white underside to their tails which are evident when 'stotting' or 'pronking' - displays designed to indicate that they are fit and healthy and not worth chasing!

The tails of birds too, can be illuminating – the long, attention-seeking tails of the male Paradise Flycatcher and Pin-tailed Whydah are designed to attract females, whilst the fan-like tails of the bee-eater family clearly aid their manoeuvrability, allowing them to catch insects in flight...and so on.

Horns, tusks and teeth

Many African animals sport impressive horns or tusks. These can be used in defence or may just be for show (to impress the ladies) or to fight off rivals. All antelope have horns, sometimes in both sexes, or in other species, only in males. They vary greatly in shape, size and the use for which they have evolved. The rapier-like horns of the oryx are used both for fighting and defending themselves from predators. The swept-back curve of the sables' horns make them a force to be reckoned with, while the twisting spirals of the kudu are really only for show. Elephants are not the only animal with tusks – the warthog sports a fine pair that are used to lethal effect against any attacker. The tusks on a hippo too are formidable weapons that are used to good effect against rivals, or as a threat display (their characteristic open-mouthed yawn). All tusks are in fact elongated teeth – incisors to be precise.

Bills

A bird's bill is perhaps its most telltale feature. A strong hooked bill will indicate a bird of prey (eagles, hawks, owls) although a hook at the end of a thin, longish bill (e.g. a shrike or coucal) is an indicator of its predatory feeding habits. The open-bill, spoonbill and marabou storks all have bills designed-for-purpose according to its diet. The amazing African skimmer has a pronounced lower mandible that it uses to 'skim' the surface of the water for small fish as it flies only millimetres above the surface. The hornbills are a family of birds of many different sizes but readily identified by their prominent bills, sunbirds (nectar gatherers) and woodpeckers too, use their bills to fill a niche as do barbets (fruit-eaters) and kingfishers. All I am saying is that, as you start to 'notice' the different bill types, so your bird-spotting will become more rewarding.

Colouring & markings

Colouring too, can be instructive in understanding how an animal fits into its environment. The white stripes that break up the body outline of kudu, nyala and bushbuck in thick bush help to keep the animal hidden in a habitat where flight is more difficult and camouflage more certain. In the open plains or desert regions, being seen is a given, but the use of colouring can help in other ways - for example: a white underbelly helps keep the animal cool by diffusing or reflecting the heat rising from the open ground during the heat of the day - springbok, impala and oryx all have distinctive white under-bellies. Interestingly, in both gazelles and springbok, there is also a solid horizontal stripe between the white under-belly and the tan coat - this acts to break up their outline when viewed from a distance, across the shimmering plains or desert sands, and so acts as a form of camouflage.

You might also find the differences in markings between sub species of interest. These are particularly pronounced in the case of giraffe

(Reticulated, Masai, Rothchild's & Thornicroft) and zebra (Burchell's, Mountain and Grevy's), although more subtle colour, and size, variations are also common (e.g. the black-faced impala of northern Namibia). In the case of the Plain's zebra, you may also notice that some populations have a brown 'shadow' stripe, whereas in others it is absent. The white circular ring seen on the common waterbuck is notably absent on the defassa waterbuck which are otherwise virtually identical.

It often appears that elephants in different parts of Africa are different colours. For example, the elephants found in Etosha in Namibia are quite different in colouring to those found around Lake Kariba in Zimbabwe or Amboseli in Kenya. This is because of the soil colour variations found in these locations. The elephants mud-bathe or 'dust' themselves regularly and in this way take on the colour of the soil type where they live!

You might also notice that the young of sable, wildebeest and zebra - all grassland dwellers - are a chestnut brown colour, very different to the adults. This presumably provides a level of camouflage when lying in long grass while their mothers graze. The young of oryx are distinctly chestnut coloured too, and perhaps this allows them to blend in to the more arid Kalahari sands.

The facial 'masks' prominent in roan, sable and gemsbok are also worth noting – perhaps you have an idea as to why these antelope share such a characteristic feature? I am yet to find a satisfactory explanation myself, although it may somehow be related to the overhead sun – perhaps an anti-glare mechanism? It is probably no coincidence that all are open plains or desert dwellers and that the only cat to have similar facial marking is the cheetah – the only diurnal cat.

It is also interesting to note that no two wild dog are alike – each has its own distinct pattern of white, black and tan that make up its multi-coloured coat. The same applies to zebra. It is thought that young zebra imprint their mother's pattern (along with their scent) into their memories and in this way they can always pick out their mother from a group. Mountain gorillas too can each be distinguished by their unique and individual nose print!

Posture

Start to take notice of posture too. Whether an animal is looking alert, relaxed, or agitated can tell you a lot. If you see a group of impala or zebra all staring intently in one direction (and not at you!) then it is very likely that they have spotted a predator nearby. If you are sitting watching a wild dog pack relaxing in the shade and some of them start to rush around, whimpering and nuzzling other members this is often the prelude to a hunt. An elephant that has its trunk raised in the air is trying to scent something – maybe you? A lone wildebeest with head held high, looking both alert and agitated is likely a territorial male displaying his status and keeping an eye out for females passing through his 'patch'. And a sable or waterbuck male raising its foreleg and tapping between a female's hind legs is just flirting!

If you see something unusual, ask your guide what it means…

Spoor (signs)

Your guide is not the only one who can detect the 'signs' left by animals. Look for hoof and paw prints (known colloquially as 'spoor'), dung or 'scat', broken branches or disturbed ground - these are all 'signs' that give an indication of what walked by or what events may have unfolded in the night. More importantly they give clues as to what you can expect to encounter up ahead. Listen to your guide as he explains how he interprets what he sees; point out those things that you notice and ask about them; and you can always study the *Animal Spoor Charts* later in this book to get some background.

Environmental factors

It is also important that you think about those factors that affect the environment around you on safari, notably the time of year, weather and habitat – even the phases of the moon.

Habitat

Take note of the habitat you are walking or driving through – it can tell you a lot about what you can expect to find. Browsers (eats leaves rather than grass) like kudu, nyala and bushbuck tend to stick to the thickets and more wooded river lines whereas zebra, wildebeest and buffalo are content out in the open grasslands. Waterbuck, lechwe and sitatunga all prefer wetland areas to varying degrees. White rhino are open grassland feeders whilst black rhino, as browsers, favour the thicker bush. Oryx and springbok are only found in the more arid desert regions whereas sable and roan antelope (a quite rare sighting on safari despite a wide distribution across Africa) occur only in savannah woodland where the more tufted perennial grasses dominate, with your best chance of a sighting generally being late in the dry (winter) season when they are forced to finally come to the permanent water sources.

Look out for fruiting trees (including seed pods) like the numerous fig, ebony, palm and acacia trees which attract elephants, monkeys, baboons and an assortment of fruit-eating birds. Flowers too have their own fan base - buffalo love the beautiful velvet flowers of the Sausage tree!

Some predators are more suited to certain habitats – cheetah are generally found in open grasslands rather than thick bush, but leopards are shy and prefer riverine thickets or rocky outcrops. Brown hyena are more adapted to the arid desert regions than their more numerous spotted cousins, whereas lions have adapted well to all but the most extreme desert or forest habitats. Rocky outcrops are ideal habitat for hyrax and klipspringer and you will seldom find a hippo terribly far from water.

Weather

Cold, wind and rain all affect animal behaviour. Elephants don't much like the cold, and on winter mornings you will often only find them in the thick bush where they will gently browse until later in the day when it has become warmer and they feel the need to move into the open or go down to the river for a drink. Wind seems to unsettle the smaller antelope and even zebra – the noise and disturbance of the wind interferes with their ability to detect sounds and smells, they become edgy and will often huddle closer to each other. Cool and overcast days can often see shy nocturnal animals out and about during daylight – honey badgers, leopard and even pangolins. The scorching heat of summer will see most animals resting in the shade of a tree or bush through the middle of the day – look deep into the shadows if you want to see that elusive lion pride. The coming of the rains at the end of the long dry season will also herald the sudden departure of the large herds of buffalo and elephant; away from the permanent water courses toward the 'interior' where surface water will once again be available and where they can disperse in search of fresh grazing.

Seasons

Nearly all animals take part in seasonal movements or migrations of one form or another. The driving force for such movements is the need for sustainable food and water. Nearly all animals need water to survive and as the dry season progresses so the animals are drawn to the permanent waters within their local ecosystems. The famous wildebeest migration in the Serengeti and Masai Mara is but a large scale model of this phenomenon. Here vast numbers of animals follow the rains in an annual cycle in search of new grass. Across the continent a similar pattern unfolds. As the dry winter months see rivers and pans dry up, so the herds of elephant, buffalo, zebra and wildebeest, along with many other species of antelope and their associated predators, migrate inevitably toward the permanent sources of water that remain. Zebra in northern Botswana migrate seasonally between the Makgadikgadi & Nxai Pans region and the permanent waters of the Savuti, Linyanti and Chobe river systems, wildebeest from Angola travel south to Luiwa Plains in Zambia to coincide with the coming of the rains, and the desert-adapted Gourma elephants of the Sahel in Mali follow a circular migration path that covers over 450 kilometers

(280 miles), moving from one water hole to the next on a route laid down over centuries…and so it is across much of Africa.

Smell & hearing

Being on safari is not only about what you see – there is a whole world of smells and sounds to identify too. Sometimes it is the fresh crisp smell of the early morning or the combined smell of dust and dung from a herd of buffalo that captures that safari moment. Or perhaps it is the roar of a lion, or whoop of a hyena, that reassures you that you are indeed in Africa.

You will find that both of these senses come into their own more when you are on foot and away from the purring motor of your game drive vehicle. And don't switch those senses off around camp either – wild Africa goes 24/7.

Being able to identify the multitudes of smells and sounds around you will without doubt add that extra dimension to your safari, and allow you to pick up the tempo of the bush without relying only on what you can see.

Smell

As any good wine buff will tell you, smell is extremely underrated in importance in our lives. Just think of the lovely fresh smell of newly baked bread, or the aroma that you get as you pass the coffee shop on the way to work – or the arresting smell of newly cut grass. Well it's the same on safari – perhaps more subtle, but nevertheless distinctive.

Hearing

You are going to hear a range of sounds you've never heard before on safari – but many of the more interesting sounds are really easy to get to grips with – like the trumpeting of an elephant or the snorts of a hippo. Impala and baboon bark, squirrels chatter and lion announce their presence with a great booming roar. Almost everything out there makes one sound or another. Bird calls are tricky though, and these will take some time to master, but can be extremely rewarding (being able to identify a sound that you hear outside your tent really does heighten the pleasure).

Night sounds are often especially striking. A lot can be gleaned from keeping an ear open through the night as you lie in bed (when you are not sleeping of course). Lions, hyena, leopard, elephants and hippo all contribute strongly to the cacophony of sounds of the African night – along with owls, nightjars, crickets and frogs. Not only does this add to your overall safari experience but will offer clues as to what you can expect to find come morning - the bark of a baboon troop in the late evening will often indicate that a leopard is on the prowl, and those hippo returning to the water after a night of feeding can provide the reminder that dawn is on its way...along with another exciting day on safari - time to get up.

Keep in mind...there are a number of aspects of life in the wild that may benefit from some explanation - do keep in mind:

Avoiding injury

Most wild animals are wary of any physical encounter – be it in catching the next meal or in defending its territory. The exceptions to the rule are a mother's instinct to defend her young and the urge to defend one's territory. Risking physical injury goes against all the rules of survival and is almost always avoided – backing away from a confrontation has left many an animal fit to fight another day.

Be pragmatic (survival is the key)

The harsh reality of survival in the wild should always be witnessed with a pragmatic outlook – a lioness who abandons her cubs to ensure her own survival is only obeying the harsh laws of nature. A zebra that kicks to death a 3 month old wildebeest calf – lost and squealing for its mother – is only protecting its own from the attention of predators which will inevitably be drawn to the squeals of the lost calf. Predators will prey on the weak, the young and the infirm – this is the law of nature.

Sleep deprivation and dehydration

Probably the two most debilitating factors in our own lives are a lack of sleep and dehydration. These can be significant factors in the wilds of Africa too. You will be pleased to know that many of the animals you will see on safari sleep a great deal – take lions for example – they can snooze for up to 20 hours a day. A pangolin sets the record – he's happiest when he gets around 22 hours sleep a day – I'm serious! But whilst den-dwellers like warthog, jackals, and aardvark are able to catch a good amount of shut-eye, spare a thought for the smaller antelope like impala, gazelles and puku who can only move into the open and wait out another night, waiting and watching for a for a lion or leopard to come looking for dinner! Some animals hardly seem to sleep at all as they spend up to 20 hours a day feeding – giraffe and elephant only catch snatches of sleep – and that's standing up (mostly). When you see buffalo, kudu, zebra and the other ungulates lying down in the shade of a tree – they're probably not sleeping, they're 'masticating' (chewing their cud like good ruminants do).

In Africa, having access to water is a daily preoccupation for most animals - especially during the drier months of the year when no rain falls and the pans and rivers dry up. A lack of food means that they lose condition, a lack of water means dehydration and death. Nearly all animals must move to permanent sources of water to meet their daily intake requirements. The larger animals, including elephant, buffalo and zebra need water on a daily basis while the desert adapted species like springbok and gemsbok (oryx) are able to go for days without drinking. Most of the smaller antelope (klipspringer, dik dik, grysbok and steenbok) are almost entirely independent of water, gaining the moisture they need from their food – foliage, shoots, fruit and berries.

Life & Death in the African bush

Finally, let me just say this: you have come to witness one of the greatest shows on earth – the pinnacle in animal evolution – and it is worth keeping in mind that all you see on safari is a result of millions of years of evolution.

There are two suggestions that I would like to make in this context:

- Contemplate the wonder of what you are seeing – such a spectacle may not be here for us to witness forever, and in some places, not for very long. Be sure to fully appreciate the things that you see on safari for you may just be the last generation to do so. We are at a point in history when Man, by sheer weight of numbers, is dominating the planet in such a way as to alter it for ever more.

- Think more deeply about evolution so that you may better grasp the utter randomness of it: that everything living is largely here by accident - "a consequence of a brutal system with no principles beside the one that every individual is striving for reproductive success".

It is humbling to think that all that we see on safari had evolved long before Man came to dominate the earth – had thrived and survived for thousands of years, in a state of absolute balance – nature at its best. You are privileged to being witness to the playing out of nature in all its untainted glory.

So do keep observing and noticing...there is a wealth of information just staring at you in the face (eyes, ears and nose)!

Animal Behaviour

An understanding of animal behaviour is important if you are looking to get the most out of your safari. What, where and why an animal does what it does? This chapter is designed to help you become more familiar with these behavioural traits, so that you can recognize them for yourself, and in this way gain an understanding of all that is taking place around you on safari. In the following section we will look at some of the anatomical adaptations and attributes that you should look out for, and what they mean – but more on that later…

It is important to keep in mind that the first rule of animal behaviour is that there are no absolutes! Although we may expound at length on what we know about animal behaviour, in truth many of these behavioural traits can vary from one region to another with variations in food and water availability, predation pressures or a combination of other factors. There are no strictly defined behavioural rules. Hyena might hunt extensively in one area but purely scavenge in another. Lions are predominantly nocturnal yet can be found hunting by day in some areas as opportunity presents itself. In describing an animal's behaviour we tend to generalise to enable us to convey a certain level of understanding. Do not be too surprised if you pick up on some behavioural variations – make a note to ask your guide about them. All individuals, including wild animals, have unique personalities; what is typical for one individual may not be so for others.

Secondly, although we often draw a parallel between animal behaviour and human behaviour, for ease of understanding or by way of explanation, we should not fall into the trap of judging animals in the wild by our own standards of compassion and fair play; the raw act of survival in the wild, and the very strong instinct to procreate, does not always lend itself to what we would consider 'good conduct'.

Who's with whom?

As with all celebrity watching, not only do we need to know who's who, but also, who's with whom? Here are some of the scenarios to look out for:

Alpha pairs (dominance hierarchy)

This scenario is found in wild dog and banded and dwarf mongoose, and even ground hornbills amongst others, and is where the members of the same species live together in a group (strength in numbers) and adopt a breeding strategy that allows only the dominant (or alpha) pair to mate and have offspring. The whole group is then involved in protecting, feeding and rearing the resulting offspring. Wild dog are perhaps the best example for you to observe on safari as their dens are often accessible and you can spend time observing their behaviour – and the pups are very cute!

Monogamous couples

Uncommon in mammals (only 3% of all mammals are monogamous), and more often found in birds, mating (or pairing) for life appears to work for the bat-eared fox, jackals, porcupine, duiker, dik dik, eagles, secretary birds, hornbills and geese (among others).

The territorial male (or female)

Being territorial is a concept easily grasped by us humans. We all like to own our own home, secure a partner and raise a family – and woe betide anyone who messes with this arrangement! Well, maybe not all of us, but I'm sure you get what I mean…

The dominant male (or coalition of males) in a lion pride will patrol and scent mark to maintain a territory, and male leopards will hold a territory that may overlap with the territories of one or more female leopards…but when it comes to other species like wildebeest, lechwe, puku & kob – the territorial system works somewhat differently. In this instance each male takes up residence on his selected patch (physical location) and awaits the approach of the female herd. He paces and defends his patch vigorously against other males and can often be seen standing sentry from a position within his territory that commands a view – waiting patiently for his turn to come around. When the herd comes closer he attempts to keep the females in his sphere of influence for as long as possible, during which time he enjoys certain mating rights. Clearly, the male that can locate and defend the best grazing has the best prospects. It's not just good looks that gets the girl!

And it's not all about mating rights – there is more going on here.

For example, the role of the dominant male lion in a pride is often misunderstood. The dominant male, or coalition of males, provides stability for the pride, fending off challenges from younger, immature or nomadic males, thus ensuring that the pride's young cubs grow to maturity and secure a future for their genes. Without his protection the pride would be fractured and young cubs would live in constant fear of being killed by roaming males. This stability is often shattered in areas where hunting takes place as pride males are often shot as trophies.

And it is not only males that are territorial. Hyena clans, led by the females, will defend their home range against other clans too. Lionesses too, will chase off unwelcome females that wander onto their pride's turf.

Many of the larger antelope are only territorial during the mating season, setting up a small territory to entice breeding females to mate, and fighting off any challengers.

Other territorial species commonly encountered on safari include hippo, waterbuck, jackals, chimpanzees and gorillas. Notably non-territorial are elephant, buffalo, cheetah, giraffe and the African wild dog. See the Attributes charts in the reference section.

Mixed herds

Although living in herds is a common safety measure for many species, mixed herds, where mature males and females stay together, is not as common as one would imagine. Zebra, gorillas (not always) and most antelope herds have a single male in attendance, whereas with elephant, the mature males come in and out of the herd when in musth (a heightened sexual state).

Buffalo have adopted the practice of mixed herds with the younger, stronger bulls vying for the attention of the 'ladies' and the older bulls 'retiring' gracefully. Baboons, although staying together as a troop, have a distinct hierarchy whereby only the most dominant 'dog' baboons are permitted to mate with 'in season' females. Monkeys and chimpanzees too, co-habit, with strict rules for the relationships between male and female. Sable and roan antelope also form mixed herds, as do wildebeest and eland.

Bachelor herds (the lads)

A number of antelope form bachelor herds, and male buffalo and elephant will almost always be seen together with at least one other male counterpart. For antelope this is likely for the same reason that they form herds in the first instance – for safety in numbers (more eyes and ears). But for buffalo and elephant it seems they just like the company!

Solitary (lonely hearts club)

Solitary behaviour is most common among cats and nocturnal animals such as leopard, caracal, civet, and the African wildcat - lion being the notable exception (they are principally nocturnal but not solitary). All of the nocturnal mongooses, genets and civets are solitary, together with the pangolin and aardvark. Bushbuck, sitatunga and steenbok too are notably solitary, coming together to mate but otherwise spending their time alone. Even hippo, when they come out of the water at night to feed, by and large forage on their own even though they spend their days together in large 'pods'.

Harems (polygamous)

Zebra stallions on the other hand, work hard to maintain a 'harem', keeping their ladies apart from other males. A number of antelope work on this basis too, with species like the impala taking time during the 'rutt' to sort out amongt themselves who will get ALL the 'ladies'. In the case of the impala however, the dominant male is often so overwhelmed with his 'duties' that he has little time to eat and will gradually weaken to the point where he can no longer hold his own against the other males seeking to depose him.

Matriarchal and matrilineal (Mum rules)

Elephants are the best known followers of the matriarchal system in which adolescent males are driven out of the family group and strong, lasting bonds are fostered between aunts, sisters and nieces. The matriarch, generally the oldest female in the family group, is the undisputed leader and is responsible for the well-being of the group, deciding where they go and when. A similar female-dominated social structure is referred to as matrilineal, and is where female members acquire their mother's social rank within the group (be it clan, troop or herd). Both hyena and baboons are matrilineal but in the case of hyena the females are dominant whereas with baboons the males dominate. Confusing perhaps, but worth remembering if you get the opportunity to watch either for any length of time.

Keeping a low profile

Sometimes it's not who's with whom but who's missing? For most expectant mothers on the African savannah, when it comes time to give birth, the mother seeks out a quiet location well away from the herd or family group (wildebeest being a notable exception). Newborns arrive virtually without any discernible scent or odour and with excellent ground camouflage. Mum then leaves the newborn hidden (simply lying down in long grass), returning only to feed and groom the youngster over the coming weeks. This will continue until she is confident that the little one(s) are strong enough to hold their own and less vulnerable to predation. The wildebeest is an exception to this rule, being born amidst the herd and then able to stand and run with its mother within an hour of being born!

Who's talking to whom?

Now we all know that most wild animals have more highly developed primary senses (sight, smell and hearing) than us Homo sapiens. However, one advantage that we do have is a much larger brain. This has allowed us to develop, among other things, a vast array of gadgets and gizmos that enable us to communicate with each other – speech, the telephone, and the internet to name a few. Although arguably less sophisticated, the wildlife you will encounter on safari have developed their own forms of communication too:

Scent marking

A great many wild animals actively scent mark as they move around. This acts like a local blog post for any animal passing by – especially to those of the same species. The message is not a complicated one either - "buzz off – this is my patch" or "Hey, I'm looking for some company tonight…how about it?"

This scent marking is done using a range of methods, such as sprayed urine or pheromones and 'musk' secreted from specialised glands found in the hoof, or in front of the eye (pre-orbital) or between the tail and rectum (perianal). Secretions from these glands have a long-lasting scent and leave behind the unique odour profile (or signature) of the owner. Such scent markings are amazingly persistent and can last for up to 6 weeks in some cases. Many of the larger antelope have hoof glands, whereas a number of the smaller antelope like the klipspringer and dik dik utilise a gland on the face near the eyes (pre-orbital). The hyena family, mongooses and the aardwolf employ anal glands (sometimes referred to as 'pasting') but the 'top gun' must surely be the civet. Their olfactory organ (a pouch-like gland between the anus and their genitals) produces an oily substance as thick as honey, which smells so unpleasant as to verge on the nauseating! Used as a defensive deterrent this can be extremely effective (with a similar strategy employed by polecats). Interestingly though, this particular quality is highly valued by makers of perfumes for its ability to 'exalt' perfumes made with it, allowing them to 'linger for longer'.

A male eland, in the course of marking his territory, uses a gland on his forehead. In the process of 'leaving his mark' he also 'collects' an assortment of leaves, grass and mud which sticks to his forehead. If you see a big bull, take a closer look. Perhaps this is some kind of 'macho' look that they think will work on the ladies? Whether this actually communicates something to other eland is hard to tell, but it certainly seems to beef up the bull's self-esteem!

Scent marking by brown hyena is possibly the most elaborate routine of all – not one but two pasting's (one white, one brown) are applied with great care on grass stems at periodic intervals throughout the night. One is long-lasting and designed to deter other hyena that happen upon their patch, with the other fading after only a few hours and intended to remind the owner that he/she has passed this way already that night!

Mutual grooming and greetings

Whereas a bunch of flowers works to send a message of love (or apology) in our world, baboons and other primates (and some mongooses) prefer mutual grooming to show their affection (and affiliation). Like domestic cats, lions within a pride will greet each other with an affectionate head/neck rub. Elephants have a similar greeting behaviour, touching each other with their trunks and even getting visibly excited at seeing an old friend. Wild dogs too will rouse the others in the pack with some excited neck rubbing and playfulness, in order to stir up some activity and encourage the group to hunt.

Bulletin boards

Less subtle is the use of dung middens! This is where an animal habitually returns to the same location to defecate. In some instances this merely acts as a territory indicator e.g. hyena and civet, but in other cases, like with rhino, they use these middens as a kind of bulletin board, coming back to check who has passed by recently, whether a female might be in oestrous or whether another rhino has left a message.

Chemical signals

One of the strongest and most sought-after signals in the animal world is the chemical signal indicating that a female is in oestrous (in heat). You will notice that dominant males, both carnivores and herbivores, never tire of smelling the rear ends of the females. This is often accompanied by a characteristic 'grimace,' known as flehmen, and characterized by opening the mouth and drawing back the lips. In this way the male 'tests' the strength of that signal (smell) using the vomeronasal organ, located at the back of the throat, and is thus able to determine whether the female is ready to be mated.

Whilst most mating behaviour is triggered by the female coming into oestrus, and in so doing attracting the attention of dominant males in the herd, a number of antelope follow a more elaborate courting routine before mating actually takes place. The male, having determined her condition by urine-sniffing and flehmen, follows behind her, making his approach by tapping between her legs with his foreleg. If she is willing to mate, the female parts her hind legs and holds her tail to one side. So if you see this behaviour on safari you now know what it's all about.

Interestingly, and while on the subject, only one or two animals in the wild are thought to engage in sex for recreational purposes – the porcupine (probably just a pseudo masochistic streak) and the bonobo (a pygmy chimpanzee that is seriously promiscuous!).

Vocal communication

The vocal repertoire in the animal kingdom is extensive too, ranging as it does from:

Whining and neighing (zebra)
Grunts and air-venting (hippo)
Hissing and spitting (small cats and snakes)
Trumpeting (elephants)
Screams (monkeys)

Hoot (owls)
Duet (birds)
Cackling (a frenzied laugh that can only be a spotted hyena)
Roar (or call) (lions, leopards)
Whoops and howls (hyenas and jackals), to
Barks (whaa who!) (baboon)

Some of these vocalizations are meant to communicate displeasure, whereas others are to attract a mate and still others are alarm calls to let you know that a predator is close by (often, that's you!). On a walking safari you will soon become familiar with the 'chickering' of tree squirrels and the warning snorts of impala and other antelope. Warthogs champ their teeth, porcupines rattle their quills and rabbits thump their feet! Each has its own way of signalling danger.

Meerkats and primates like the vervet monkey, have even developed a range of alarm calls that distinguish between threats from the air (eagles), on the ground (snakes) and other carnivores. Each threat requires a different 'escape' response, and so these distinguishing alarm calls allow them to react in the most appropriate manner for each situation!

During the early stages of the mating season, known as the 'rutt', impala employ a deep resonating bark. This is a time when aspiring young (and older) males attempt to secure a group of females for their harem. Males' dash about making a distinctive 'rutting' bark that is both loud and out of tune! This is seemingly intended to send a strong message to any other aspiring males – "watch out – I'm big, I'm tough and I'm hard to bluff!"

Territorial male lions and leopards (and females on occasion) will regularly call in the early evening and through the night as a warning to others that a particular territory is occupied. These calls are one of the distinctive sounds of the African night. It is specifically against the regulations in most National Parks to play a recording of lion calling, as this can be very dangerous. Any territorial male within earshot will certainly come running to investigate, becoming agitated and extremely aggressive in its search for the 'interloper'!

When threatened, lions will growl aggressively; rhino will snort; and elephant trumpet to indicate their displeasure – all vocal signals to be heeded.

Infrasound (a sound with a frequency too low to be detected by the human ear) is used by elephants to communicate between them. When observing elephants you might notice that at times a family group will very suddenly stop and remain perfectly still, and then without any apparent signal, start feeding and moving about once more, all in unison. This is an example of low frequency communication between the matriarch and the rest of the group. Giraffe and rhino are also thought to communicate using infrasound.

The 'tummy rumble' that we so often hear when around elephant doesn't come from the stomach as one might expect, but is rather a reassuring sound made with the vocal cords.

Visual communication

Visual communication, in its many guises, is also significant. The animals you will see on safari do not use facial expressions, as we know them, but rather employ a range of somewhat exaggerated poses and postures to get their message across…

Submission and aggression

Submissive behaviour in the form of downcast eyes, ears pinned back, or head lowered keeps lower ranking individuals from being 'put in their place' by a more dominant member of the group. Snarling and bristling (arching the back and raising the hair on the neck and tail) are more aggressive signals that say "look how big I am – don't waste your time". Intimidation is a big part of the dominance/submissive dynamics within a group. Dominant members are continually reinforcing their position whilst lower ranking individuals use submissive behaviour to keep out of trouble. When meeting an adversary the same conventions apply. Even an animal the size of an elephant flaps out its huge ears to give the impression that it is much larger than it is. Only once the ears have been pinned back and the head drops down do you know that the 'display' is over and you are now being charged for real!

As mentioned previously, even the position of a baboon's tail communicates its status within the baboon hierarchy. In monkeys, the position of the tail sends definite signals to others, ranging from confident when held up over the back, to fearful when held in a horizontal position. A dominant male in a troop of vervet monkeys has another way of communicating its social status – it flashes its bright red penis and blue testicles in a display of genuine attitude!

Zebras will draw back their lips and expose their formidable teeth as fair warning to rival males – and they know how to use them! Hippos also employ a similar 'display' strategy to intimidate any challengers, opening their huge mouths wide and showing off their fearsome ivory.

The stare

Staring is common too. When two animals come upon one another unexpectedly they more often than not stop and stare at one another – not to see who will blink first but more likely in an attempt to intimidate the other before deciding whether to back off or hold their ground. Staring can be offensive or defensive – crouching and advancing while staring is offensive, arching the back and gaping is more defensive. Monkeys will sometimes reinforce the stare by raising their eyebrows and flashing its white eyelids – very disconcerting! If this doesn't work they will open their mouths, pull back their lips and expose their teeth in a snarl. Charming!

Posturing

Mock attacks and posturing are also defensive in their own way. A lion or elephant that mock charges you, is really trying to warn you off. When they are really intent on harming you they will just keep coming. The trick is to know which is which!

Movement of the body up and down or rocking from side to side (as seen in monkeys) is also a way of creating the illusion of a mock attack without moving forward. Sneaky!

If all else fails then running away is always an option - and one that is taken more often than not.

Size matters

In its own way, the size of an antelope's horns or an elephant's tusks also sends a visual message to any would-be challengers: - "Don't mess with me!" But the elaborate horns found in male kudu, impala, waterbuck, lechwe, reedbuck, nyala and bushbuck have more to do with the domestic issue of territorial dominance, than defence against predators. Here, horn size is an indicator of strength (and size) as a means of intimidating other males. In sable, oryx (gemsbok), eland and roan the horns, found in both sexes, have a more defensive role (against predators).

More visual signs

As an alternative to the chemical signals mentioned above, female baboons and chimpanzees in oestrous (and to a lesser extent monkeys) blatantly 'advertise' their condition to all and sundry with a remarkable pink anogenital swelling (bare swollen bum). Clearly, it pays to advertise as the female becomes increasingly popular as the swelling gets bigger and pinker!

Other behavioural traits

There are also some issues of day to day behaviour that you should know about...

Nocturnal or Diurnal?

Many guides will assume you know which animals are active at night (nocturnal) and which prefer to be out by day (diurnal). Try to get to know which is which by referring to the Animal Attributes section later in this book.

I mention this not so much to stop you looking out for nocturnal animals by day, but more to help you look in the right places and at the right times. Hyena, honey badgers, and porcupines are all predominantly nocturnal but will start to become active toward last light and so you may see them around dusk, or possibly around their den sites during the day.

Then of course there are those that only like to be out and about at twilight (dawn and dusk and moonlit nights). These are referred to as crepuscular, of which the serval and bat hawk are good examples.

Terrestrial or Arboreal?

Most of the animals you have come to see on safari live on land – right? Wrong! A number are, in fact, what is referred to as arboreal – they prefer to spend their time foraging and living their lives in the tree tops. The tree squirrel is an obvious one (although you will most likely see them scampering along the ground trying to get to the nearest tree!). The genet is another. Most monkeys, gallegos (bush babies) and chimpanzees are also considered arboreal. Hippos, although they spend a large part of the day in water, are considered to be terrestrial. So too are baboons even though they roost in trees at night.

Browsers or Grazers?

What distinguishes a browser from a grazer? A browser is a herbivore that feeds on plants other than grass, primarily foliage (leaves). Kudu, giraffe, gerenuk and klipspringer are strictly browsers. Wildebeest, sable and hippo are all grazers, eating mainly grass. But many animals switch between the two according to the seasons - including impala, elephant and eland.

How do they know to do that?

Instinctive vs Imprinted vs Learned behavior

Instinctive, imprinted and learned behaviour are all distinctly different patterns of inherited behaviour. The distinction between each is rather interesting. When a spider spins its web, it knows instinctively where to position the web and what shape it should be. This is an example of instinctive or innate behaviour. There is an important difference between such instinctive behaviour and what is imprinted or learned behaviour. Learned behaviour is a consequence of observing and copying, an experience that is acquired during an animal's lifetime. Imprinted behaviour is a form of learned behaviour that takes place in very young animals – for example, the imprinting of the shape, sound or smell of their mother. A young wildebeest must have a strong imprint of its mother and stick close by her side in order to stand a chance of survival. But it is only learned behaviour that allows an animal to adapt to changing circumstances – the ultimate key to success.

Why do they do that/why is it that?

If you are going on safari for the first time you can be forgiven for being curious about certain behaviours that you witness. So you can be ahead of the crowd I have tried to answer some on the more common observations/queries:

- **Why do warthogs turn around and go down their burrows backwards?**
  Warthogs have a formidable set of tusks that protrude from their snout. In order to 'come out fighting' they reverse down their burrows. It also means that if they want to make a fast 'getaway' they can accelerate much faster going forwards than backwards, and thus exit the burrow at speed.

- **Why do hippos splatter their dung with their tails when**

defecating?
For males, this is how they mark their territory.

- **Why do elephant, buffalo and warthog all enjoy wallowing in mud?**
Wallowing serves a dual purpose - both as a means to keep cool and to remove or protect the animal from insect bites. Older buffalo, warthog and elephant have only sparse hair covering their bodies. This makes them vulnerable to ticks and other biting insects. After wallowing, the dried mud helps to protect their skin from these annoying insects.

Elephant love a dust or mud bath for the same reasons. Birds too will lie with wings spread on the hot, dusty road – dusting themselves and exposing their feathers to the sun – all techniques used to persuade those pesky parasites to take their leave. Zebras, like the domestic horse, will have particular 'dusting' areas that they use regularly. They genuinely seem to just enjoy rolling on their backs and kicking their legs in the air!

- **Why do wildebeest (and impala and other herd species) calve together over a few short weeks each year?**
This is simply a strategy to overwhelm the predators by sheer numbers and ensure that a higher percentage of calves grow to a more defendable size.

- **Why do some female antelope have horns but some do not?**
There doesn't appear to be a hard and fast rule on this, but it is generally true that in larger antelope, like eland, sable and oryx (gemsbok), both sexes have horns – this could be to give them the capacity to defend themselves, and their young, from larger predators (much like buffalo). An exception to this seems to be the smaller antelope, like impala and duiker, who rely more on speed and agility to make their escape and so females have little need of horns, whereas the males use them for fighting other males.

- **Why do chimpanzees sometimes carefully fold or roll leaves**

before swallowing them whole?

It appears that chimpanzees, and other primates, have learned how to self-medicate. The leaves are designed to pass through their digestive system whole, and in so doing, push out any internal parasites like worms.

In other examples of self-medication, monkeys will rub their fur with particularly pungent plants to provide a level of insect repellent. Elephants are also thought to seek out leaves or bark of particular trees to cure themselves of certain ailments. Clever stuff!

- **Why do sparrow weavers always build their nests on the western side of the tree?**
  This is because their nests are not constructed merely to raise their young, like most birds, but are actually used as places to roost at night (this is their home). As such, especially in winter, it helps if the nests face west, garnering the last of the sun's warmth before the cool night sets in.

- **Why do people always say that the rock dassie is the elephant's closest relative?**
  This is because they share a common ancestry going back some 4 million years. They appear to be the only survivors of a particularly unusual evolutionary line that share the dubious characteristic of being the only mammals whose penis and testicles are contained within their bodies.

- **Why do warthogs have warts on their face?**
  These so called 'warts' consist of hard skin and dense connective tissue and are thought to protect the eyes and face when fighting! Males have 4 warts or lumps, 2 beneath the eyes and 2 further down the snout, and females only 2 beneath the eyes.

- **Why do lions commit infanticide?**
  A dominant male lion, or a coalition of two or more brothers, when taking over a pride, will invariably go out of their way to kill any young cubs sired by the displaced male(s). There are two reasons

for this: firstly, this will immediately bring the females into oestrous so that they can mate with them, and in so doing pass on their own genes: and secondly, such an action terminates the previous males gene dominance and accelerates their own – an important aspect in evolutionary success. New pride males will also drive out any sub-adult males from the pride or kill them before they can become competitors. This drive to pass on their genes and to enforce their reproductive dominance is very strong. A dominant male will also not hesitate to kill leopard, cheetah or hyena cubs on sight and will actively seek them out – satisfying the urge to drive out or kill any competition.

Lions are not the only animal to participate in infanticide – mountain gorillas and leopards will similarly kill infants when taking over a group or territory.

- **Why do lions roar predominantly in the early evening (and hyena too)?**
  One possible explanation is that after the sun sets each day a temperature inversion takes place, with warmer air rising off the land and being replaced by cooler air – this effectively creates a 'ceiling' of warm air that assists in bouncing sound waves back down (off this ceiling), and so allowing sounds to travel further. So if a lion wants to advertise its presence in a territory, early evening is a good time to gain the maximum effect. It is also the time of day when they shake off their slumber and start to get active! A male lion's call can travel roughly 5 kms (3 miles) which gives him an effective territorial diameter of around 10 kms. Calling the early morning is common too - here the reason may just be that the air is clearer with sound travelling furthest.

- **Why do some trees have thorns whereas others do not?**
  As a general rule, fine-leaved trees have thorns whereas broad-leaved trees do not. The leaves of fine-leaved trees are also more nutritious than those of broad-leaved trees, and as a consequence, up to half of all leaves produced by fine-leaved trees are browsed by

giraffe and other browsers. By contrast, the main consumers of broad-leaved trees are actually insects – especially caterpillar larvae. In this instance, thorns would offer little protection against such larvae but hairy leaves and digestion-inhibiting tannins do. Hairy leaves act in the same for larvae way as thorns do against browsers, as a physical barrier. Raising tannin levels, whilst costly in terms of energy use, is a very effective deterrent. By way of explanation; many trees are able to increase the amount of tannins in their leaves when they detect an attack. Such raised tannin levels, whilst making the leaves less palatable, also work to deactivate the digestive enzymes needed to break down the cellulose in the leaf. Such an increase in tannin levels is also able to be transmitted between trees as a wind-born scent, alerting other trees nearby. Animals soon learn to avoid plants with high tannin content, and will often consciously 'browse into the wind' to counter the latter effect. As a result, less than ten percent of the leaves in a broad-leaved savannah are eaten by browsers, like kudu and bushbuck. By contrast, up to half of all leaves produced by fine-leaved trees are browsed - the best known and most widespread example being the acacia, with its small compound leaflets. The manufacture of tannins would prove too 'expensive' and would adversely affect the plants structural growth. It is 'cheaper' for them to replace the leaves they lose than to defend them in this way. Instead they use thorns, which are relatively 'cheap' to produce. Thorns do not prevent browsing, they merely slow down the rate of consumption to a level the plant can tolerate and encourages the animal to move on before too much damage is done.

- **Why do bats hang upside down?**
  Bats hang upside down because their legs are too weak to hold their body weight upright. Bats are the only mammals capable of flying, and to fulfill this particular niche they have had to develop extensive, but lightweight, membranous wings. This need to reduce body weight has also necessitated the underdevelopment of the one thing that was not of prime importance – their legs. To be

able to hang upside down they have also had to develop a
regulatory system that prevents blood from pooling in their head
when upside down. Fascinating stuff.

"I never knew of a morning in Africa when I woke that I was not happy" -
Ernest Hemingway

Animal Physiology

The African bush is a living tapestry of evolutionary splendour – from the lofty giraffe to the diminutive elephant shrew. Each design has a niche, each attribute a key to its survival. The only thing that is constant is change. Evolution. Charles Darwin himself is reputed to have remarked that "it is not the strongest of the species that survives, nor the most intelligent, but the one most able to change". The notion of the 'survival of the fittest' only applies on an immediate day-to-day basis. Over time those that adapt – survive. The diversity of animal species in Africa is testament to this!

Each animal walks this earth because it has developed traits and physical features that have enabled it not only to survive, but thrive. We've talked a lot about what makes animals behave the way they do – now it is time to get to know more about what makes one animal physically different from another – and why that might be.

Let us take a look at some of the more universal physiological adaptations that are of interest...

Animal Senses (sight, sound & smell)

Each individual animal has developed a set of senses that best meets the needs of its specific habitat and lifestyle. Moles have very poor eyesight because they spend most of their time underground, but they are especially attuned to the vibrations that go on around them. A bat-eared fox, with its huge ears, has acute hearing that enables it to locate beetles and grubs lying underground. A hyena can pick up the scent of carrion from nearly eight kilometres (5 miles) away.

Let us take a closer look at each of the senses of sight, hearing and smell...

Sight

Different animals see things in different ways – some only see black & white, others in full colour. Some have wide stereoscopic vision whilst others use narrow binocular vision (like us). Some animals have compound eyes whilst others have single-aperture eyes like our own. Each has evolved for a purpose.

What other animals 'see' is very unlike our view of the world. Each species has different uses for what it sees – a cat is more interested in detecting movement, and judging speed and distance, than concerning itself about the colour of its prey. Primates on the other hand, rely on colour vision to select which fruits are edible or ripe.

Most insects are equipped with pairs of compound eyes; each made up of thousands of simple light-sensitive lenses designed more to detect movement than colour (or resolution). Yet some insects, bees for example, can see blue and green, thus allowing them to recognise specific flowers. Bees, along with ants and other invertebrates, use their ability to see polarized light (light that has been reflected back off shiny surfaces like water or sand) to precisely navigate their way back to their nests. We cannot see polarized light.

Spiders' eyes are less complex than those of insects and are fixed on their heads, looking in different directions to give a wider view. They are very sensitive to light and can see in one tenth of the light that we need, reacting instantly to the smallest of movements. But they can only see for about 15 cm (6 inches) and so have no real appreciation of the larger world around them!

Primates like gorillas, chimps and monkeys, together with wild dog, jackals and all the cats, can see in colour. Giraffe are thought to have at least some colour vision. Buffalo have only partial colour vision – they cannot see red – whereas zebra have full colour vision. Elephant and hippo have little use for colour vision and may have sacrificed colour for more light-sensitive black and white vision better suited to feeding at night.

Fish can see some colours, and some fish can even see infra red light at wavelengths invisible to humans. This helps them to see in murky water, where the longer wavelengths of infra red are scattered less than the shorter wavelengths of our visual spectrum.

Nocturnal cats (thus excluding the cheetah) can see in light only a sixth as bright as needed by humans. At the back of their eyes all nocturnal animals have a layer of reflective crystals, called the tapetum lucidum, which bounces light back through the retina to improve the amount of light that is received by the brain. It is this reflected light that makes a nocturnal animal's eyes glow when a spotlight is shone on them at night. The tapetum is also found in spiders, butterflies and moths.

All predators, including cats and eagles, have narrow binocular vision, like humans, that allows them to judge depth and distance and thus enables them to pinpoint their prey with accuracy *. However, they have an almost 270 degree blind spot beyond their peripheral vision.

Antelope, zebra and wildebeest on the other hand, with eyes set on either side of their heads, have a much wider arc of vision with virtually no blind spots in which to be surprised by predators, but they have only a very narrow band of binocular vision, directly in front of their face. They have no depth perception at all over most of their field of vision. So if you want to get up close to a group of zebra, buffalo or impala you should always approach them by walking toward them in a shallow spiral or at a slight diagonal, never straight towards them. Because they are not able to judge that you are getting closer, this is less threatening to them and they are less likely to run off even as you get closer! Similarly, you may see zebra, wildebeest or other antelope staring fixedly at a predator that appears somewhat too close for comfort. It is only by staring straight at them that they can judge how close they are!

Birds of prey, whose sight can be up to 8 times keener than ours, have the additional benefit of coloured filters that help to sharpen and add contrast for long-distance vision.

Stay with me…

To a predator, the immediate detection of movement is more important than colour. The detection of movement and colour is a function of two different types of light detectors in the retina. These are called rod and cone receptors. The outer zone of the retina is made up of rod receptors which detect movement, even in dim light. The inner zone contains many cone receptors which are used to detect detail and colour, but they only work in bright light. The combination of rods and cones makes the eye efficient under all lighting conditions.

Nearly all mammals have eyes equipped for some form of colour vision, but each will vary greatly in their ability to use it. Dogs can be trained to recognise colours but normally behave as though they see only tones of grey. Their colour vision is rather indistinct. Like many other mammals, they use their eyes mainly to detect movement, rather than to see detail. A dog will see leaping rabbits 150m away, but will not recognise a motionless rabbit 20m away! For this they rely more on their acute senses of smell and hearing.

In the human eye there are three types of colour receptors, or cones, these three cone types we call 'red', 'green' and 'blue'. Consequently, for humans, all colour hues that we can see can be produced by mixing red, green and blue light (three-dimensional colour). This is how a colour television set works - a mixture of three wavelengths that produce several million 'colours'. Most mammals, other than primates, have only two cone types, and thus have only two-dimensional colour vision (more like a faulty colour TV set). It is hard to imagine but animals with 4 and 5 dimensional colour vision do exist.

Bees, like humans, have three receptor (cone) types, although unlike humans they can also see ultraviolet light. This UV vision is useful in locating the fruit, flowers and seeds on which they feed. In UV light their foods contrast better against their backgrounds and so stand out for easy location.

In birds, sight has reached a level of perfection found in no other animal. Their vision is sharp and accurate and most have exceptional colour vision.

All bird species are thought to have at least four cone types and so have four dimensional colour vision, including UV. This UV vision is used in two ways – firstly, to hunt its prey -the UV enabling them to detect their prey - and secondly, in mate selection. It has been shown that a bird's plumage appears significantly different when viewed under UV lighting. It is thought that this is a definitive factor in mate selection, and an example of how differently birds see each other, compared with how we see them.

Because of the position of their eyes in their head, and the fact that their eyes are virtually fixed in their sockets, birds must turn their heads to alter their field of vision. They are thus able to focus on close objects better with one eye than with two. You will notice this phenomenon when a bird wants to look directly at you – it turns its head to one side!

Overall, of all the senses, sight is the only one where humans fare better than most other mammals – more specifically, the ability to see fine detail in good light (day-light). But when it comes to hearing and smell we are definitely behind most other mammals.

* A predator's vision is aided by the fovea, a small area of the retina where photoreceptors are especially densely packed. It is the fovea that provides the visual detail, being served by 50% of the nerve fibres in the optic nerve – carrying information to the brain. The fovea is

measured by 'cycles per degree' – a term used to describe how clearly an object can be seen. Humans come in at 30 cycles per degree and are considered to have good visual acuity, better than many other mammals including cats at only 9. But we are nowhere near as sharp-eyed as raptors, which have an exceptional ability to see detail, as much as 160 cycles per degree.

Hearing

Sensitivity to sound varies widely with different animal species. Many can hear sounds well beyond our range of hearing. Sound is measured in hertz (Hz), with humans having a range of between 60 and 20,000Hz. Dogs can hear sounds as high as 45,000Hz – the explanation behind the dog whistle. Cats and mice can detect sounds which are higher still and rely on this faculty a great deal as an early warning system. Some bats come in at an amazing 210,000Hz.

At the other end of the scale, elephants are able to detect sounds as low as 16Hz (known as infra sound). They use infra sound to communicate with one another, in a seemingly silent code not audible to humans. Infra sound also has the characteristic of being audible over large distances and is used to monitor earthquakes. In the same way, it is thought that elephants can detect when rain has fallen many miles away - they can actually hear it!

Smell

For many mammals, and insects, their sense of smell is by far the most important of the three senses. Many animals have developed an acute sense of smell and often rely most heavily on this sense for confirmation that all is well, or otherwise. Even though a buffalo may be looking right at you, and is seemingly aware of your presence, only when it picks up your scent does it startle and run off (hopefully in the other direction).

It is the antennae of insects that are used to detect odours and chemical scents emitted by flowers, fruits, animal dung or a receptive mate. These odours and scent signals help them to find food or a mate. The feathery antennae of the male Emperor Moth can detect the pheromones produced by the female from up to 10kms (6 miles) away! Now you know how those flies seem to appear out of nowhere as soon as you take out your sandwiches!

Many mammals can detect odours at such low concentrations that it is difficult to comprehend, and will respond to scent signals that humans cannot smell at all - at whatever concentration.

Most ungulates, including buffalo, along with lion and other carnivores have another attribute that man lacks. In the roof of the mouth is what is known as the vomeronsal or Jacobsen's organ, which is designed to detect air-borne chemical signals (or smells) to determine whether a female is in heat (oestrus). This 'grimace' is very distinctive and represented by the curling back of the upper lip and wrinkling of the nostrils while opening the mouth - known as flehmen. See the earlier section on *Chemical Signals under Animal Behaviour.*

Keeping out of trouble

You might be tempted to feel sorry for all those poor defenseless impala (and gazelles) that get preyed upon by a myriad of predators – not least of which include all the big guns - lion, leopard, wild dog, cheetah and hyena. But don't despair - they have a few tricks of their own, as do insects, birds, and plants too. All have evolved their own ways of keeping out of trouble...

Speed and deception

You will notice, especially in the smaller antelope like gazelles, which have strong, powerful hindquarters, cloven-hooves, and the long slim legs of an athlete – ready to sprint away at speed. This, plus the agility to jump and change direction rapidly, means that only the fastest predators, with sufficient endurance, can possibly hope to catch them.

Sight, Sound & Smell

All antelope have protruding eyes set to the side of the head to provide for wide-angle vision (almost 360 degree visibility). What we refer to as stereoscopic vision. This enables them to detect movement in all directions. They also have large rotating ears to increase their hearing capability and large nostrils to maximize their sense of smell.

Early warning systems

By living together in herds for extra vigilance, and mixing with other alert animals, like baboons, antelope like impala are alert to any danger and when accompanied by another excellent 'early warning' system – oxpeckers – they are difficult to sneak up on!

Camouflage

Both predator and prey use camouflage to good effect. While most savannah species rely on speed to escape, most browsers who live in thicker, wooded areas rely more on camouflage and nerve. If you look at the colouring of kudu, bushbuck, bongo and nyala – they all share a tell tale characteristic - they all have vertical stripes that run down their body. This acts to break up their outline and so make them harder to detect in the dappled light of their wooded environment. Their first instinct when they detect a predator is to stand stock-still and, as the predator's eyes rely more on movement than definition, they will often go undetected.

Even for impala and gazelle, which live mostly in the open, camouflage has its place. The newborns of these species, and even those of buffalo, wildebeest and zebra, are all fawn in colour. This earthy colouration, combined with a lack of scent, allows these youngsters to remain unseen by simply lying low, close to the ground and hidden by grass while their mothers feed nearby.

We all know about the ability of chameleons to blend in with their surroundings – but did you know that some frogs can change colour in a similar way?

Defence mechanisms

Some animals, notably the striped polecat, civet and aardwolf, can eject a powerful, vile scent from their anal glands that is so repulsive that it acts as a very effective deterrent!

The porcupine's quills, held erect in a huge halo that doubles its size and then rubbed together to make an ominous rattling sound, combined with the stamping of its hind feet is generally enough to put most attackers off!

Hedgehogs on the other hand, merely roll themselves up into a tight ball, offering only a covering of sharp spines to any tormentor.

Feigning death is not an uncommon tactic either.

Plants too have developed a host of defense mechanisms – from thorns and hairy leaves, to poisons and digestion-inhibiting chemicals. Thorns do not prevent an animal from browsing but they do slow down the rate at which this takes place. The main consumers of tree leaf in broad-leaved savanna's, where the nutrient-poor soils result in less nutritious leaves, are insects – hence hairy leaves are more prevalent. Trees do not only embrace physical defenses, they are also adept at employing chemical defenses, from sticky resins and waxy cuticles to strychnine's, cyanide's, pyrethrums and tannin's (phenols) that they manufacture specifically to deter herbivores. As soon as a browser starts to feed, the tree will begin to raise the tannin levels in the leaves making them less palatable. Some trees will also emit chemical signals (ethylene) into the air that alert other nearby trees to begin tactical manoeuvres to ward off the onslaught – quite amazing!

More anatomical specialisations and adaptations

Both the bat-eared fox and serval use their larger-than-life ears to listen for their prey underground or in the long grass.

The honey badger has a thick, loose skin that helps to protect it from bee stings and snake bites.

The klipspringer's coat hair is hollow and quill-like yet elastic, and by standing on end traps air around the body. This provides an excellent insulator and regulator for coping with the extremes of temperature found in its habitat of rocky outcrops and mountainous terrain. In addition, the klipspringer's tremendous agility up and down rock faces can be attributed to their tiny hoofs which have evolved to become cylindrical in shape - giving the impression that the animal is walking on tip-toes!

Desert adaptations

The ground squirrel, found in hot arid regions, fans out its tail and holds it above its head to provide shade in the heat of the day (like a parasol?).

The fog basking tok tokkie beetle of Namibia has adapted its behaviour to survive the arid and waterless Namib Desert – this involves perching on a dune crest at dawn, facing west and doing a headstand! Moisture-laden breezes rolling in from the cold Atlantic sea mix with the hot, dry desert air producing a fog that condenses on the beetle's uplifted back, allowing droplets to trickle down to a grateful mouth!

Not only that, but these surface beetles have also developed bigger bodies and longer legs than their cousins in colder climes. The thick body shell, incorporating the hardened fore wings, helps in maintaining a bearable internal temperature and in limiting moisture loss through evaporation. Long legs enable the beetle to scamper rapidly across the surface without the body being barbecued on the scorching sand. Scampering creates a wind flow over the body surface which cools the beetle as air is pushed ('breathed in') through holes along its side - the tok tokkie beetle having no lungs.

The name tok tokkie derives from the Morse-code like sounds that these insects make when tapping the ground with their abdomen in order to attract a mate. The drumming patterns are species-specific so you would have to learn the different tunes to know which is which. Try tapping a little tune of your own and see what happens...

The oryx (or gemsbok) is yet another desert-adapted species. It is able to raise its own body temperature to alleviate the need to perspire. Its muzzle contains an intricate network of blood vessels through which blood is cooled by the moisture of its nasal passages, thus protecting its brain from the excessive desert temperatures. This heat transfer reduces the temperature of the brain-bound blood by about 3°C. When the thermometer registers 42°C, most animals die. Yet the gemsbok plods steadily on through the unrelenting heat of the arid desert, despite a body temperature of 45°C (11°C above normal). What's more, it can do so for hours on end without apparent harm. Being hotter than its surroundings, it actually sheds body heat by conduction and radiation into the atmosphere, thanks in part to its light grey-fawn coat.

Adaptations amongst birds

It is worth discussing, albeit briefly, the many special adaptations that make birds so unique (they can fly after all) and remarkable. Firstly, setting birds apart from all other animals, are the feathers; each with a specific function: flight feathers for the tail and wings, contour (or vaned) feathers to protect, waterproof and insulate the body, and soft down feathers designed to trap air and keep the bird warm. The skeleton, including wings and legs, have hollow light-weight bones. A bill replaces teeth and jaws. Specific bill, wing and tail shapes reflect the need for agility, manoeuvrability, or specific prey. Almost a third of a bird's body weight is made up of powerful wing muscles, attached to a purpose-designed keel on the breastbone. The lungs are linked to a specialised network of thin, bag-like air sacs throughout their body (these air sacs cannot actually extract oxygen the way lungs do, but they help by storing air, and controlling the flow of air through the lungs, this enabling birds to receive oxygen when breathing in and out).

One of the most distinguishing features amongst birds is the enormous diversity of bill (beak) shapes and sizes, each designed to fill a particular niche – from the extended lower mandible of the African skimmer to the upside down bill of a Flamingo – not to forget the spoonbill and open-billed storks.

Interestingly though, despite a bill seemingly designed specifically for catching fish, not all kingfishers eat fish! In fact, most prefer insects. Only the pied, giant, malachite and half-collared kingfishers hunt predominantly fish.

Some other examples include:

- The African harrier hawk (or Gymnogene), a large bird of prey, has adapted to feeding on vertebrates and fledglings. It has developed double-jointed knees to enable it to clamber around the branches of trees, reaching into holes and crevices in search of food.

- The breast feathers of sand grouse are uniquely designed to allow for the absorption of water. In this way they are able to soak their belly feathers in water, and then fly back to their nest - sometimes up to 50kms away – where the chicks carefully strip the water from the individual feathers.

- With large protruding eyes and an aerodynamic shape the bat hawk is a specialist killer that ventures out only at dusk and dawn. To witness this specialist bat-catcher in action is an amazing sight indeed. With aerial maneuverability and speed the bat hawk sweeps across the night sky plucking bats out of the air, feeding them directly into its mouth in mid-flight whilst pursuing the next.

Melanism, Leucism and Albinism

Melanism is the occurrence of an increased amount of dark pigmentation of skin, feathers, eyes or hair, resulting from the presence of melanin. It is the opposite of leucism, which occurs because of a lack of melanin or other types of pigmentation to a lesser or greater degree. This brings about a variety of colour variations, either as patches or light sections or merely a generally lighter coloration than normal. Albinism is the complete lack of pigmentation caused by a genetic mutation (inherited if both parents have the albino gene). In leucism the eyes and soft parts are normal in colour whereas in albinism, eyes or soft parts are very pale in colour, even a fleshy pink due to underlying blood vessels showing through.

Interestingly, melanism has been found to be linked to beneficial changes in the immune system. It is understood that genes for melanism in felines may provide resistance to viral infections and that a viral epidemic may explain the prevalence of black leopards in Java and Malaysia, and the relatively high incidence of black leopards and black servals in the Aberdares region of East Africa. Previously, black furred felines in the Aberdares had been considered a high altitude adaptation due to absorbing more heat, and in other regions as an adaptation to aid hunting after dark.

"What is man without the beast?
For if all the beasts were gone
Man would die from a great loneliness of spirit
For all things are connected
Whatever happens to the beast, also happens to the man,
Whatever befalls the earth, befalls the sons of the earth."
Chief Seattle 1854

What's in a name?

You are undoubtedly going to be bombarded with a host of unfamiliar names and descriptive terms while on safari. These names and categorisations are used not only to identify the animals in question, but also to communicate the many facets about their lives. The topic can even be rather fun. For example, did you know that the collective noun for warthog is a 'sounder' of warthog? It's also a 'crash 'of rhino and a 'journey' of giraffe! See the list of collective nouns later in this chapter.

What's in a name?

Have you ever wondered why the two species of rhinoceros are referred to as Black and White rhino when clearly neither is black nor white, but more a grey colour? It appears that when the first settlers drove their wagons north from the Cape of Good Hope they spoke of the then very common rhinoceros they encountered as the wyde rhino – "wyde" being the Afrikaans word for "wide" and pronounced "vhite", and describes the wide upper lip that is prominent in the white rhino. The English-speaking folk who came after thought they were saying "white", and so the name stuck. Now we have to assume that when the next 'uitlanders' (foreigners or non-Afrikaans immigrants) came upon a rhino that had a narrow, hooked upper lip they must have decided that the two rhinos would make a nice 'set' (like salt & pepper) and called this one the black rhino! It's a true story – I promise!

Then of course there are the scientific names of the animals themselves – not to be confused with their everyday common names! Please do not despair – mammals and birds are very seldom referred to by their scientific name on safari (only trees seem to suffer this affectation!) – but, it is interesting and fun to know the origins of such names, to understand the hierarchy and what it all represents. For a further explanation on the subject of scientific and common names please refer to Appendix A toward the back of this book.

Scientific and common names are, however, just the beginning. It has also useful to place the different animals into categories that can tell us more about each animal's lifestyle and origins. Getting your mind around some of these terms is important in gaining a better understanding of the lives of the animals you will encounter on safari. Let us start off with the major categorisations and later, under Animal Behavior, we will look at a few other categorisations that you might find useful.

Ungulates, Ruminants, Herbivores, Carnivores & Primates

Ungulates, which include all antelope, buffalo, giraffe, rhinoceros, zebra and elephant, are hoofed animals that walk on tiptoe! It's true if you think about it. Think of a sable, kudu or impala – look down at its feet and what do you see? Its hooves of course! But look carefully – each hoof is in fact split in two. What you are looking at are in fact two digits or toes – the 3rd & 4th digits to be precise. Look again – up the leg from the hoof are the vestiges of digits 2 & 5. These are called false hooves.

Interestingly, ungulates are split into even-toed and odd-toed ungulates. Out of the 200 ungulate or hoofed mammals, all but 17 are even-toed. Odd toed ungulates include rhinoceros and elephant (3 toes) and zebra (single hoof – like a horse).

Nearly all even-toed ungulates are **ruminants**. Non-ruminants include elephant, hippopotamus and rhinoceros.

Ruminants are distinguished by a unique digestive system which features a four-chambered stomach (rumen, reticulum, omasum and abomasum) for the efficient digestion of plant matter. Non-ruminants on the other hand have a single large stomach. Ruminants and non-ruminants therefore differ in how they process the food they eat. This is significant – stay with me!

Ruminants are able to regurgitate their food so as to chew it into a fine 'cud' and, along with multiple stomach chambers; this is significant in aiding digestion efficiency. As a result, their energy conversion is remarkably efficient. By comparison, the non-ruminants have a single stomach (or hind gut) which cannot extract as much nutrition. This leads to the need to consume more food. To obtain more bulk the non-ruminant eats material which is coarser and easier to consume in bulk. The effect of this being that body size becomes a factor. The longer a bulk-feeder can keep a meal in its (single) stomach the better chance it has of digesting it properly. An elephant will take up to two and a half days to digest its food. The longer its food is kept, the bigger the storage vat that is required and the bigger the frame needed to carry such a large container. This leads to a tendency in non-ruminants to grow large as we see with elephants and hippopotamus.

All ungulates, be they ruminants or non-ruminants, odd or even-toed, are all **herbivores** – an animal whose diet consists of plant food.

Carnivores, as we know, prey on living things (like herbivores).

Omnivores on the other hand, including genets, civets and the honeybadger, eat most anything - insects, invertebrates*, fruit, frogs, reptiles, birds and small rodents including mice, moles and bats and are referred to as Omnivorous.

Primates are more like us – they eat a selective array of fruits, vegetable matter and meat. Gorillas are essentially vegetarian. Actually they are folivores, which means they eat leaves, stems and shoots. Chimpanzees are classified as frugivores – meaning they eat predominantly fruit, but they do also hunt monkeys and small forest antelope.

You may also come across the name pachyderm. This is a term used informally within the safari industry to describe elephants, and sometimes for rhino and hippo. This is in fact an obsolete Order of mammals used to describe an artificial grouping of unrelated animals, but who share the anatomical characteristic of having a "thick skin".

* An **invertebrate** describes any animal without a spinal column. The group includes 97% of all animal species — the exceptions being fish, reptiles, amphibians, birds and mammals (all the ones of most interest to us on safari!).

Collective nouns - pod, herd, pack!

On your safari you will hear groups of animals referred to by a selection of somewhat unusual names – here are a few of the collective nouns that you may come across:

A *huddle* or *pod* of hippo
A *sounder* of warthog
A *pack* of wild dog
A *parade* of elephants
A *cackle* or *clan* of hyena

A *skulk* of jackals

A *journey* or *tower* of giraffe

A *parliament* of owls

A *muster* of storks

A *float* of crocodiles

A *deceit* of lapwings / plovers

A *lounge* of lizards

A *cloud* of bats

A *rank* of impala

A *wake* of vultures

A *shrewdness* of monkeys

A *prickle* of porcupines

A *swarm* of bees

An *army* of caterpillars

An *armoury* of pangolins

A *whistle* of puku

A *crash* or *stubbornness* of rhino

A *leap* of leopards

A *coalition* or *bond* of cheetah

A *rumpus, congress* or *troop* of baboons

A *pride* of lion

A *implausibility* or *herd* of wildebeest

A *funeral* of marabou (storks)

A *colony* of ants (or termites)

A *plague* of locusts

A *descent* of woodpeckers

A *dazzle* or *zeal* of zebras

A *belligerance* or *herd* of buffalo

A *band* or *business* of mongooses

A *cete* or *colony* of honey badgers

A *flamboyance* of flamingos

A *covey* of quail or partridges

A *flight* of doves

A *raft* of ducks

A *stand* or *grove* of trees

A *constellation* of stars

A *confusion* of guinea fowl

And if you thought some of these are a bit of a stretch, consider a *murder* of crows and an *unkindness* of ravens?

Rabbit or Hare?

Even though rabbits and hares might appear to look the same to the untrained eye, in fact they are a completely different species, and have more differences than similarities.

The essential difference between rabbits and hares is that rabbits burrow and hares do not. As a result of this *single* behavioural difference each species displays a host of adaptations that has evolved to differentiate between them - notably:

Rabbits are born completely helpless, naked and blind (in their burrow) while hares, born in the open, come into this world fully furred, able to see and are almost immediately mobile. In fact, hares can survive on their own after only one hour from birth!

Needing to be able to escape quickly should they be discovered by a predator, hares have a broader air passage (from the nostrils to the trachea) to assist in a faster oxygen intake. They also have longer hind limbs than rabbits allowing them to be more agile and faster (for a quick getaway).

Living in the open, without access to a burrow, hares need to be more wary and have evolved longer ears, good camouflage and are scentless to evade detection.

Rabbits are very social animals; they live in colonies. Male rabbits even fight within a group to become the dominant male. The dominant male rabbit then mates with most of the females in the area. In opposite, hares live a mostly solitary life. They come together in pairs only for mating. There is almost no fighting among hares - they just pair off.

Rabbits and hares also have different diets. While rabbits prefer soft stems, grass or vegetables hares eat more hard food: bark and rind, buds, small twigs and shoots.

Baby-rabbits are called kittens while baby-hares are called leverets.

On safari you will see only hares. Those shouts of rabbit, rabbit are quite incorrect. So now you know!

Fireflies and Glow worms

One of the more fun, after dark attractions on safari, especially for children, are those flying insects that glow in the dark – fireflies. But do you know the difference between a firefly and a glow worm? They are in fact both beetles, and in most species both males and females grow wings and morph into the brown, elongated shaped insects we call fireflies. But in some species the females remain in a larva state and never develop wings – these we call glow worms. Interestingly, these beetles actually glow at all stages of their life cycle, even the eggs. The flashing you see after dark is the result of a protein and enzyme reaction in their bodies that releases energy in the form of a greenish-yellow light (bioluminesce). This intermittent 'glow' is an essential part of courtship. Each species has its own flashing pattern, produced by the males. A receptive female of the same species will then answer with a similar flashing pattern, so that the two can find one another and mate.

Grubs, maggots and nymphs?

As a further illustration of the intricacy of naming conventions, you might also find it interesting to know the names used to describe the larval stage of different insects (or not!):

Insect species	Larval stage
Grasshoppers & cicadas	nymph
Butterflies & Moths	caterpillar
Dragonflies & Mayflies	naiad
Beetles, bees & wasps	grub
Flies	maggot
Mosquitoes	wriggler

Scientific & Common names

While on safari you will see a wide assortment of flora and fauna, from mammals to fish, trees, reptiles and birds. Mostly, we get along just fine referring to each by a 'common' name. But this can cause some confusion for the safari-goer as there are often a number of common, or should I say 'colloquial' names for many trees, flowers and birds depending on the region or country you are visiting. By way of an example, the fairly widespread tree, *Faidherbia albida,* is alternatively referred to as the apple-ring acacia, winter thorn, acacia albida or Ana tree - depending on where you are and who you ask!

To add to this confusion is the fact that each will have several different names in the many local languages of each country (in our example above – the Tonga name for an Acacia Albida is Musangu). So in order to be more precise, and to avoid confusion in identifying each, a system of classification, known as Taxonomy, has been universally accepted to provide what are referred to as 'scientific' names.

A scientific name is generally of Latin or Greek origin and is expressed in two parts. Firstly its Genus, depicting its relationship in the classification hierarchy, and secondly, the species, which is a grouping of specific characteristics. The species is always expressed in lower case, with both the Genus and species in italics. It is common practice, where an animal is mentioned, be it mammal, bird, tree, or insect, that it will have in brackets next to its common name, its scientific name (in italics) e.g. apple-ring acacia (*Faidherbia albida*).

The organization (or hierarchy) of all living things can be seen like a pyramid, or family tree, with seven major levels or categories: **Kingdom, Phylum, Class, Order, Family, Genus, and species**. At each level the members share common attributes with other members in that classification. By way of example, the full scientific name of a serval (*Felis serval*) would be:

Kingdom (Animalia), Phylum (Chordata), Class (Mammalia), Order (Carnivora), Family (Felidae), Genus (Felis), species (serval)

Of all these groups, only a species actually exists in nature. The rest have been devised purely to show how the different species are related to one another. Some names are more revealing than others: for example, the protea family of flowering plants found in South Africa is named after the sea god Proteus, who could assume many different forms! The fish eagle, *Haliaeetus vocifer*, is descriptive of the bird itself: Haliaeetus - a fish-eating eagle and vocifer as in vociferous, for these are extremely vocal raptors; with its haunting cry being one of the most evocative sounds of the African bush.

A sub-species generally refers to a population which could potentially inter-breed with other members of its species but are prevented from doing so by geographic separation. For example there are a number of giraffe sub-species – Rothschild's, Masai, Reticulated and Thornicroft. These are sometimes referred to as different races.

When it comes to both common names and scientific names you will find that some early explorers were wont to give their names to the animals they recorded, or have had them named in their honour – hence we have Burchell's zebra (*Equus burchelli*), a Burchell's Coucal and Burchell's Starling, named after the explorer and naturalist William Burchell. Bizarrely, the explorer Francois Levaillant named two colourful birds after his Khoi Khoi servants, Narina and Klaas - hence the Narina trogon and Klaas's cuckoo! Other examples include Jameson's Firefinch and the Mountain Gorilla (*Gorilla beringei*), named after the German, Captain Robert von Beringe – reputed to be the first European to shoot and kill one.

Most safari guides will occasionally make use of scientific names, especially in reference to trees. As it was a requirement for them to learn these in guide training they now feel obligated to burden you with them too! Many are impossible to pronounce and often shed little light on the situation for non-Greek or Latin scholars. Unless there is a specific reason to mention the scientific name – to help to explain a characteristic about that animal perhaps or to highlight the association between one tree and another – they are just showing off! Just ask your guide to switch the sub-titles back on (hopefully he will take the hint).

You will seldom hear anyone call a bird by its scientific name –

there is enough confusion between the ever-changing (English) common names as it is! It appears that over time the East African ornithologists and their southern African counterparts somehow managed to adopt different family names for many of the bird groups, e.g. Plover vs. Lapwing, Dikkop vs. Thick-knee, Khorhaan vs. Bustard, Francolin vs. Spurfowl and Lourie vs. Turaco etc. To make matters even more confusing, the powers that be seem embolden enough to even challenge some rather long-standing favourites for no apparent reason – some proposed changes have included Terrestrial Eagle for the Secretary Bird and Short-tailed Eagle for the Bateleur Eagle – neither of which were popular! Unfortunately, there has been a spate of name changes in recent years, and I am not certain I am fully up to date with them all myself!

Naming conventions

Some clarification on the different designations for wildlife reserves may also be useful:

National Parks vs. Game Reserves vs. Conservancies and Private Game Reserves

You might be confused by the various designations given to conservation areas in different countries. What differentiates a National Park from a Game Reserve or private concession? Who owns these wildlife sanctuaries and where do local communities fit in? In broad terms, the following best encapsulates the major classifications you will encounter on safari:

National Park

A National Park is an area set aside by government statute for the preservation and protection of wildlife and for the benefit of the people of that country and is characterized by the following:

- No hunting is permitted.

- No permanent human habitation.

- It is open to the public

- It is generally a 'managed' environment i.e. it has fences, water points and research is ongoing.

Game Reserves

The distinction between a National Park and a Game Reserve (in a general sense) is that within a Game Reserve hunting may be permitted under a licensing system. In addition, the traditional inhabitants of the area may be allowed to continue to have access, or to have grazing rights for their livestock, and in some cases to live within its boundaries. The distinction between a Game Reserve and a Private Game Reserve is the obvious – the former is a government classification as it relates to state land, and the latter is privately owned. (See below for more on Private Game Reserves.)

Game Management Area (GMA) or Safari Area

This is a designation used in a number of countries to include areas set aside specifically for hunting and they act as buffer zones between National Parks, Game Reserves and farm land under the authority of the local chief or council.

Private Concession Areas

This is a designation given to an area that has been provided to a safari operator for their exclusive use or, if within the boundaries of a National Park, permission to establish a safari camp or lodge in a particular location with non-exclusive traversing rights in a pre-determined radius from that site. Such concession areas are also more commonly being negotiated with local communities on community lands.

Private Game Reserves & Conservancies

Such a designation is generally given to tracts of privately owned land which had previously been used for agriculture but that has now been given over to the protection of wildlife. Game fences are erected and species re-introduced or encouraged to thrive. Through related tourism ventures, paying clientel are able to view, or hunt, the wildlife as they would in other wildlife protected areas.

The role of such reserves, in terms of their contribution to conservation, cannot be over emphasized. In recent years there has been a great deal of interest in the creation of privately owned reserves and conservancies, outside the auspices of government. These private reserves are to be welcomed and bring a number of advantages to conservation in general, along with better utilization of marginal farming land. Many have been extremely successful in breeding, and bringing back from the brink, endangered species. Research is often a positive by-product and the involvement of local communities has also been given priority. All represent positive change.

Intensive Protection Zone (IPZ)

An IPZ is just that – a designated area, generally with a radius of 5 to 10kms, within a National Park ort Game Reserve where special protection is given to a specific species e.g. rhino, and where a number of that species has been relocated and protected from the threat of poaching.

Wildlife ownership

Each of the above designations assumes that the right of ownership of wildlife rests with the state. The state in its benevolence sets aside certain areas for the protection of its wildlife – as we have seen above. However, more recently, community involvement has become the key to spreading the conservation message. In some countries this has seen the ownership of wildlife transferred from the state to the land owner – an important change which encourages landowners to consider wildlife as a resource to be valued. After all, it is the people and local communities, who live alongside these animals, who need to see the value that the wildlife represents – whether this be in terms of the money raised through hunting or other non-consumptive (photographic) tourism ventures.

The growth of game farms/ranches in South Africa serves as an example: in 1965 there were only four wildlife-fenced properties in the country (all near Kruger) - by 2005, with wildlife ownership having been transferred from the state, there were more than 10, 000 properties in the nine provinces countrywide.

Wildlife Corridors

There is much talk in recent years about the need to create "wildlife corridors" that will allow wildlife, and especially elephant, to move between existing wildlife reserves. This may take the form of fence removal, extension of boundaries or even the creation of much larger "Peace Parks" that transcend national boundaries – see http://www.peaceparks.org/

Community Based Tourism Projects

Independently negotiated Community Projects are also becoming more and more a part of the overall make-up of conservation efforts in many countries throughout Africa. Vast tracts of land are in the hands of local communities. In circumstances where this land has not been completely turned over to agriculture, lease arrangements have been struck between safari operators and the local community. As well as providing employment the local community can expect to receive a percentage of the profits, or a set fee, from hosting visitors, either from hunting or photographic activities. In this way the local community is encouraged to protect the habitat and the wildlife that are the attraction for tourists.

One such community program originated in Zimbabwe and has gone on to become the model for many other countries on the continent - named CAMPFIRE (Communal Areas Management Program for Indigenous Resources). CAMPFIRE has developed into an important conservation strategy, ensuring that significant financial earnings revert to rural communities for their benefit whilst securing habitats for wildlife.

But enough about naming conventions...in the next chapter we will take a look at some of Africa's biggest names..

The African Elephant

Before we talk about the many animals you have come to see on safari I would first like to introduce you to the African elephant. No other species more encapsulates this continent. A formidable giant, which despite its great strength, shows intelligence, gentleness and empathy.

Rather than offer up facts and figures I have chosen to list a series of interesting facts about elephants that I hope you will find more engaging, and in this way give you an insight into this remarkable animal:

African elephant (*Loxodonta africana*)

- The elephant's trunk is a fusion of its nose and upper lip and comprises approximately 40,000 muscles. The trunk is incredibly versatile, sensitive enough to pick up a blade of grass at ground level and strong enough to rip the branches off a tree as high as 6m (20ft) off the ground. The trunk is also used for drinking – the elephant can suck up to 14 litres of water at a time and then blow it straight into its mouth! It uses its trunk to spray dirt and mud on its body, which will dry and act as sunscreen. The trunk is a multi-purpose tool capable of stripping off bark, breaking branches, uprooting shrubs and is dexterous enough to pick up pods, fruits and even single seeds using the two 'fingers' at its tip. And that's not all – with nostrils at the end, the trunk also acts as its nose!

- An elephant heart beats at an average of 28 beats a minute – compared to the average for humans at around 70.

- Elephants have a lifespan similar to humans – up to 60 years.

- Their tusks are elongated upper incisor teeth (not canines). Some adults lack tusks (genetically) and some have only one (perhaps the other has broken off). About one third to a quarter of the tusk is housed within the elephant's skull. At birth a small milk tooth, known as a 'tush' is already in place. The full tusk grows behind this 5cm long tooth, breaking through at around one year old.

- An elephant's tusks grow throughout its life, although they may wear down or sometimes break due to extensive use or in clashes with other elephants. Most elephants favour one tusk over the other (left or right tusked just as you are left or right handed) and so the most used tusk is usually shorter as it is worn-down by regular use.

- The heaviest reliably recorded tusks were a pair weighing individually 102.3 kg and 107.3 kg. These tusks came from near Mount Kilimanjaro in Tanzania (Smithers' Mammals of Southern Africa).

- An elephant will have up to 6 sets of molars in their lifetime. Once the last set start to wear down the elephant is unable to chew its food properly and hence extract sufficient nutrients. An already inefficient metabolism will slowly starve the animal until it dies.

- The movement of the molars in chewing its food is unusual in that the action is forward and back rather than from side to side like most herbivores.

- Elephant ears are very large, making up 20% of its surface area, flat and roughly the shape of the African continent, often torn and tatty and with holes in them. The thin, smooth inside skin of an elephants ears are laden with blood vessels and when flapped, cool the blood as it passes through a web of vessels inside the ear, bringing down the body temperature by up to 3 degrees Celsius.

- The wrinkles in an elephant's skin helps them to cool down their bodies. The creases and pleats of the skin create a larger surface area through which heat can be released, whilst helping moisture to be trapped for longer periods to aid cooling. In this way an elephant can release up to 75% of its body heat through its skin.

- An elephant's front feet are roughly circular, with five blunt toenails whereas the hind feet are oval and have four blunt toenails (see *Spoor Charts*).

- The front feet are larger than the back feet since the front feet support the very heavy head and tusks of the elephant. The speed at which an elephant is moving can be accurately gauged by the relative positions of the front and back spoor. When moving at a leisurely pace the back track falls behind the front. As the animal picks up speed the gap between the front and rear tracks closes; when moving at top speed the rear track actually overtakes the front and the toes scuff the ground.

- Elephants are in fact walking on tip-toe on a cushioned pad (sole) made up of elastic like tissue. This allows elephants to move amazingly silently for such a large animal.

- An elephant's height (to the shoulder) can easily be determined from the size of its footprints – for females the calculation is 5.5 x the length of the hind footprint, and for males it is 5.8 x.

- Elephants have only one basic gait: an ambling walk (and do not actually 'run'). When in a hurry they will take longer, quicker strides reaching speeds of up to 30km/hr. Due to their vast size they cannot jump.

- The tail of an elephant is thin and up to 1.5m (nearly 5ft) long. It ends in a whisk of long, thick hairs which are sometimes collected and used to make bracelets.

- Elephant bulls have wider heads than females and in profile they have a more rounded forehead. Their tusks too are usually larger and thicker than the females.

- An elephant's skull is not solid bone. It consists of a lightweight honeycomb structure which assists in cooling the blood that passes to the brain. It also lightens the weight of the skull allowing the elephant to keep its head up. This is in contrast to hippo or white rhino whose heads are so heavy that they seldom raise their heads to shoulder height!

- Elephants will sleep for 4 to 5 hours a night (often lying against a termite mound) and often rest (standing up) in the hottest times of the day.

- They spend most of their lives feeding as they have a rather inefficient digestive system. Only around 40% of their food is assimilated, compared with over 65% for a ruminant (e.g. buffalo, giraffe and all antelope).

- Elephants must therefore select the most nutritious and palatable of the plants which are available through the changing seasons. They tend to concentrate on grasses and herbs in the rainy season and on more woody plants (leaves, branches and bark) in the drier months.

- Elephants will feed for up to 20 hours a day when food is scarce (a lot less when nutritious green grass and leaf is more abundantly available), with an adult bull able to eat up to 300kg (over 600lbs) of vegetation in a day and drink over 200 litres of water. They are important agents of seed dispersal through their dung. As many as 1200 acacia seeds have been counted in just one ball of elephant dung.

- Elephants dig for water in dry river beds and mine for sodium, calcium and potassium at natural mineral licks – other animals follow their lead and so benefit from the elephants' ingenuity.

- Elephants are competent surveyors too, and many a road has been sited along ancient elephant trails that wander through the mountains.

- The elephant is not only a symbol of Africa, but its fate is entwined with the fate of wild places throughout Africa. Found in varying habitats the elephant has adapted itself from arid deserts to dense forests, and from thick woodland to open grass plains. Because of their sheer size and need for vast quantities of forage, elephants have an enormous impact on their environment. But that impact is not necessarily negative. Elephant are often referred to as Africa's architects, being responsible for the destruction and removal of trees and the opening up and transformation of woodland into grassland. Such habitat modification can benefit a vast array of antelope and in turn the predators that feed on them.

- Elephants are fond of bathing. Generally this is done after drinking and can be either mud wallowing or a dust or mud bath using their trunks to spray themselves. This is sometimes followed by a good rub against a nearby tree.

- Elephants can swim considerable distances and, when in deeper water, will use their trunks like snorkels. When the opportunity arises they like nothing better than a good 'splash', submerging themselves completely and even trying a tumble or two – water can really bring out the child in them!

- Elephants have a structured social order, staying together in family groups of related females of between 6 and 20 individuals. The females spend their entire lives in tight family groups made up of mothers, aunts, sisters, older daughters and younger offspring including immature males (up to about 13 years old). The leader of each group is normally the oldest and most experienced cow, she is known as the matriarch. All activity, direction and rate of movement are set by the matriarch, with the herd following her lead at all times. These family units in turn form kinship groups which comprise loosely affiliated family units that, although separate, are often within range of each other.

- Leadership and experience plays such a crucial role in elephants' social structure that a female's lifespan extends beyond her ability to bear offspring – most unusual in wild animals and a characteristic shared only by man.

- They will form large herds of over 100, and up to 400, at certain times of the year with such gatherings often associated with peak mating activity. This is usually during times of good rains and abundant food, later breaking up to calve and forage in smaller units during the drier months.

- Cows are in oestrous for only 3 to 6 days at a time. They may mate 3 or 4 times in a day and with more than one bull. The gestation period is 22 months and the cows give birth to a single calf of between 90 and 120kg. Twins are extremely rare.

- The brain of an elephant is only 35% formed at birth, and like humans they take many years to take on life's experiences. Youngsters have little control of their trunk in the early months and are quite hilarious to watch at the waterhole or when attempting to imitate Mum's dexterity with her trunk. Baby elephants form playgroups, with other youngsters from their kinship group, to play and learn.

- Female elephants have a single pair of mammary glands, located on the chest immediately behind the forelegs (unusual for non-primates).

- On reaching sexual maturity a male elephant will be ousted from the family group and will wander alone until joining up with other 'bachelor' males to form a loose association. They will only rejoin the herd when they have attained sufficient size and experience to compete for mating rights against older bulls.

- The term 'musth' (an Indian word meaning 'intoxicated') in mature bulls describes a heightened sexual state as a result of rising testosterone levels. This is indicated by the copious secretions from the temporal glands, located on the side of the head, aggressive behaviour and by a swollen and partially extended penis which drips continuously. A bull in 'musth' is not to be taken lightly – keep your distance!

- Elephants are definitely 'touchy, feely' animals, with elaborate greeting rituals which include scenting, touching, rumbling sounds and on occasion, placing their trunks in each other's mouths. In day to day interactions they constantly touch one another and will express themselves using gentle rumbling sounds to full blown trumpeting.

- It is thought that elephants are able to 'listen' with their feet by picking up ground vibrations through the soft pads!

- Whole books have been written on their various posturing antics which include 'standing tall', 'head-shaking', 'ears out', 'testing the wind' and the old favourite – the 'mock charge'. See if you can recognise them on safari.

- Elephants, like dolphins and whales, are intelligent animals with complex social structures and the capacity to experience fear, joy, tenderness, happiness and excitement. Elephants have a much more developed hippocampus that most animals; this region of the brain is responsible for emotion and spatial awareness. Elephants commonly display grief, compassion, playfulness, cooperation, and excellent learning abilities.

- Elephants have been shown to recognize themselves in a mirror – an indicator of self-awareness. Humans, great apes, and dolphins are the only other animals known to possess this form of self-awareness. Researchers report that all of these animals lead socially complex lives and display empathy (concern and understanding of another's feelings).

- Elephants are even thought to grasp the concept of death in a way not seen in other animals – they will stroke and sniff at bones with seeming compassion and even attempt to bury their dead by throwing dirt, leaves or branches over the body of a fallen comrade.

Forest elephants

When you think of the African elephant you are probably imagining a savannah elephant. It is a huge animal, standing almost 12 feet tall at the shoulders (3.6m), with large ears in the shape of the African continent and tusks that are long and curved. It lives in mixed woodland and frequent open grasslands.

But when a DNA identification system was set up to trace where poached ivory was coming from, scientists found that African elephants consisted of two very different species. DNA evidence shows that about 2.5 million years ago two genetically different strains of elephants evolved in Africa. The forest elephant, now known as Loxodonta cyclotis, found its niche in the equatorial forests of central and western Africa. Here they have lived hidden from view and practically forgotten.

Forest elephants look very different from their savannah cousins. Their bodies have adapted to living in dense forests. Their ears are small and rounded and their tusks are straight and thin, since curved ones might get caught in the under brush and vines of the forest. They are also significantly smaller so they can move around the dense forests more easily (standing a modest 2.2m). The lower jaw is longer, giving the forest elephant a long, narrow face. There is also a pinkish tinge to the ivory.

(Source: www.blueplanetbiomes.org/)

Desert-adapted elephants

There are only two known populations of desert-dwelling elephants in the world – one can be found in Damaraland, in the far north-west of Namibia, and the other in Mali in West Africa. The Namibian desert elephants are uniquely adapted to the extremely dry and sandy conditions of their environment - having smaller bodies and larger feet than other elephants, and having learned to adapt their diet and movements to take advantage of the meagre vegetation on offer in this arid region. The desert-dwelling elephants of West Africa live in the Gourma region of the Sahel, an ever-narrowing strip of land that lies between the desert in the north and the savannah in the south. The Sahel in West Africa is a near-desert wasteland of sparsely vegetated plains and endless miles of sand dunes. To survive in this extremely harsh landscape the Gourma elephants follow a circular migration path that covers 450kms (280 miles), moving from one water hole to the next. No other group of elephants is known to follow such a pattern. They must travel long distances between water holes, sometimes as far as 100 to 150 kilometres (60 to 95 miles). In some years the water holes dry up quickly after the end of a very short rainy season. An error in judgement - arriving at a spot with no water, for instance - could lead to the death of the herd. The 325 to 350 elephants in this region of Mali is one of West Africa's largest populations. Researchers with Save the Elephants, a non-profit research organization conducting elephant studies in Kenya, South Africa, and Congo, as well as Mali, were able to pinpoint the elephants' numbers and migration corridors using GPS technology. Led by a matriarch, the female elephants and their young travel an average of six miles (10kms) a day, "up and down mountains, in and out of forests, deserts, savannahs, across remote places," said Iain Douglas-Hamilton of Save the elephants. The Bull elephants travel independently and meet up with the rest of the herd around Banzena, the region's most reliable water source, from March to May. Amazingly, the elephants seem to be able to hear rainfall from great distances and respond accordingly said Douglas-Hamilton: "when rain falls, they hear it and go within 24 hours, heading for where the rain has fallen. Rain has a very low infrasonic signal and the elephants hear it over great distances" he said. (Source: National Geographic – September 2002 & February 2003)

The Ivory Story

Elephant tusks are similar to human teeth, consisting of a central core of pulp, covered in dentine and encased in bone-like cementum. The internal dentine, making up 95% of the tusk, is the substance commonly referred to as 'ivory'. It is a combination of mineral-based connective tissue and collagen proteins, making it very strong. Only elephant tusks have a cross-hatch pattern when viewed in cross-section, and the term ivory is generally only applied to this material.

Once referred to as 'white gold' ivory has always been valued by man as a decorative article being an excellent material for carving. Elephants have been hunted for their tusks for centuries.The Old Testament records that King Solomon ordered his throne to be made of ivory as long ago as 1000BC. The ivory trade peaked in the 19th century when ivory was considered a symbol of wealth and status. Prior to the introduction of plastics, ivory was used for billiard balls, piano keys, dice, bagpipes, buttons, brush handles, letter openers, fans, and and prized as 'hankos' (personal seals) in parts of East Asia (most notably Japan and newly rich China).

The Convention on International Trade in Endangered Species (CITES) oversees international trade involving rare animals. A total ban on ivory trading was imposed by CITES in 1989 after elephant populations in several African countries were devastated by poaching. In the 1980s an estimated 100,000 elephants were being killed per year and up to 80 per cent of herds were lost in some regions. In Kenya, the population plummeted by 85 per cent between 1973 and 1989 whilst those in Uganda and Sudan plummeted by 90%. Since the ban the elephant has recovered well and there are now thought to be over 600,000 elephants surviving in Africa compared to the previous 1.5 million. However, throughout the 1990s, privately-run carving and ivory distribution operations emerged and flourished unchecked in

China, and to this day large amounts of ivory continue to be imported into, and exported out of China.

In 1997, and again in 2007, the ban was lifted to allow Namibia, South Africa, Zimbabwe and Botswana to sell its ivory stockpile in one-off auctions to Japan under strictly monitored conditions. There has been, and continues to be, a great deal of controversy surrounding these decisions. The contention being that ivory from such sales continues to feed the demand for ivory and thus goes against the very reason for banning trade in ivory in the first place. This demand in turn fosters continued poaching and trade in illegal ivory.

The countries most affected by increased elephant poaching include Sudan, Central African Republic, Democratic Republic of Congo, Chad, Kenya, Tanzania, Zimbabwe, Zambia, Malawi, Mozambique, Nigeria, Cameroon, and Mali. A complete ban on ivory trading is still strongly supported by a number of these countries, including Kenya and Mali whose elephant populations are most under threat from poaching. Conversely, in countries like South Africa and Botswana, where their elephant populations are mushrooming beyond what they consider an ideal stocking capacity, there is much debate surrounding the need (or otherwise) of culling elephants to reduce numbers in order to lessen their impact on the environment. This is a topic that is taken up in the section AFRICA – Conservation issues later in this book. Clearly, there is much emotion and soul searching in the debate and perhaps there is no single answer for the different situations found in each country.

Today it seems that the elephant is most at danger in the forests and savannah of West Africa along with the Hippo, whose numbers have been reduced alarmingly in recent years. That said, on a continental level, elephants are certainly less endangered than cheetah, Wild dog or rhinoceros.

"Now, more than ever, when the elephants are so very vulnerable, their social family fabric torn to tatters, should the world SAY NO TO IVORY, no matter in what form. Each and every one of us can, and should, at least do that. Every piece of ivory is a haunting memory of a once proud and majestic animal, that should have lived three score years and ten; who has loved and

been loved, and was once a member of a close-knit family akin to our own; but who has suffered and died in unspeakable agony to yield a tooth for a trinket. Something so symbolic of death and suffering can never be beautiful." - THE ELEPHANT DEBATE by Daphne Sheldrick D.B.E. : 1992 UNEP Global 500 Laureate

Some Elephants of Distinction

Ahmed was the only elephant protected by a presidential decree in Kenya's history. He was thought to have had the largest known tusks on a living elephant at that time and was considered a living symbol of the awareness of conservation. Even with round the clock protection by armed guards, there were numerous attempts on his life. He even sported a bullet hole on his right ear. With such a bounty on his head, and despite many attempts on his life, he was to die a natural death in 1974 aged 55 years. He was truly a survivor. His amazing tusks were recovered and can now be seen at the Nairobi Museum in Kenya.

A herd of elephants that roam a private estate outside Hwange National Park in Zimbabwe is the only herd to receive the patronage of a head of state and are fondly referred to as the **Presidential Elephants**.

Over thirty years ago seven impressive elephant bulls, all with tusks weighing more than 50 kg each (110lbs), were identified in Kruger National Park in South Africa and promoted as an example of the successful conservation work being done in Kruger. These bulls, named: Dzombo, Joao, Kambaku, Mufanyane, Ndlulamithi, Shawu, and Shingwedzi became known as the **Magnificent Seven**, a reference to the 1960 Hollywood film of the same name. Kruger's elephants, with their large tusks, have been a source of inspiration around the world. While many of Africa's elephant populations have seen the genes of their largest tuskers depleted by ivory hunting and poaching, Kruger's legends live on to this day. The tusks and skulls of all seven elephants are now housed in the elephant Hall at Letaba Camp in the park. (Source: www.sanparks.co.za/)

Jumbo the Elephant was a 19th-century male African elephant born in the French Sudan (present-day Mali). Jumbo was exported to a zoo in Paris; then transferred in 1865 to the London Zoo in England where he became famous for giving rides to visitors, especially children. In 1881, Jumbo was sold for US$10,000 to P. T. Barnum, who took him to America and exhibited the elephant at Madison Square Garden, and around the country. It is this elephant's name that spawned the common word, "jumbo", today meaning large in size. It is likely a variation of one of two Swahili words: jambo, which means "hello" or jumbe, which means "chief". On Jumbo's death, at a railway siding in St Thomas Canada, his skeleton was donated to the American Museum of Natural History in New York City, where it remains to this day, and a life-size statue was erected in 1985 in St. Thomas to commemorate the centennial of the elephant's death.

"We admire elephants in part because they demonstrate what we consider the finest human traits: empathy, self-awareness, and social intelligence. But the way we treat them puts on display the very worst of human behavior." – Graydon Carter, Editor of Vanity Fair

The Big Cats (lion, leopard & cheetah)

Lion (*Panthera leo*)

- The lion is one of 4 big cats – the others being tigers, jaguars and leopards. The lion is the second largest cat after the tiger, with males weighing up to 250kg and females up to 180kg.

- At one time the lion used to occur right across Africa, Western Europe and all the way to India and even in the Americas (lions are still found in the Gir Forest of southern India).

- Lions are the only social (or non-solitary) African cat with prides of up to 30 members, made up of related females, their offspring (including a number of immature males), and of course the dominant pride male(s). In fact, they are a truly sociable cat that relies extensively on group co-operation both in hunting and raising their young.

- The status quo within a lion pride does not remain the same for very long. The dominant males are usurped, lionesses get injured or killed, terrible losses of cubs are suffered and juvenile male lions get pushed out of the pride.

- When tackling larger prey, like elephant, giraffe and full grown buffalo, it is the co-ordination of the females in a pride, and on occasion the males, which tips the scales in their favour. Whilst the females do the majority of the hunting, it is the role of the dominant male(s) to secure a territory for the pride and ensure the survival of the young cubs.

- The male lion has a prominent mane of thick, dark-coloured hair, giving it a regal appearance that has earned it the title of 'king of beasts'. They are the only cats to have a mane, suggesting that it is linked to their unique social system (as the only non-solitary cat) with mane colour being associated with sexual maturity and health - it is said that darker and fuller manes attract more female attention!

- Male lions are territorial, scent-marking key points of their territory with urine, patrolling the boundaries regularly and roaring to warn other lions of their presence.

- Competition between males to head a pride is fierce, and dominant males (or coalitions) will reign on average for only 2 to 5 years. Their lives are extremely arduous and fights for possession of the pride are vicious, often resulting in serious injury and even death. In the wild a male lion will live for only 8 to 14 years.

- When a lioness comes into oestrus, and finds a mate, the pair will couple up to four times an hour for a period of one or two days, with each mating lasting for less than a minute.

- Lionesses tend to stay with the pride in which they are born. This makes the group a collection of sisters, aunts, mothers and grandmothers who have grown up together. Males are expelled from the pride in which they were born once they reach maturity (3-4 yrs old). They usually form coalitions with other males (often relations) with whom they hunt and scavenge for food until they can challenge for a pride of their own.

- Unusually, a lactating female will allow cubs who are not her offspring to suckle indiscriminately, showing no preference for her own. In this way, the mortality rate of lion cubs, although very high, is reduced.

- Lions use darkness, long grass and coordinated ambush strategies to good effect when hunting, although it is debatable whether they take the wind direction into account. Most hunts take place during the cooler hours, often between dusk and dawn.

- Lions can eat as much as 25 percent of their bodyweight at one time, gorging themselves and then going without food for up to 3 to 5 days. A male lion can eat as much as 50kgs in a single sitting, gorging themselves into near immobility when the occasion arises.

- A lion's tongue is covered with tiny backward-curved hooklets that allow them to literally strip the meat from bones.

- Lions are also the only cats to have a tuft at the end of their tail.

- A lion spends up to 20 hours a day sleeping!

- Despite the regal 'king of beasts' tag, lion have no compunction about stealing the kills of others and will readily eat carrion (the carcass of a dead animal).

- Lions are not as fastidious about their grooming as are the smaller cats and are often infested with ticks and bloodsucking flies, and can give off quite an odour!

- Lions are very adaptable in their choice of habitat and are found in very arid regions, woodland and open savannah, but are absent from equatorial forests.

- The Barbary lion, thought to have been the largest of the African lion sub-species, is now extinct. It was the Barbary lion that fought gladiators, mauled Christians at the Coliseum in Rome and protected the Tower of London in the Middle Ages. Together with the Barbary leopard and Atlas bear (a sub-species of brown bear), also extinct, these three animals were once found in the Atlas Mountains of North Africa, from Morocco to Libya.

Leopard (*Panthera pardus*)

- The most secretive, elusive and cunning of the large carnivores.
- Easily recognizable by its spotted coat pattern of circular rosettes *.

Their soft, beautiful fur is much sought after in traditional African cultures as a symbol of authority, and thus favoured by kings and chiefs.

- Extremely powerful, leopards are capable of killing prey much larger than themselves, with a swift single bite to the base of the neck or by clamping down on the windpipe and suffocating its prey.

- Extremely agile, they are capable of remarkable leaps, climbing trees with ease, and are also very adept swimmers.

- With strong forelegs and neck a leopard can carry prey three times its own weight into a nearby tree. Here it will cache the kill, returning nightly to feed on it, thus denying competing carnivores and scavengers the opportunity to steal the kill. This habit allows leopard to hunt less frequently than ground-dwelling cats, such as cheetah, which often lose prey to marauding lions or hyenas.

- Leopards are very opportunistic animals and have an extremely varied diet. They will consume protein in almost any form, from small rodents to antelope twice their own weight. Their main diet consists of over 30 different species including: medium sized antelopes such as reedbuck, impala, and Thompson's gazelle and the young of larger species like Topi, Hartebeest, wildebeest and zebra as their primary food sources, with hares, birds and small carnivores rounding out the list. They have even been known to include the occasional baboon in their diet.

- They favour rocky and/or densely bushed habitat, such as that found along rivers and kopjes (rocky outcrops).

- Very solitary and predominantly nocturnal, both males and females mark out their own territories, although male territories tend to be bigger and overlap a number of female territories.

- Both sexes produce a deep rasping cough to advertise their presence. Leopards also growl, roar and purr.

- They have a lifespan of only 10 to 15 years in the wild although they have been known to live to 25 years in captivity.

- Cub mortality is high at 40 to 50%.

- The whitish tip of the mother leopard's tail is held upright during forays on the ground. This erect tail posture is thought to provide the cubs with an eye-level visual marker, helping them follow their mother through the tall grasses and shrubs.

- An adaptable species with regard to human invasion of its habitat, and capable of living in very close proximity to urban areas.

- Although under threat, they are widespread throughout Africa south of the Sahara, with more than 20 subspecies.

* For the novice, there is a tendency to mistake leopards for cheetah and vice versa. The trick is to think less about the 'spots' and more about body shape. The cheetah is long-legged and slight, with a small(ish) head and distinctive black tear ducts, and is seen more during the day than at night.

Cheetah (*Acinonyx jubatus*)

- The name cheetah is derived from the Sanskrit word "Chitraka" meaning "speckled or spotted one". The cheetah once ranged across Asia and India but today can only be found in Africa.

- Throughout history cheetahs have been trained for hunting, with many civilizations depicting them in their art and in written records. Cheetahs were so popular in India that Akbar the Great was said to have kept a stable of 1,000.

- The million-year-old fossilised remains of a cheetah have been found near Bulawayo in Zimbabwe, a testament to its ancient lineage.

- They are the most specialised of the cats and occupy an ecological niche not exploited by any other carnivore, hunting the fastest antelope in the open grass plains in broad daylight.

- Built for speed, it has long, slim, muscular legs, a small, rounded head set on a long neck, a flexible spine, a deep chest, large nostrils, and hard pads on its feet for traction plus a long tail that acts like a rudder when at full speed. It can accelerate to 70kms/hr is 3 seconds and can sprint at over 100 kms per hour (60 miles/hr); compared to a lion's top speed of 60kms/hr.

- Their claws are blunt and unsheathed (and despite still possessing the mechanism, do not retract) and act like spikes on an athletics track.

- Distinctive black 'tear tracks' running from the inside corner of each eye to the mouth may serve as an anti glare mechanism for daytime hunting.

- Cheetahs have a high concentration of nerve cells, arranged in a band at the centre of their large eyes. This arrangement, called a "visual streak", significantly enhances the sharpness of their vision and together with binocular vision, aids in seeking out prey. On safari, you will notice that cheetah will often take up an elevated position, on a termite mound or similar, in order to scan the savannah (both for prey and foe alike).

- The cheetah is basically a solitary animal. At times, a male will accompany a female for a short time after mating, but most often the female is alone or with her cubs.

- Females will have up to 5 cubs, with the family group remaining together for up to 2 years.

- Cheetah cubs sport long blonde strands of hair over their backs, very similar to that of a Honey Badger, one of Africa's most feared small animals. Coincidence – maybe!

- Cheetahs do not roar like lions, but they can purr, hiss, whine and growl. They also make a variety of contact calls; the most common is a birdlike chirping sound when calling their cubs (or siblings).

- They are very prone to having their kills stolen by other larger predators – especially by lion and hyena.

- Never numerous, cheetahs have become extinct in many areas, principally due to shrinking habitat, loss of species to prey upon, disease and a high rate of cub mortality. In some areas 50 to 75% of cheetah cubs die before they reach 3 months, as they are highly susceptible to disease at this age and succumb to lion and hyena pressure.

- An aberrant form, the King cheetah (*Acinonyx rex*), the result of a recessive gene that must be present in both breeding adults, occurs in parts of southern Africa. It is bigger in size and the spots on the upper body have coalesced into bars, giving it a distinctively darker and very striking appearance.

Large Herbivores (buffalo, giraffe, rhino, hippo, zebra)

Besides the elephant, Africa has a number of large herbivores to fill out this ecological niche:

Buffalo (*Syncerus caffer*)

- Buffalo are one of the most widespread of the African ungulates (hoofed animals) and are to be found throughout Africa south of the Sahara, save for large tracts of southern Africa where they have been displaced by farming.

- Buffalo live in mixed herds comprising cows, calves and mature bulls. Older bulls leave the herd to live in small bachelor groups known as "dagga boys".

- The main source of food for lions, buffalo herds can number in the hundreds and are one of the most successful African mammals. They are highly gregarious but non territorial.

- Buffalo tend to be non-migratory, inhabiting a home range which is largely exclusive to that group.

- Buffalo have earned a formidable reputation amongst hunters and conservationists and are considered unpredictable and extremely dangerous if cornered or wounded.

- Sight and hearing of buffalo are both rather poor, but their sense of smell is well developed.

- When walking, buffalo move one leg at a time, with three feet always on the ground.

- Buffalo horns, found in both males and females, are hook-shaped and formidable weapons that are used effectively in their defence against lions. In males, the horns broaden across the forehead, meeting in the middle to form a heavy shield known as the 'boss'.

- Apart from their horns, one of the buffalo's most distinguishing features is the large, droopy ears fringed with long hair on the edges and situated below the horns.

- A wide incisor row and massive molars coupled with a strong prehensile tongue enable buffalo to feed on coarse grasses, taking a pioneering role as a bulk feeder and reducing grassland to the height preferred by more selective feeders like zebra and wildebeest.

- Buffalo are very water dependent and through the dry season can always be found near a water source. Their favoured drinking times are morning and late afternoon. Mud wallowing is also typical. During the hottest time of the day, herds will typically rest and ruminate, although they often prefer resting in the open rather than in shade.

- They are particularly susceptible to drought and are prone to disease, including anthrax and rinderpest. But they are resilient and have a remarkable capacity to recover their former numbers quickly when conditions improve.

- Buffalo get some relief from pests through a symbiotic relationship with oxpeckers which remove biting and sucking insects from their skin. The sudden flight and alarm calls of oxpeckers serve as a good indicator of unseen buffalo for people who are walking in the bush – take heed.

- Females have their first calves at age 4 or 5 years old and will usually calve only once every two years. Calves are suckled for around 6 months and during this time are completely dependent on their mothers. There is a strong bond between mother and calf and between related females in a herd. The distinct distress call of a young buffalo triggers a mobbing attack that is often successful in deterring or repelling attacks from lions.

- Buffalo bulls remain with the herd until too old to fight for the attention of the breeding females. These ousted bulls band together in groups of 2 to 6 and are referred to as 'dagga boys'. The term 'dagga' is a reference to the coating of mud (dagga) that these older bulls use to combat biting insects, which are an annoying feature as their coats lose hair with age. Between the biting insects, lack of female company and the attention of lion these 'dagga boys' can be extremely irascible and unpredictable and should be avoided.

- Like the elephant, a much smaller forest sub species of buffalo is found in Central and West Africa.

Giraffe (*Giraffa camelopardalis*)

- The word "giraffe" is thought to come from either the Arabic word, "zirafah", which means "the tallest of all", or "xirapha" meaning 'one who walks fast".

- It is truly a unique animal; the genus *Giraffa* containing only the single species!

- Although mostly silent giraffe do cough or snort in alarm, cows seeking their lost calves bellow, and they have also been heard moaning, snoring, hissing, and making strange flutelike sounds at night!

- They have excellent eyesight and are even thought to have full colour vision.

- They are the tallest quadrupeds, reaching a height of up to 5.5m (over 18ft) and the males can weigh nearly 1200kg.

- Their sturdy front legs appear much longer than the rear pair, because their backbone angles down toward the rump. But in fact, all four legs are almost the same length.

- When a giraffe walks (or ambles), you will see that the legs on the same side of the body move together, rather than in a bipedal manner like a cow – take a look. But when galloping, the front legs move together and the back legs move together, like a running rabbit!

- They can gallop at nearly 60 km/hr (37 miles/hr) but can hardly jump at all.

- It is the only animal born with 'horns', and even these are unique; known as ossicones, they are in fact formed from ossified cartilage as opposed to living bone. At birth they are not attached to the skull, but folded flat under the skin. They soon assume their erect position and grow slowly as they ossify (turn to bone), eventually fusing with the skull but remaining covered in skin and fur. It is only the males that begin to lose these beautiful tufts of fur on the tip of the 'horn' because of fighting, or 'necking'.

- They are gregarious by nature but have no social structure. They form loose, open herds but no lasting bonds.

- They are not in the least territorial and range freely. As territories are areas that animals will defend, it might explain the giraffe's broken social structure and possibly their gentle nature.

- Giraffe can live for up to 25 years in the wild.

- They have a fairly long gestation period (pregnancy) of nearly 15 months.

- Like most mammals, including humans, a giraffe's neck has only 7 vertebrae.

- They have a prehensile (adapted to grasping or holding) tongue up to 45cms (18 inches) long, together with extremely flexible upper lips, to facilitate the selective stripping of the most succulent leaves. Interestingly, and unusually, the tongue is black (a bluish purple). They have no front teeth in their upper jaw.

- They have a long tufted tail used for swatting flies.

- Young male giraffe 'spar' in a ballet of gentlemanly conduct, seeming to play out the ritual in slow motion while each waits its turn to strike the other with a thundering blow of the head. In adult males these fights become deadly serious.

- They require less sleep than almost any other mammal, averaging less than 4 hours a day and generally for no more than a few minutes at a time while standing, but will occasionally lie down to rest and ruminate.

- Baby giraffe's are, on average, nearly 2 metres tall (6 feet) when born and will nearly double their height in the first year.

- In order to drink giraffe need to spread their forelegs wide, and virtually straddle the water's edge, before lowering their long necks to drink. In this somewhat awkward position they are very vulnerable (and hence their extreme caution when drinking).

- To prevent it passing out when it lifts its head up after drinking, giraffe have a series of one-way valves in their neck to control the rush of blood from the head.

- Giraffes drink water if it is available but can go weeks without it (even longer than camels); getting enough water from dew and the foliage they eat. They have never been seen to bathe.

- The giraffe has the largest heart of any land mammal, weighing over 10 kgs, used to pump 60 litres of blood around its body every minute at a blood pressure, and heart rate, twice that of an average human.

- Giraffe defend themselves against predators by a downward and forward chop (with great force) with the front hoof, normally only one but sometimes both feet together. They also kick out backwards and sideways with one back leg, aiming the hoof at the intended target.

- Male giraffe (bulls) tend to feed at full stretch in the higher part of the tree, whereas the females (cows) tend to bend their necks to browse the leaves, at or below two metres. This is possibly due to the fact that the males' heads are considerably heavier than those of the females, and lowering the head too much is a strain.

- Males can be recognized by the lack of tufts or hair covering the 'horns' – this hair has been worn off by the males in their jousting competitions as they grow up. Their coat markings also tend to darken in colour with age.

- Calcification of the skull in males takes place throughout its life and can lead to a skull weighing as much as 7kg at age 15 giving it a distinct advantage over younger bulls when determining dominance.

- Giraffes chew bones to help meet their need for large quantities of calcium and phosphorous. This phenomenon is known as 'osteophagy'.

- It is likely that on safari you will come across only four of the nine recognised sub-species of giraffe – Rothschild's, Masai, and Reticulated (all found in East Africa) and Thornicroft (endemic to the Luangwa Valley in Zambia). Each can be distinguished by the unique markings or patterns of their coats.

- The giraffe currently sits on the IUCN's Red List as a species vulnerable to extinction. The global population has plummeted by up to 40% in the last 30 years, with reduction in habitat being the main factor in their plight.

- The savannah giraffe's forest-dwelling cousin, the okapi (*Okapia johnstoni*), is found in West Africa. They share a similar body shape but not the extended neck, and have much in common – the same ambling walk, a prehensile tongue adapted for selective browsing, fur covered horns, specialized teeth and tongue, a ruminating four chambered stomach, and the need to straddle the forelegs in order to drink (indicating that this limitation existed before the giraffe's neck and limbs became elongated), an extended gestation period and a shared habit of defending themselves against predators by kicking.

"Out on safaris, I had time after time watched the progression across the plain of the giraffe, in their queer, inimitable, vegetative gracefulness, as if it were not a herd of animals but a family of rare, long-stemmed, speckled gigantic flowers slowly advancing." - Isak Dinesen, Out of Africa

Rhinoceros - Black (Diceros bicornis) & White (Ceratotherium simum)

- In 1840 the hunter and artist, Captain William Cornwallis Harris, described the black rhino as "a swinish, cross-grained, ill-favoured, wallowing brute, with a hide like a rasp, a mud-begrimed exterior and a necklace of ticks and horseflies." – take that!

- Another observant hunter records "…the average rhinoceros is an odd mixture of timidity, inquisitiveness, stupidity and nervous irritability" Charles Maberley – *The Game Animals of Southern Africa*.

- They have extremely poor eyesight, and probably cannot

distinguish a stationary object beyond 15 metres! However, they have excellent hearing and an acute sense of smell. In fact, the nasal passages are bigger than their brains.

- The horns, one short and one long, whose structure resembles that of a horse's hooves, are composed of soft keratin on the outside, similar to our own hair and fingernails, while at its centre there are dense deposits of melanin and calcium. These horns are not attached to the skull like the true horns of antelope. The horns grow continuously and if cut off will re-grow.

- Rhino sleep soundly (good to know when tracking rhino on foot). They sleep both at night and through the heat of the day, either lying down or standing.

- Rhinoceros can live for up to 50 years.

- They are thought to be able to eat plants that are toxic to other animals (including noxious weeds and the leaves of the fever berry tree) and in times of drought, or notably in the case of the desert-adapted rhinos of Namibia, can survive up to 5 days without water.

- Both courtship and mating are remarkably prolonged and presumably this is where the myth of the rhino-horn as an aphrodisiac originated.

- They have 3-toed feet, being an odd-toed ungulate, and are more closely related to horses and zebras than the hippopotamus. They love to wallow and dust bathe to cool off and rid themselves of biting insects.

- Reproduction is relatively slow with a gestation period of 15-16 months and a calving interval of between 2 and 4 years. As a result, calves seldom have peers to play with.

- They can reach speeds of up to 45kms/hr (around the same speed as Usain Bolt over 100 metres).

- Males will defecate in the same spot – referred to as a midden – as part of their scent marking rituals. This is followed by scraping the soil with the back feet and urinating in a backward spray between the legs onto nearby bushes. This acts as a signpost for other male rhinos to check and acknowledge – just like an outdoor bulletin board!

- Despite declining numbers, and a continued onslaught by poachers, the rhinoceros has become a symbol of the struggle, and success, of African wildlife conservation. The fight continues.

DIFFERENCES BETWEEN BLACK & WHITE RHINOCEROS

- Black rhino (*Diceros bicornis*) are considered to be very cantankerous. Cows with calves are especially dangerous and will charge under almost any circumstances. The white rhino (*Ceratotherium simum*) are relatively complacent.

- Black rhino are browsers (hence the hook-lip) and feed on leaves, whereas white rhino are grazers (featuring a distinctive broad, square lip) and eat grass.

- The choice of food, and hence its habitat, by each species of rhinoceros has an interesting behavioural association. When a black rhino and calf are disturbed and take flight, the mother will keep the calf in front of her so that she does not lose the calf in the thick bush. In contrast, the white rhino and calf, as grazers, are found more in open grassland with tall grass. The white rhino calf follows behind its mother as it would not be able to see where it is going in the long grass.

- Black rhino have smaller heads and a more pronounced nuchal hump (the lump above the shoulders) whereas the white rhino has a larger head with the neck muscles attached in such a way as to them to feed in a relaxed manner with their heads down (in the same way as hippo). It is this feature that is the most obvious difference between the two species – a head-down versus the head-up posture in black rhino.

- The black rhino is no taller than a buffalo but is nearly twice as heavy (reaching 1000kg), whereas the white rhino is twice the bulk again at over 2000kg.

- Black rhino are considered more solitary, whereas white rhino, with the exception of adult bulls, are quite gregarious.

- Black rhinos are not considered territorial as they live in overlapping home ranges which are not defended. Fights between males are rare because they usually avoid each other (see scent marking behaviour above). Fights usually only occur when two bulls are courting the same female. When a female comes into heat the smell of her urine changes and it is this that the males detect whilst patrolling.

- Conversely, male white rhinos are both solitary and territorial.

- These prehistoric creatures were once widespread throughout the continent. Early European explorers recorded sightings of as many as 150 in a single day. Over time the rhinoceros has been brought to the brink of extinction due to habitat loss, excessive hunting and, in more recent times, to satisfy the demand for rhino horn in Asian medicine and as prized dagger handles in Yemen.

- Today the best locations in which to find rhino are probably Kruger, KwaZulu-Natal and the eastern Cape reserves in South Africa, Lake Nakuru, Meru and Laikipia (including Ol Pejeta and Lewa Downs) in Kenya, Ngorongoro and Mkomazi Reserve in Tanzania, Etosha in Namibia, North Luangwa in Zambia, Majete Wildlife Reserve in Malawi, and Matobo Hills in Zimbabwe. A number of reintroduction programs are currently under way in Botswana, South Africa and other parts of Africa. This should result in both an increase in overall numbers and the return of the Black and the White rhino to regions where they were once abundant.

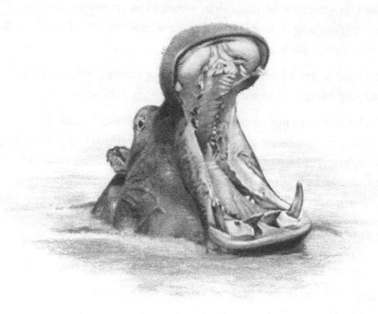

Hippopotamus (*Hippopotamus amphibious*)

- The name hippopotamus comes from Greek and means 'river horse.' They are not related to horses however, but share a common ancestry with whales.

- The basic unit of hippo society is called a 'pod' and comprises females with their young, controlled by a dominant bull. The groups are territorial, each occupying a specific stretch of river – defended and demarcated by the male splattering dung on rocks and bushes. He does this by using the telltale wagging of his flat, bristle-fringed tail, like windscreen wipers, as he defecates.

- Although hippos are generally seen in large groups immersed in water by day, come nightfall they are solitary - going out on land to feed – each on their own.

- Their nostrils, ears and eyes are situated on the top of the head allowing them to see, hear and smell while remaining totally submerged except for the top of their heads.

- Their nostrils close when they submerge and it is the sound of expelled air as they open their nostrils when surfacing that is so distinctive. They also 'spin' their ears as they surface to get the water out!

- If necessary, a hippo can remain submerged for up to 6 minutes.

- Although ungainly looking, hippo can run on land at an astonishing 30kms per hour (20 miles/hr).

- Besides the cacophony of sounds we hear from hippo while they are in the water, they also use clicks and whistles under water – similar to dolphins. Above water, hippo vocalise through their nostrils, reaching up to 120 decibels (equivalent to a jumbo jet passing overhead). They can also hear and make sounds above and below the water at the same time.

- With its resonating grunts, splashing and air-venting the hippo is one of Africa's noisiest animals, yet on land it is virtually silent.

- Hippos have lost virtually all their hair (as hair does not function as an insulator in water) and they no longer have sweat glands to help them cool off (the water does that for them). This makes them vulnerable to the hot midday sun if caught out of the water for any length of time. However, they do have numerous glands under the skin that produce mucus that acts like a sun block. This turns a reddish brown on exposure to the air and accounts for the pinkish colour that you can sometimes see when they are out of the water. This secretion is also thought to have anti-biotic properties and may go a long way to explains why the many cuts you can see on their skin do not become infected, despite living in water.

- Their naked skin is very permeable and fluids are lost very quickly, meaning that they can become dehydrated when out of water for extended periods or as a result of too much sun.

- They do not actually swim under water but rather run along the bottom, and whilst not considered good swimmers, can be remarkably graceful under water.

- Because of its sedentary life and good insulation (fat) the hippo uses only small amounts of energy in relation to its size, and thus requires less food than you might expect (although a third the size of an elephant it requires only a sixth the amount of food). When times are good however, an adult hippo will eat up to 40kg of grass in an evening.

- When grazing, hippos crop the grass with their broad muscular lips and grind the grass between two rows of molars.

- The hippo's formidable canines are part of the 'yawning' displays that act as a threat to rivals. Hippos are extremely aggressive fighters and deaths from fighting are not uncommon.

- Only the dominant male in a pod will mate with the females. Apart from whales and dolphins, hippos are the only African mammals that mate in water.

- Baby hippos are able to suckle under water, coming to the surface to breathe. They are also born bottom first (the breech position) which is extremely unusual for mammals.

- Originally thought to be related to pigs, DNA proof now suggests that hippos are most closely related to whales and dolphins - not too surprising considering all of the above.

- The common hippo, which weighs up to 2600kg (over 5500lbs), can be found in virtually all of Africa's major river systems, whilst the pygmy hippo (up to 280kg) is found only in West Africa.

- The pygmy hippo is a shy, solitary, forest dweller and is hunted for its meat. It is now thought to be threatened with extinction in its natural habitat due to de-forestation and excessive hunting.

Plains zebra (*Equus quagga*)

- Extremely gregarious, plains zebra live in small cohesive groups typically comprising a stallion, a harem of several mares and their offspring. Single males unable to secure a harem, form small bachelor groups.

- Females establish a dominance hierarchy within the herd. When moving, the group is led by the dominant female and her foal, followed by other females in order of dominance, with the stallion guarding the rear.

- Stallions will defend their harems from predators, including hyena and wild dog, with aggressive kicks from the hind legs.

- Not strictly territorial, zebras have loosely organized home ranges within which they move seeking grazing and water. In particular areas they migrate seasonally in search of better grazing, and like wildebeest they will congregate in large migratory herds.

- The zebra's striped pattern of black and white has generated a good deal of discussion over the years – see the discussion points below – *So why do zebras have stripes?*

- They have a very distinctive high pitched neighing 'Kwa-ha-Kwa-ha' alarm call followed by a snort.

- A newborn zebra has a fluffier coat with brown stripes and is short-bodied and long-legged.

- Zebra adults are only about four feet tall at the shoulder!

- Zebra are almost exclusively grazers and their hindgut fermentation digestive system allows them to extract energy and nutrients from coarse, low-quality grasses. They are thus less sensitive than other grazers to poor food quality and can maintain body condition on very poor forage. They are the only grazer to have both upper and lower incisors; enabling them to snip the grass blade (rather than yanking it out). Zebras always look fat and flourishing -the only indication that an animal is in poor health is if the mane, which is short and always stiff and upright, has flopped down.

- Their main predators are lion and hyena. However, they are dangerous prey as they can lash out viciously with a kick that can break a jaw or even kill – the number of zebra with scarred rumps testifies to the effectiveness of these defensive kicks.

- In addition to the plains zebra (*Equus Quagga* – formerly *Equus burchelli*) there are two other distinct species: the Grevy's zebra (*Equus grevyi*), and the mountain zebra (*Equus zebra*). Each species having a stripe pattern that is distinct from the other species.

- The Grevy's zebra is named for Jules Grevy, a president of France in the 1880s and who reportedly received one from Abyssinia (Ethiopia) as a gift.

- Today, Grevy's zebra are found in the semi-desert of northern Kenya, east of the Great Rift Valley and north of the Tana River, although their range does extend into neighbouring parts of Ethiopia and Somalia. The Plains zebra is the most abundant and

widespread, occurring throughout the tropical grasslands of east
and southern Africa. Mountain zebras are found only in Namibia
east of the Namib Desert and in South Africa's Cape Province.

- Unique to the Grevy's zebra, foals are left in 'kindergartens' which
  are guarded by the dominant stallion while the mothers go to
  water.

- An interesting sub-species of the plains zebra, called Crawshay's
  zebra, is endemic to the Luangwa Valley in Zambia and
  noteworthy for having a unique tooth structure, narrower stripes
  and its lack of a brown 'shadow' stripe as is common to the plains
  zebra.

- The quagga (*Equus quagga quagga*), the southernmost subspecies of
  zebra from South Africa, is now extinct. It occurred in large
  numbers south of the Orange River at the beginning of the
  nineteenth century, but Boer settlers decimated the population for
  meat and hides. The quagga had disappeared from the wild by 1878,
  and the last zoo specimen died in 1883.

So why do zebras have stripes?

There are a number of theories on this including:

1. When panicked by a predator zebra bunch together as they race
   away from the danger, their combined stripes causing a 'dazzle'
   effect and thus make it difficult for the predator to single out an
   individual or 'target' animal.

2. As each individual zebra has its own unique stripe pattern, it just
   may be that these patterns are intended purely as a means of
   recognition between individuals and between a foal and its mother.

3. There is some evidence that the stripes help to confuse the blood
   sucking tsetse fly or, at the very least, make the zebra less of a target
   (research indicates that tsetse and other parasitic, blood-sucking
   flies avoid striped surfaces and prefer instead to land on uniform

colours). The theory behind this is that as insects are capable of seeing polarized light, and because light reflecting off dark colours is polarized (in the same way as water) but off white colours it is unpolarized, the zebras striped pattern (and mix of polarized and unpolarized light) acts to confuse the tsetse fly and in this way causing them to leave zebras alone.

4. It has also been suggested that as lions see in black and white, and hunt predominately at night or in low light, a zebras stripes create an optical illusion that helps to conceal the zebra by breaking up its outline and body shape, and even distorting distance.

5. An alternative theory suggests that the stripes serve as a thermoregulatory mechanism, with micro-cooling taking place between the hotter black stripes and the cooler white stripes.

Canids (wild dog, jackal, bat-eared fox)

Africa also boasts a small number of mammals of the dog family:

African Wild dog (*Lycaon pictus*)

- The Latin name for the species, *Lycaon pictus*, means "painted wolf," referring to the dogs' mottled coat. Although distantly related to wolves, both being canids, they have only four toes on their front feet whereas the wolf has five (they lack the 'dewclaw' – a raised fifth digit).

- They are a quite distinct species and cannot reproduce with any other canid, including domestic dogs.

- Each dog has a unique pattern of brown, black and white but all have a white section at the end of their tail and a predominately black muzzle. Puppies are born with a black and white coat that begins to change to a distinctively patterned coat of black, tan, dark brown, and white at about a month old. Each dog's coat pattern is unique.

- Wild dog fur differs from other canids, consisting of stiff bristle-hairs and no under-fur. They lose their fur as they age, with older dogs becoming increasingly 'hairless'.

- They rely a great deal on their highly social behaviour and communal social structure (pack) for hunting, defense and reproduction. Pack size varies from 3 to 30 individuals, although large packs will tend to split up into smaller units for long periods.

- Once wild dogs reach maturity it is the females that leave the pack to seek out other breeding opportunities, while the males stay behind to form the nucleus of the pack.

- Whilst some social carnivores keep the peace by using aggressive posturing to keep subordinates in line, wild dogs do the opposite, with exaggerated submissive posturing and greeting ceremonies reinforcing the pack social structure.

- A wild dog pack is characterised by a dominant (or alpha) pair, with only the dominant male and female mating and able to reproduce (although 'mistakes' do occur!).

- The pups from the dominant pair, numbering up to 10 or more (the largest of any canid), are cared for cooperatively by the entire pack, thereby enhancing the survival prospects of the litter. Members of the pack will return to the den following a hunt to feed the pups (and the mother or carer) by regurgitating meat from the kill.

- Wild dogs are considered to be crepuscular hunters, which means they will hunt mainly in the early morning and evening, but will often hunt into the night when the moon is full and the weather is clear.

- They undertake a ritualised social frenzy (accompanied by considerable whining and excited twittering) in preparation for a hunt, generally in the early morning or late evening.

- Team work along with endurance forms the basis of their hunting technique and wild dogs boast one of the highest success rates of all the large predators (70-80%). A wild dog pack may even have a 'resident' hyena that follows them like a shadow, feeding off scraps and leftovers - a reflection on their hunting prowess.

- The wild dog skull is heavy, with strong muscles and modified upper incises that give a very powerful bite. Sharp canines are used to grip prey once caught. The carnassial (paired upper and lower teeth) pass by each other to slice meat. These teeth enhance the shearing capacity so that prey can be consumed quicker. What's really interesting about these sectorial teeth is that they have self-sharpening abilities.

- They are unusual also in that they allow the youngest in the pack priority access at a kill – a social behaviour not practised by any other large carnivore.

- They show little or no fear of man and will tolerate vehicles and safari participants, even on foot, at close quarters.

- Wild dogs, although not strictly territorial, will avoid clashing with another pack. They range widely, thus requiring extensive wildlife habitats in which to survive. It is thought that fewer than 3,500 remain in Africa today. They are to be found in isolated pockets in Kruger National Park in South Africa, the Zambezi Valley, Laikapia in Kenya, the Selous Game Reserve and Ruaha National Park in Tanzania, South Luangwa National Park in Zambia, Moremi/Selinda/Linyanti in northern Botswana, Hwange National Park in Zimbabwe, Niassa Reserve in Mozambique, and have been reintroduced into a number of private reserves in South Africa.

- African wild dogs once numbered more than 500,000 across Africa, with packs of up to 100 not uncommon. They have been badly affected by habitat loss and persecution by farmers, and are at persistent risk of diseases spread by domestic dogs, including canine distemper, parvo virus, rabies and anthrax.

- They are now extinct in 25 of the 39 countries where they once roamed.

Jackals (Genus *Canis*)

- Three species of jackal can be seen on safari, the black-backed (*Canis mesomelas*), side-striped (*Canis adustus*) and the golden jackal (*Canis aureus*) - with the black-backed more numerous, and seen more often, as they are more diurnal (active during the day) than the other two.

- They are resourceful, intelligent, wary and cunning, using their sharp eyesight and acute sense of smell to scavenge and hunt. They can best be described as opportunistic omnivores, constantly traversing their territories in search of prey or carrion. Having curved canine teeth and quick, nimble reactions they are well adapted for hunting small mammals, birds, reptiles and insects.

- With fused leg bones and an easy gait, jackals are capable of maintaining speeds of 16km/hr (10mph) for extended periods of time, allowing them to cover large distances in search of food.

- They are among the few mammalian species in which the male and female mate for life (monogamous). Mated pairs are territorial, and both the female and male mark and defend the boundaries of their territory. In black-backed jackals, the young from one year's litter often act as 'helpers', suppressing their own breeding ambitions and remaining with their parents for a year or more in order to help them raise the next litter and thus increases the survival rate for this species.

- Litters number up to six but usually average two to four. Sometimes pups will stay with their parents and help raise their younger siblings.

- Jackals are highly vocal. Family members communicate with each other with a screaming yell and yapping, or a siren-like howl when a kill is located. They also utter a repeated yapping when tailing a predator; a call that sometimes betrays an irritated lion or leopard.

- Jackals display a remarkable array of social traits such as ritualised submission and dominance behaviour (much like domestic dogs).

- They have a lifespan of only 8 to 10 years in the wild.

Bat-eared fox (*Otocyon megalotis*)

- The bat-eared fox's name derives from its enormous ears, which are large in proportion to its head like those of many bats.

- They feed primarily on insects including termites, scorpions and spiders. Their specialty is to hunt for succulent, subterranean beetle larvae which they detect with their radar-like ears, pinpointing the position and then digging with their front paws.

- In a threatening posture a bat-eared fox will fluff out its fur and tail and arch its back in an attempt to make itself look larger (just like a domestic cat). To escape from predators, it relies on speed and an amazing ability to dodge and turn at speed.

- Bat-eared foxes make use of an underground den to raise their pups. Pups reach their full adult size by 3 months and stay with their parents until they are 7 months old. Unlike other canids, the male undertakes most parental care duties (principally guarding and grooming), while the female forages for food that maintains her milk production.

- Adult foxes are unusual in that they are playful as adults in the wild – a trait not often seen in other predators.

- The Cape fox (*Vulpes chama*), endemic to the Cape region of South Africa, prefers the semi-arid regions of southern Africa including the Karoo and Kalahari. It is nocturnal and even smaller than the bat-eared fox at between 3 and 4kg (6 and 9lbs) and only 45 to 60cms (2ft) long, excluding a long bushy tail.

- The Simien fox (or jackal) a.k.a. Ethiopian Wolf (*Canis simensis*) is a small, reddish, fox-like wolf. It is one of the rarest and most endangered of all canids. The numerous names reflect previous uncertainty about its taxonomic position, but it is now thought to be related to wolves, rather than the foxes or jackals it resembles. It is found only in the Afro-alpine regions of Ethiopia above 10,000ft (3,000m). Only about seven populations remain, totalling an estimated 550 adults.

Smaller cats & other carnivores

Not to be forgotten are the smaller cats and other carnivores which you will (hopefully) come across on safari:

Caracal (*Caracal caracal*)

- Though sometimes known as the African lynx, due to its short tail, tufted ears and long hind legs, the caracal is now thought to be more closely related to the African golden cat (*Caracal aurata*) and serval (*Leptailurus serval*) than to any members of the lynx genus. Its taxonomy remains a matter of debate.

- The word caracal means 'black ears' in Turkish. A quite spectacular cat, the caracals most distinctive feature is the long black tufts on the back of the ears together with a distinctive feline 'masked' face.

- The caracal is the origin of the expression 'put the cat among the pigeons'. In ancient India and Iran, trained caracals were released into arenas containing a flock of pigeons. Wagers were then placed on how many birds the cat would take down in a leap.

- Essentially an animal of dry regions, the caracal has a wide habitat tolerance and is widely distributed (with its historical range mirroring that of the cheetah). They are found in woodlands, savannah and acacia scrub throughout Africa; jungle scrub and deserts in India; and arid, sandy regions and steppes in Asia. While drier open country is preferred, they are absent from true desert and are usually associated with some form of vegetative cover. They range up to 2,500m and exceptionally 3,300m.

- It is the largest member of Africa's small cats (weighing up to 20kgs/44lbs), and is a formidable hunter due to its speed and agility.

- Mostly nocturnal, caracals prey on a variety of small mammals and birds, with the most common being guinea fowl, francolin, rodents, hares, hyrax, and small antelope.

- Caracals are remarkable jumpers, their powerful hind legs allow them to leap more than three metres (9.8 ft) into the air to knock flushed birds down with their paw, or to catch birds on the wing.

- They can survive long periods without drinking. During the hot hours of the day, they rest in crevices, and hunt mainly in the cooler morning, night and evening hours.

- Vocalizations are few, mainly growls and spits in anger, and a loud barking sound used to call their partners.

- As with other desert animals, their sight and hearing are very good and they have a moderate sense of smell.

- Like most of the smaller cats, the caracal is not often seen on safari and a sighting is worth savouring.

Serval (*Leptailurus serval*)

Often overlooked, the serval is a beautiful small cat that, although widespread, is unfortunately not seen with any regularity on safari.

- Servals are characterized by their tawny, black-spotted coats, long neck and long legs to see over the savannah grasses. They have large oval ears set close together and an acute sense of hearing that is used to pinpoint their prey – mainly field mice.

- The colouring behind the ears is also interesting – black with distinctive white markings that flash prominently when the ears are pricked up. It is thought that this may be a signal to their young to keep back when following an adult that begins to stalk its prey.

- Its main habitat is grassland savannah. Being water-dependent it is not found in arid regions or deserts.

- They are primarily crepuscular (active in the early evening and at first light) although nocturnal hunting, on moonlit nights, is not uncommon. In the Serengeti, where their prey, Nile rats, are active during the day they too have become diurnal.

- A highly specialised rodent predator, serval hunt exclusively on the ground (unlike the caracal which can leap high into the air to pluck a guinea fowl from a tree). They walk slowly through tall grass and listen for telltale movement. Using their relatively tall vantage point, and their large ears, they can accurately fix the position of their potential victims. They will spend up to 15 minutes standing perfectly still, listening, but with their eyes closed. Then they pounce, leaping high in the air with all four feet off the ground. Their prey is stunned or killed as the cat hits them with its forefeet and follows through with a killing bite. Serval can also detect prey underground and dig and hook them out. They are very efficient hunters with a success rate of around 50%.

- Servals lead solitary lives and come together in pairs only for a few days when the female is in heat. Females raise the litter alone.

- Serval have a variety of vocalizations, including a high-pitched cry used to call other serval. When angry they snarl, growl and spit. When content they purr.

- The serval is sometimes preyed upon by leopard and other large cats, but more dangerous for this cat are humans; having been extensively hunted for its attractive fur.

- A totally black variant is quite common in the Aberdares region in Kenya – a gene mutation referred to as melanism.

African Wild Cat (*Felis silvestris lybica*)

- The African wildcat is the ancestor of the domestic cat and is widely distributed across the continent (absent only from closed tropical forest) with a variety of coat colours to help it blend into its environment (basically a pale striped tabby).

- The wildcat is solitary, primarily nocturnal, and terrestrial. Their diet consists of rodents (mainly), hares, birds, reptiles, amphibians, insects and other invertebrates. Wildcats seldom scavenge carrion.

- A striking characteristic is the wildcat's long legs. When the wildcat is sitting upright, its long front legs raise its body into an almost vertical position. This characteristic pose, which is almost impossible for domestic cats or crosses, can be seen in the ancient Egyptian bronze mummy cases and tomb paintings. Even when walking the wildcat's long legs and high shoulder blades give it a distinctive action; it moves more like a cheetah than a domestic cat.

- The biggest threat to wildcats are domestic cats, with hybridization becoming widespread. Feral cats also compete with them for prey and space, and there is a high potential for disease transmission.

- Not to be confused with the less common black-footed cat found only in southern Africa (and seldom seen on safari).

Honey Badger (*Mellivora copensis*)

- This little animal holds the reputation of being one of Africa's most fearless and ferocious animals. Although heavily built with a broad head, powerful jaws and long claws, this diminutive beast stands just 30cm (12 inches) tall.

- The Honey Badger is black in colour but with a distinctive silver-grey mantle. It has small eyes, no external ears and short legs. It is unusual in that its ears are enclosed in its skin, with an opening that can be closed to keep out dirt when it is digging.

- A successful hunter, scavenger and forager with an extremely keen sense of smell, the honey badger eats a variety of foods including the young of large mammals, rodents of all sizes, birds, reptiles (including snakes), amphibians, fish, insects, fruit and carrion.

- Its loose, thick skin allows it to withstand bee stings and bites from its prey – even venomous snakes lucky enough to succeed in biting a honey badger are thwarted by its apparent ability to fall into a comatose state, emerging after an hour or so apparently none the worse for wear!

- Known for its fondness for honey (hence the name), folklore celebrates the relationship between the honey badger and the honeyguide. This small dull-coloured bird leads the badger to bees' nests, whereupon the badger breaks open the hive and the two share in the spoils.

- In the same way a human will use smoke to subdue bees before harvesting honey, the honey badger uses its protruding anal glands to fumigate bees and other biting insects before attacking their nests. Backing up to the opening of the hive, the badger will rub its anal pouch all around the entrance, swirling its tail, sometimes even performing handstands while releasing a profuse secretion with a suffocating odour which is reputed to leave the bees stupefied!

- With their slow reproductive turnover (a single cub born every 16-18 months) their relatively high adult and cub mortality (only half the cubs reaching independence) together with their extremely large home ranges, the honey badger is of particular concern from a conservation perspective.

Mongooses, Genets and Civets (Family *Viverridae*)

- The Viverridae family, which includes mongooses, genets and civets, is a good example of the diversity that exists within a single taxonomical family classification. They are considered the most primitive of all living carnivores having survived over 50 million years.

- They are mostly terrestrial (except for the genet) and nocturnal (except for the dwarf and banded mongoose which, being active by day, are more social and form large family groups for safety - a good example of how group cooperation can improve a species' chances of survival).

- Each dwarf mongoose group is led by a dominant female and her male consort, usually the oldest animals in the group. The rest of the group is composed of family members - generally older offspring of the dominant pair. Each year the female will produce three litters of young, with two to four infants in each litter. The dominant female spends little time with her young other than suckling them. Subordinate females tend to the infants. The babysitters change often during the day, and even subordinate males will relieve them and take a turn, thus allowing the babysitters an opportunity to forage for food.

- Mongooses, genets and civets are mainly carnivorous - consuming small rodents, reptiles and young birds but can include fruit. The more diminutive dwarf mongoose mainly feeds on insects like termites, locusts, beetles, grubs, larvae and spiders.

- Mongooses are notorious for their fearlessness and ability to attack and kill snakes.

- An oily secretion scraped from the perineal gland of captive civets was once refined and used to enhance the fragrances of some of the most expensive perfumes! This secretion, called 'civet' is used to mark their territories and has a remarkable ability to retain its smell for long periods of time.

Nile Crocodile (*Crocodylus niloticus*)

- Crocodiles, alligators and the gharial (or gavial) are the last of the ruling reptiles, the Archosaurs, which dominated the earth's history for over 150 million years. The Archosaurs reached their heyday during the Jurassic era (190 -130 million years ago) and have changed very little in the last 65 million years.

- The fact that crocodiles have not changed much over millions of years does not mean that they are not advanced reptiles. Unlike other modern reptiles, crocodiles have efficient four-chambered hearts like mammals (and birds), especially efficient for oxygenating their blood and enabling them to stay under water for long periods. Their gular pouch (a flap of skin under their chin) blocks water so that they can eat prey under water as well as on land. Their clawed feet help them to be excellent climbers and their vertical pupils, that open wide in low light, make them formidable nocturnal hunters. They also have behavioural adaptations, including caring for their young, which makes them more advanced than snakes, lizards, or turtles. In fact, their well-developed senses, existence of a four-chambered heart and the fact that they care for their young, all point to them being more closely related to birds than other living reptiles.

- The Nile crocodile is reputed to be resistant to all known diseases: it seems they cannot become ill or infected. Even when a severe wound is exposed to infected water, the crocodile is able to produce a protective layer of fat, which insulates their system against the elements. This is a remarkable fact and may well explain the success of these ancient creatures – amazing!

- Crocodiles grow continuously throughout their life, living for up to a century and reaching lengths of over 6 metres (18ft).

- Up to 80% of a crocodile's weight is made up of muscle and thick armour-like skin. This armoured skin has, in fact, a delicate sense of touch that's among the most acute in the animal kingdom. The small, spotted bumps that cover the skin are full of nerve endings that make their hides even more sensitive than human fingertips to pressure and vibrations in the water (and on land).

- They normally dive for only a couple of minutes, but will stay underwater for up to 30 minutes if threatened; and can stay under water for up to 2 hours if they lie inactive on the bottom.

- Being cold-blooded, crocodiles have an ectothermic metabolism and thus control their body temperature through external means. They tend to bask in the sun to raise their body temperature, especially through the cooler winter months, and go back into the water to cool off in summer. This also means that energy is not wasted in maintaining body temperature, and allows crocodiles to survive a long time between meals — though when they do eat, they can eat up to half their body weight at one time.

- Crocodiles are well adapted as predators, with few natural enemies once they grow beyond hatchlings in size. Their teeth, about 30 to 40 in each jaw, are set into sockets in the jawbones and interlock when the mouth is closed. In crocodiles, the fourth tooth on each side of the lower jaw protrudes when the mouth is closed; in alligators, these teeth are not visible.

- As the crocodile floats it is almost completely submerged, its protruding nostrils and eyes and a portion of its back being the only parts visible. When stalking its prey it will lunge out of the water gripping the prey in its massive jaws, and then dragging the victim below the surface. Once dead, the crocodile will begin to feed by rotating its body whilst gripping the prey in its jaws, tearing its victim apart.

- The jaws of crocodiles are powerful enough when closing to crush the bones of small animals, but are so weak when opening that they can be held together by hand!

- As many as 90 eggs, the size of goose eggs, are buried a few feet below the surface of sandy banks along rivers or lakes. The female guards the nest for 3 to 4 months before the eggs hatch, urinating regularly on the nest to keep the eggs moist, while being incubated by the heat from the sun. Once hatched, the young hatchlings are carried down to the safety of the water in their mother's gular pouch. She will guard her babies for over a year after they have hatched. Even though a female crocodile is a force to be reckoned with, many small crocodiles fall prey to animals such as marabou storks, herons, ibis, turtles, and even catfish. Less than two percent of all Nile crocodile eggs hatch and grow to maturity.

- Crocodiles are vital to the riverine ecosystems. Over 70% of their diet is fish – most specifically, catfish. If crocodiles were to vanish from the ecosystem, the catfish population, with their voracious appetites, would multiply and potentially wipe out other fish species that are, in turn, food sources for over 40 different types of birds.

- Crocodiles can be quite vocal, producing sounds ranging from hisses when disturbed or confronted to fearsome roars and bellows, usually during the mating season.

- The phrase 'to weep crocodile tears' is indeed a myth. Crocodiles do have glands which produce tears to lubricate the eyes as humans do, but they do not cry. Whatever emotion they experience when devouring their prey you can be certain it is not remorse!

- Along with the widespread Nile crocodile, Africa has two other crocodile species; the slender-snouted and dwarf crocodile, both found only in West Africa.

The Big 5 (& Little 5)

Whilst on safari you will undoubtedly hear the term 'the Big 5' *. This is a label that has its origins in the big game hunting fraternity, and refers to the five species considered to be the most dangerous of the large mammals to hunt, namely: elephant, black rhino, buffalo, lion and leopard (and not necessarily in that order!).

There's no argument that the members of the Big 5 are fearsome and dangerous, and it is to be expected that all visitors to Africa have them at the top of their wish list, but they are really only the tip of the assegai (so to speak!). Sightings of the mischievous honey badger, or an encounter with a family of bat-eared foxes are both equally as exciting, and perhaps more fascinating in many ways - not to mention a host of other predators, scores of antelope species I(both large and small)...and not forgetting the birds, trees, and insects to be encountered on safari (more on these in the following chapters).

While the Big 5 are certainly a draw, it would be remiss of me not to at least bring to your attention some of the more diminutive, and less heralded, species that you can see on safari. In contrast to the Big 5 the following chapters feature a selection of other groupings, each with their own interesting features, and all adding to the unique diversity that sets Africa apart.

* You will also hear the term 'Small 5" – this refers, in deference to the Big 5, to the elephant shrew, buffalo weaver, leopard tortoise, rhino beetle, and ant lion.

The Little 5

Not to be outdone, we also have the Little 5 . Typically, all members of this group are antelopes of small stature and rather shy. All have pre-orbital glands (near the eye) which are used to mark their territories, with only the males in this group growing short, straight horns. Look out for them and see if you can pick up on their more individual characteristics as detailed below.

Klipspringer (*Oreotragus oreotragus*)

- The only antelope that lives in and around rocky outcrops or *kopjes* (pronounced "copies"). They are nearly always seen in pairs and standing in a characteristic pose on top of these rocky boulders.

- A short body, massive hindquarters, and sturdy long legs enable the klipspringer to jump from rock to rock with great agility, yet it walks in a stilted manner and runs in jerky bounds even on level ground. It stands on the tips of its truncated hooves as if on tip-toe. It has a thick, speckled 'salt and pepper' patterned coat with shades of grey and rust that allow it to blend in well with the rock *kopjes* on which they are found. The coat hairs are air filled, brittle, and lie loose over the body.

- A strict browser and territorial, with large dung middens and black, sticky pre-orbital gland secretions placed on grass stems and twigs marking the territory to any would-be trespasser.

Dik Dik (*Madoqua kirkii*)

- Named for the sound they make when alarmed, they are distinguished by an elongated snout, a pale ring around their eyes and a tuft of hair on their crown. Their soft coat is grey or brownish above and white below.

- Dik-Diks stand just 30–40cm (12-16") at the shoulder and weigh just 3–5kg (7-11lbs).

- They form monogamous relationships within defined territories and are hunted primarily by monitor lizards, eagles, pythons, and smaller cats such as leopard and caracal.

- A browser able to live without water, its tiny nostrils and swollen snout are possibly adaptations to reduce water loss.

Grysbok (*Raphicerus sharpei*)

- The grysbok (pronounced ghreysbock) stands about 20" (45cm) at the shoulder and weighs only 7–11.5 kg (15-25lbs). Its distinctive coat is a reddish-brown streaked with white; its throat and underside are off-white.

- Their habitat is rocky hill country. They are solitary nocturnal browsers and spend the day in the protective cover of tall grass or shrubs. They are extremely timid and will run away at the first sign of anything unusual.

Oribi (*Ourebia ourebi*)

- Oribi are graceful, slender-legged and long-necked antelope found in open grassland almost throughout sub-Saharan Africa, although not common.

- The back and upper chest is yellow to orange-brown. The chin, throat, chest, belly and rump are white. The tail is short and bushy.

- Primarily grazers, oribi prefer to eat short grasses but will browse on leaves, foliage and young shoots during the dry season. They typically inhabit open grasslands or thinly bushed country, preferring habitats with short grasses on which to graze, interspersed with tall grass which provides cover from predators and the elements. Oribi are highly water-dependent and tend to avoid steep slopes.

Steenbok (*Raphicerus campestris*)

- Steenbok resemble small oribi, standing less than 2 feet (45–60cm) at the shoulder. Their coat is typically rather orange, any shade from fawn to rufous. The underside, including chin and throat, is white, as is the ring around the eye. Ears are large with 'fingermarks' on the inside. They have a long black bridge to the glossy black nose, and black circular scent-gland in front of the eye. The tail is usually invisible, being only 4–6 cm long.

- Steenbok are typically solitary, except for when a pair come together to mate. However, it has been suggested that pairs occupy consistent territories while living independently. They stay in contact through scent markings so that they know where their mate is most of the time. Scent marking is primarily through dung middens.

- At the first sign of trouble, steenbok typically lie low in the vegetation. If a predator or perceived threat comes closer, they will leap away and follow a zigzag route to try to shake off the pursuer.

The Shy 5 (aardvark, meerkat, porcupine, pangolin, elephant shrew)

The Shy 5 are a collection of the lesser noticed, and seldom seen, nocturnal species found in Africa:

Aardvark (*Orycteropus afer*)

- The name aardvark comes from Afrikaans, its literal translation means 'earth pig'.

- Despite its pig-like snout, the aardvark is in no way related to pigs - in fact, their DNA shows them to be more closely allied with elephants!

- With the body of a pig, ears of a rabbit, tongue of an anteater and tail of a kangaroo, this creature is in fact the only species in its taxonomic 'Order'.

- Although the aardvark, which is endemic to Africa, shares some similarities with the South American anteater, the two are not related.

- The aardvark has a short neck connected to a massive, almost hairless body with a strongly arched back. The legs are short – with the hind legs being longer than the front ones. The head is elongated, with a long, narrow snout and nostrils that can be sealed (to keep out dust and ants when digging). The long, tubular ears are normally held upright but can be folded close to the head. The short but muscular tail is cone-shaped and tapers to a point. The thick claws on the forefeet are long and adapted for digging.

- Aardvarks are mostly solitary and nocturnal. They have very poor eyesight but a keen sense of smell. They are specialized in eating termites and will spend the night foraging, apparently aimlessly, moving from one termite mound to another, dismantling the hills with their powerful claws. Having exposed the nest, the termites are trapped by the aardvark's long protractile tongue (up to 30cms (1ft) long), which is covered with a thick, sticky saliva.

- Aardvarks can be found wherever there are sufficient termites for food, access to water and soft, sandy soil. If the soil is too hard aardvarks, despite being speedy and powerful diggers, will move to areas where the digging is easier.

- Aardvarks may dig themselves new burrows almost nightly, especially during the rains. Their burrows, often in termite mounds, can be over 10m long and have several entrances. They change burrows frequently, providing opportunity for subsequent residents including ground squirrels, hares, civets, hyenas, jackals, porcupines, warthogs, monitor lizards, and even birds who use the abandoned aardvark holes as shelter.

Meerkat (*Suricata suricate*)

- Best known for their shared responsibility to the group (sometimes referred to as a gang). Meerkats post sentries to look out for predators while the rest of the gang forages nearby. Not only this, but they have even developed a range of distinctively pitched alarm calls that signal to the gang whether the threat is from above (perhaps an eagle) or terrestrial (e.g. a jackal)!

- Generally meek but boisterous, aggression is only shown toward trespassing rivals. Then, back arched, fur fluffed tail rigid and mouth agape, the meerkat hisses at its aggressor. So impressive is the show that even jackals will back off. On winning an inter-gang war, the victors perform a bouncy war dance, hug each other and defecate en masse!

- As avid burrow diggers, the meerkats' territory will be dotted with a network of bolt holes and tunnels. In the tunnels the ambient temperature is about 14°C lower than on the surface in summer

and about the same amount warmer in winter. This fact is critical
to the meerkats' survival. They are metabolically adapted to shed
heat quickly but susceptible to the freezing winter nights in the
desert. During the day they enjoy a midday siesta in the shade and
will always retire before sundown to huddle together for added
warmth during the night, emerging only when the winter sun is on
the burrow. Once outside, they perch upright, sunning their chests
and soaking up the sun's warmth. Only when a respectable working
temperature is reached do they set off in search of sustenance.

- When foraging, meerkats rapaciously scour every nook and crevice,
  locating their prey using their ultra-keen sense of smell. Potential
  meals are unearthed by feverish digging, with the forager's head
  almost disappearing in the hole and its tail obscured by flying sand.
  In half an hour a meerkat can excavate a hole ten times its own size!
  It is not unknown, however, for the intended victim to depart
  quietly amid all this frenzy!

- A meerkat's staple diet is insects and their larvae. The menu may
  also include beetles, locusts, termites, spiders, lizards, geckos, some
  rodents and small birds. Unsavoury millipedes are eaten only in
  desperate times, but small snakes and scorpions are happily taken,
  thanks to immunity to their venom.

Porcupine (*Manis temminckii*)

- The word porcupine means 'quill pig' in latin; however, porcupines are not related to pigs at all.

- Heavy-bodied, slow-moving and nocturnal, this is Africa's largest rodent.

- The porcupine is, of course, easily recognized by its most notable feature—its quills. These are found along the back, tail, neck and shoulders. Quill length on different parts of the body varies, from 1 inch (25mm) up to 12 inches (30cm). Usually the quills lie flat against the body, but if danger threatens, the porcupine raises and spreads them.

- Porcupines warn potential enemies by stamping their feet, clicking their teeth and growling or hissing while vibrating its battery of quills to produce a characteristic 'rattle'. If an enemy persists, the porcupine turns and runs backward until it rams into its attacker (the hindquarters are the most heavily armed with the quills directed to the rear). The quills then lodge in its attacker as a reminder to keep its distance!

- Porcupines primarily eat roots, tubers, bark and fallen fruit, but have a fondness, too, for cultivated root crops such as cassava, potatoes and carrots.

- Porcupine quills are a favourite ornament and good luck charm for safari-goers, and along with guinea fowl feathers are favoured 'souvenirs' when out walking on safari.

- Porcupines are one of the few animals known to participate in recreational sex - on an almost daily basis!

Pangolin (*Hystrix cristata*)

- Pangolins are ancient mammals. The earliest pangolin fossils date back to the Eocene epoch, 35 million to 55 million years ago, shortly after the dinosaurs went extinct.

- The name pangolin is derived from the Malay word "pengguling", which loosely translates to "something that rolls up". They are also sometimes referred to as 'scaly anteaters'.

- Pangolins have small heads and long, broad tails. They are toothless and have no external ears, although their hearing is good. Their sense of smell is well-developed, but their sight is poor. Their bodies are covered with large, triangular, overlapping scales on their backs, sides, outer sides of their limbs, and their entire tail thus providing good protection against predators.

- Pangolins have a range of defence mechanisms to call on – starting with the ability to roll themselves up into a tight ball whenever they feel threatened - resembling a large pine cone. The armour-plated scales, worked by powerful muscles, are capable of inflicting very serious injury to anything caught between them. Added to this armoury are the anal scent glands which can emit a strong, foul smelling secretion that you really don't want to experience!

- Pangolins are nocturnal and remain in their burrows during the day. They are known to sleep up to 20 hours a day, venturing out only to eat.

- They locate prey using their incredibly good sense of
  smell, breaking open logs and termite mounds with their large,
  powerful claws and use their exceedingly long, slender tongues
  25cm (10 inch) to lap up the insects on which they feed. Large
  salivary glands coat the long tongue with a gummy mucus to which
  ants and termites stick. They can also close their ears and nostrils
  when feeding to keep biting insects out.

- As pangolins have no teeth, the gizzard-like stomach is specially
  adapted for grinding food. This process is helped along by the small
  stones and sand that pangolins consume for this purpose.

- An infant pangolin, when it begins to accompany its mother outside
  the burrow, rides on the base of her tail. If the mother senses
  danger, the baby slips under her and is protected when she rolls up
  her body.

- A shy and secretive animal, the pangolin is a very popular character
  in African folklore and thought to be a purveyor of magic and
  charms. They are also highly sought after for their meat, and are
  considered to be a suitable gift for a king or chief.

- Pangolins are not closely related to any other living mammals
  (although often confused with the South American armadillo), and
  their ancestry is not known. Four species of Pangolin exist in Africa;
  the giant pangolin, the white-bellied or tree pangolin, the black-
  bellied or long tailed pangolin, and the most widespread, the
  ground pangolin.

Elephant shrew (Genus *Elephantulus*)

- Elephant shrews are small, quadrupedal, insectivorous mammals
  resembling rodents or possums, with scaly tails, elongated
  (flexible)snouts, large ears, and rather long legs for their size, which
  are used to move in a hopping fashion like rabbits (and hence also

known as jumping shrews).

- This common English name comes from a fancied resemblance between their long noses and the trunk of an elephant, and an assumed relationship with the shrew family. Recent evidence suggests that they are more closely related to a group of African mammals that includes elephants, hyraxes, and aardvarks.

- There are more than a dozen recognised species of elephant shrew widely distributed across central, east and southern Africa. Whilst they prefer to live in forests, closed-canopy woodlands, and thickets, usually with a floor densely covered by leaf litter, they can be found in almost any type of habitat, from the Namib Desert to boulder-strewn outcrops in South Africa, to thick forest.

- Active through the daytime elephant shrews are wary, well camouflaged, and adept at dashing away from threats. Several species make a series of cleared pathways through the undergrowth and spend their day patrolling them for insect life. If disturbed, the pathway provides an obstacle-free escape route.

- Elephant shrews are not highly social animals, but live in monogamous pairs, sharing and defending a home territory they mark using scent glands found on the underside of the tail. Although they live in pairs, the partners are mostly solitary and seldom seen together, and even have separate nests.

- Female elephant shrews undergo a menstrual cycle similar to that of human females and the species is one of the very few non primate mammals to do so. The mating period lasts for several days. After mating, the pair will return to their solitary habits.

- The female will give birth to litters of one to three young several times a year. The young are born relatively well developed, but remain in the nest for several days before venturing outside. After only a few days, the young's milk diet is supplemented with mashed insects, which are collected and transported in the cheek pouches of the female. The young then slowly start to explore their environment and hunt for insects.

- Due to its small size, the elephant shrew has a number of natural predators - snakes, lizards, birds of prey and a host of omnivorous mammals all prey on the elephant shrew and its life expectancy in the wild is only around 4 years.

The Ugly 5 (hyena, wildebeest, warthog, marabou, vulture)

The Ugly 5 is a somewhat whimsical listing of animals that include the hyena, marabou stork, vulture, warthog and wildebeest. The list provides a fun alternative when the Big 5 are proving difficult to see. Of course, beauty is in the eye of the beholder - you might think the Ugly Five are rather gorgeous.

Spotted hyena (*Crocuta crocuta*)

- Of the three hyenas (spotted, brown & striped), the spotted is by far the largest and most numerous. The aardwolf too is part of the hyena family, but differs markedly in its diet – eating predominantly termites.

- Sometimes referred to as the laughing hyena – a reference to the excited, cackling 'laughter' they exhibit when around a carcass. It is thought that the pitch and note frequency (or tone) of a hyena's laugh is an indication of its age and social status. Possibly the most vocal of all the predators, this is only one of a variety of vocalizations they employ in communicating with one another - with the lazy whoop of a distant hyena being one of the most eerily familiar sounds of the African bush.

- Much maligned and misunderstood, hyenas are highly intelligent, inquisitive, bold and cunning hunters of the night.

- Usually thought of as opportunistic scavengers hyena are also effective and skilful predators, often hunting in groups and capable of bringing down animals many times larger than themselves. By teaming up they are also able to take kills away from large predators, including lion.

- They are exceptionally efficient, able to consume their entire prey, including the skin and virtually the entire skeleton. The spotted hyaena has extremely strong jaws with a bite strong enough to crush the bones of any prey. They also boast a specialised digestive tract capable of extracting fat and protein from bone itself. The only parts of prey not fully digested are hair, horns and hooves (these are regurgitated in the form of pellets)!

- The skull of a hyena can weigh over 3 kgs, primarily to support the muscle structure required to operate the incredibly powerful jaws.

- Their sense of hearing and smell are exceptional and they can smell, or hear, other predators hunting or feeding on a carcass from up to 10 kms away.

- They have amazing stamina and will lope at a steady pace for up to 5kms (3 miles) without displaying any signs of fatigue.

- Spotted hyena social structure is comprised of territorial clans of between 6 and 40 related individuals that defend their home ranges against intruding clans. They have a complex matrilineal social structure led by a dominant female (females are larger and more aggressive than males and are absolutely dominant over them). Female offspring inherit their mother's social rank within the clan.

- The centre of clan activity is the den, where the cubs are raised and individuals meet. The den is usually situated on high ground in the central part of the territory. Its above-ground entrances are connected to a series of underground tunnels.

- Litters are small – 1 or 2 cubs but sometimes up to 4. Cubs are born with their eyes open and their teeth fully erupted – unusual in carnivores, but giving them the capability of killing their siblings in same-sex litters shortly after birth – an uncommon attribute in mammals. Hyaena mothers only have two teats, so if she produces more than two offspring, life is a fight for survival from the very beginning. Many weaker cubs do not make it past the first few weeks after birth.

- The cubs have almost black coats when young and remain in the den for a year or more (an unusually long time for carnivores) – possibly as protection from other predators, especially lions, and other hyena. Hyenas, unlike jackals and hunting dogs, do not bring back food and regurgitate it for their young and so suckling is often the only way as most kills, or scavenged meals, are a long way from the den. At about a year, cubs begin to follow their mothers on their hunting and scavenging forays but until then, are left behind at the den with a babysitting adult. The mother's milk is one of the richest of all terrestrial carnivores and assists with this prolonged nursing period.

- Hyenas mark and patrol their territories by depositing a strong-smelling substance, produced by the anal glands, on stalks of grass along the boundaries. 'Latrines,' places where members of a clan deposit their droppings, also mark territories.

- Hyenas are highly social animals that communicate with one another through specific calls, postures and signals.

- When encountering one another after a separation each hyena will sniff the genitals of the other – the lower-ranking individual will get an erection; if they are of comparable status, both will.

- Often mistakenly thought of as hermaphrodites (possessing both male and female reproductive organs) due to females appearing to have a penis – see It's just not true! later in this section for a full explanation.

- When looking for hyena spoor (signs of their presence) one of the tell tale indicators is their droppings, which are a chalky white, this is due in part to the amount of calcium (from the bones they eat) in their diet.

- African legend and folklore associate the hyena with witchcraft and the supernatural and they are much feared. Cultures all across the African continent believe that some witches can turn themselves into hyaenas; while others believe that hyaena are owned by witches and to kill a hyaena is very dangerous, for if its owner finds out, they will kill the hunter with witchcraft.

Blue Wildebeest (*Connochaetes taurinus*)

- There are two species of wildebeest, the blue wildebeest (or brindled gnu), found throughout southern and east Africa, and the near extinct black wildebeest (or white-tailed gnu), found only in South Africa.

- Because of its appearance and spirited behaviour, Dutch settlers in South Africa named the animal *wildebeest*, meaning 'wild beast'. It is also known as the 'gnu'. This name, from a Khoi Khoi language, is likely based on their imitation of the grunt-like noise that the wildebeest makes.

- Often referred to as Africa's clowns, wildebeest do have some strange antics and can often be seen loping away, bucking and shaking their heads in an outburst of disgruntled virility.

- It is sometimes said that when God made the wildebeest he used only left-over parts: the mane and tail of a horse, horns of a buffalo, and the brain of a pea!

- Latecomers in the evolutionary storybook, wildebeest belong to a tribe (or sub-family) of antelopes, called *Alcelaphines*, which reached their peak two million years ago. Now only seven species survive. Yet *Alcelaphines* remain one of the most numerous and widespread bovid (cloven-hoofed) tribes. They are also the most migratory. Other relatives include bontebok, blesbok, topi / tsessebe and hartebeest.

- Paleontologists have discovered that *Alcelaphines* evolved from impala-like ancestors less than eight million years ago. The fossil record shows rapid changes, explaining why these closely related species look so different from each other. This was made possible by the hollow horns and forehead which evolve easily to suit different needs and environments.

- With a large box-like head, their broad muzzles and wide incisor rows are adapted for close, rapid grazing of short grass, in contrast to selective grazers, with a narrower mouth. Constantly on the move, the wildebeest are the nomads of Africa, forming large migrations in search of good grazing and water.

- The best known of these migrations occurs in the Serengeti and Masai Mara ecosystem of East Africa, although a similar, but not as large, migration occurs between Angola and Luiwa Plains in western Zambia. The grazing and trampling of the grasses by such large herds helps to stimulate grass growth, and their droppings recycle nutrients back into the soil.

- Wildebeests might look strange and sometimes appear to act strangely, but they are in fact ingeniously adapted to their nomadic lifestyle. Their awkward shape, with long forelegs and a sloping back, enables them to progress easily from a walk to a slow canter, which helps conserve energy when travelling over long distances. They have a distinctive and somewhat peculiar, head high, rocking gait. Zebras by comparison, and other animals with equal length fore and hind legs, are forced to break into a more energy-sapping trot in order to quicken their pace.

- Wildebeest cows give birth to a single calf in the middle of the herd. They do not seek a secluded place as do most antelopes. Amazingly, about 80 percent of females calve within the same 2 to 3 week period, creating a glut of potential meals for predators. Because of this, more calves survive the crucial first few weeks.

- Calves are born an attractive tan colour, and can stand and run within minutes of birth. The calf immediately and instinctively begins to follow its mother, staying close to her to avoid getting lost or preyed upon. Within days, it can run fast enough to keep up with the adult herd.

- There are five recognised sub-species of the blue wildebeest, each displaying varying shades of grey (body), beard colour, or size difference – each geographically separated from one another: Cookson's found in the Luangwa Valley in Zambia; Nyasa or Johnston's found in southern Tanzania and northern Mozambique; the western and eastern white-bearded found in Kenya and

Tanzania.

Warthog (*Phacochoerus aethiopicus*)

- The warthog is a tough, sturdy animal. Neither graceful nor beautiful, warthogs are nonetheless remarkable animals. Short, rotund and not especially pretty, these spirited characters have a good turn of speed and can put up quite a fight when cornered.

- Sparse bristles cover the warthog's body, although longer bristles form a mane from the top of the head, down the spine, to the middle of the back.

- The warthog has poor vision (though better than most other African wild pigs, such as the bush pig and forest hog), but its sense of smell and hearing are good.

- A particular characteristic of the warthog is its habit of lifting its tail vertically in the air when it runs – giving the youngsters something to follow when running away through long grass.

- They possess an impressive set of tusks that are used exclusively in defence. The lower blade is rapier sharp and fits tightly against the thicker upper tusk (the one for show) to fashion a formidable tearing and gouging defensive weapon.

- The warthog is mainly a grazer and has adapted an interesting practice of kneeling on its calloused, hairy, padded knees to eat short grass. Using its snout and tusks, it also digs for bulbs, tubers and roots during the dry season.

- They are capable of living in arid conditions without water for several months of the year. They have a higher-than-normal body temperature which reduces the need to cool the body and subsequently conserves moisture in much the same way as camels and desert gazelles.

- Warthogs live in family groups of a female and her young. Sometimes two families, often comprised of related females, will join together. Males normally live by themselves, only joining a group to mate.

- Warthogs sleep and rest in holes or burrows. Although they can excavate their own holes, they normally use those dug by other animals, like aardvarks. These burrows are important for a warthog's thermoregulation. Having neither fur nor fat, warthog lack both protection from the sun and insulation from cold. Sometimes warthog will line their holes with grass, probably in an attempt to keep warm.

- Female warthog have only four teats, so litter sizes are usually confined to four young. Each piglet has its 'own' teat and suckles exclusively from it. Even if one piglet dies, the others do not suckle from the now available teat!

Marabou Stork

With a face that only a mother could love the marabou is consider *the* ugliest bird in the world. There is really no competition! A large wading bird with black cloak-like wings over a white chest and underparts, and long, skinny white legs (almost like you would imagine an undertaker!) and a long, thick bill. To cap it off, excuse the pun, it's head and neck are bare although sometimes crowned with white fluffy 'hair'. The sexes are alike, but full maturity is not reached for up to four years.

Despite its unsightly appearance it does play an important role in the ecosystem as a scavenger, eating carrion alongside vultures, catfish by the mouth full and even locusts given the opportunity. They also eat a range of other insects, baby crocodiles, nestlings, small mammals, frogs and fish (in receding pools where fish become concentrated).

It is known to be quite ill-tempered, not very vocal, although it does indulge in bill-rattling courtship displays. It breeds in colonies numbering from 20-60 up to several thousand pairs, often nesting alongside other species.

It is considered to have the largest wing-spread of any living bird.

Vulture

To round out the Ugly 5 is of course - the vulture. This is a large scavenging bird that feeds, as you will know, on the remains of dead animals. It is widely distributed around the world, and found on every continent excluding the Antarctic and Australia.

- But how do vultures find these dead animals? With well developed sight vultures are constantly searching the landscape looking for any indications of a meal. But they are also watching out for the tell-tale signs from other vultures, and more often from the ubiquitous Bateleur eagles. These eagles fly at heights of between 50 and 100 metres above the ground and are often the first to spot a kill or deceased animal carcass (in part too because they are scanning the veldt from early morning whereas vultures need to wait for the ground to heat up and thermals to develop before they are able to become airborne). Having spotted a carcass the Bateleur eagle will descend to the ground. The hooded and lappet-faced vultures, while cruising at around 200 metres, notice this and come in for a closer look themselves. Monitoring this behaviour are the high-flying white-backed vultures who are able to detect such patterns from as far as 60 kms away. This pyramid system allows hundreds of vultures to converge on a carcass within minutes of the first bird arriving.

- Within the vulture community, specialisation and niches are an important element in defining their individual roles in nature. The commonly seen hooded vulture, with its small head and sharp beak, is adept at removing even the smallest pieces of flesh from a carcass whilst the larger white-backed vulture, with its long powerful neck and strong hooked bill, is better suited to reaching into the carcass and ripping out large chunks of meat. Neither of these birds is capable however, of opening up the hide of a recently deceased animal – this is the role of the lappet-faced vulture which, with its heavy-set bill and strength, is further specialised in tearing sinew off bone. Each has its place.

- As the caretakers of the bush, vultures fulfil an important sanitisation role in nature. In case you were wondering, vultures are in fact very clean animals and take great care to preen their feathers and wash themselves regularly.

- Thanks to unique features in their haemoglobin and cardio vascular systems, vultures can soar to great heights, where a lack of oxygen would kill most other birds. The highest flight ever recorded was a Ruppell's vulture, which crashed with an airplane at 37,000 feet (11,278m).

- Vultures have developed an extremely tough digestive system which acts to destroy the majority of the dangerous bacteria they ingest and helps them not get sick from feasting on rotting flesh. Their diet may be filled with toxic bacteria and putrid faeces, but vultures are apparently immune to these deadly microbes.

- Vultures are classified into two groups, Old World vultures and New World vultures. The Old World vultures are found in Asia, Europe and Africa and use their spectacular eyesight alone in order to find food (carrion). The New World vultures, like the condor, are found in the Americas, and tend to be slightly smaller than the Old World vultures, and rely more on their excellent sense of smell in order to detect food.

The Mighty 5

The Mighty 5 is an attempt to bring attention to some of the 'smaller species of significance' which might otherwise get lost in the plethora of 'bigger' and more glamorous subjects. The Ant Lion, Dung Beetle, Termite, Army Ant and the world's flying ace, the Dragonfly are my choices for the Mighty 5:

The Ant Lion (*Neuroptera myrmeleontoidea*)

- The African ant lion, despite its diminutive size, is an impressive predatory insect. In its adult stage it resembles a dragon fly, but in the larva stage this little creature is a vicious predator, capturing its prey (mainly ants) in a funnel-shaped cone in the sand. The larva, resembling a small termite, lies hidden at the bottom of its sandy 'pit' and waits for its prey to stumble into the trap, lunging out of hiding to capture and eat the unsuspecting morsel using its over-sized pincer jaws.

- If you are out walking on safari and see loose sand, take a look around for small funnel-shaped pits about 20-30mm across (an inch or so) – these tiny creatures are to be found throughout the continent and can be caught quite easily using a small piece of grass (your guide will show you how).

- Ant lions undergo a metamorphosis similar to that of a caterpillar, and as fully grown adults are known as lacewings.

The Mighty Dung Beetle (*Scarabaeinae coprinae*)

- Another fascinating sight when out in the African bush is that of a dung beetle hard at work rolling his ball of dung across the sand.

Using his (actually it's a her!) stout forelegs and the front of her shovel-shaped head as scrapers, the beetle collects suitable bits of dung from a dung pat, which she compresses and rolls into a ball. Head down, she pushes the sphere with her hind legs, travelling backwards! Occasionally, you may see two beetles with the ball, the second one assisting, walking alongside or riding on it (that's the male – getting in the way!). The ball is rolled away from the dung mass and then buried, either to be eaten by the adult or stored as food for the larva, which hatches out from a single egg laid in the dung. When the larva hatches, it eats away at the dung for several weeks until it is fully grown, and then pupates within the now hollow sphere. The pupa then breaks out of the chamber and moves up to the surface.

- They may place up to three balls on top of each other before closing the top of the hole and then leaving the larvae to hatch, feed and change into their adult form!

- Not all dung beetles make dung balls – in fact most species just dig a hole directly below the dung pat, pack it with dung and lay several eggs in cells or hollows in the dung.

- Other, larger dung beetles, pack a layer of clay around the dung ball to protect the food source of their prospective larvae. These clay balls can reach the size of a cricket ball and are almost indestructible!

- This obscure form of breeding is a vital element in maintaining a balance in the ecosystem. Dung beetles are responsible for re-cycling the tremendous amounts of dung deposited in the African bush every day. Not surprisingly, they are widespread through Africa and highly thought of.

- Dung beetles belong to the family *Scarabaeidae* and are better-known as scarab beetles. About 35,000 species of scarabs have been formally described by scientists so far, of which 7,000 are dung beetles. The dung-rolling scarab beetle was considered sacred by the ancient sun-worshipping Egyptians.

The Formidable Termite (*Macrotermes sp.*)

- Here is an ant-like creature just 5mm long who, together with hundreds of thousands of other hard-working termites, undertakes its assigned tasks in complete harmony for the good of the colony. Together they construct a vast underground network of tunnels and chambers to store and grow their food, with a state-of-the-art temperature regulation system the envy of many. They feed and raise the next generation of termites efficiently and with care. All this without a government, laws, taxes or the internet! Did I mention that they are also blind?

- Termites, like bees, have an extraordinary social structure that features different castes - from reproductive "kings & queens" (best known for their pre-nuptial winged flight in large numbers during the rains); fierce "soldiers" which defend the colony; and thousands of blind "workers" who clean the nest, forage for food and cultivate extensive fungus gardens to provide food for the colony.

- Termites are indeed one of the more amazing, and often unnoticed, creatures of the African savannah. Found in great numbers, these little creatures lead fascinating lives and have a considerable impact on their surroundings. It is estimated that they are responsible for removing up to 30% of all plant matter (leaves, grass and wood) – more than all the elephant, buffalo and wildebeest combined!

- Working predominantly at night, these colourless insects gather wood or grass, returning this plant material to a central termitaria (or termite mound - made from soil, plant matter, dung and saliva) where it is stored in chambers up to 2m below ground. On this masticated and pulped store grows a fungus on which the termites live. These fungi gardens require a constant temperature and the colony achieves this by constructing a tower or chimney-like structure that rises from the ground to a height of up to 5 metres. This structure acts as an air-conditioning unit, with vents being opened or closed as required to maintain a constant temperature inside.

- Termites are essential in maintaining the ecological balance, featuring prominently in their relationship with a multitude of other animals and birds: a) as a source of food for aardwolf, pangolin, aardvark and a host of birds, b) as a place of shelter (holes dug by aardvark) for warthog, porcupine, mongoose, hyena and wild dog to name a few, c) being responsible for recycling of grass and other plant matter on which they feed, d) bringing to the surface important trace minerals through their underground excavations, and e) forming micro-habitats of thickets used by a host of wildlife species including leopard, who hide their cubs in the dense undergrowth.

- But termites have a deep, dark secret; researchers from the Natural History Museum of London have determined that termites are actually a highly social form of cockroach. Although they appear more similar to ants, genetic testing has definitively determined that they have indeed evolved from cockroaches.

So the next time you come across a big termite mound on safari - treat it with the respect and admiration it deserves!

The Fearless Army Ant

- One of the most intriguing sights on a walk in Africa comes in the form of a large black ant. When on a raid these army ants form up in a military-style column in their thousands. Such columns can be 10 to 20 metres in length and about 30cms (1ft) wide. Place a foot in their path and the response is a distinctive hissing sound accompanied by a particularly strong and intimidating scent.

- These are nomadic ants which have no permanent nest or home and prey on other insects – predominately the near defenceless termite. They will use a hollow log or decaying stump for a temporary shelter or merely interlock their bodies in a protective dome over their queen and her young.

- With formidable pincers they are capable of lifting over 50 times their own weight, advancing on their target in vast numbers and attacking swiftly and without mercy. A raid by army ants on a termite colony is a dramatic and bloodthirsty affair. Termites guarding the mound are quickly overpowered and put to the sword and the invaders swarm in through openings designed to allow the nest to 'breath'. The battle inside the termitaria is carried out with precision and a steady stream of termite bodies are carried off triumphantly to their nearby encampment.

- In parts of Zimbabwe the army ant is called a Matabele ant. The Matabele (or more correctly – Ndebele) are an offshoot of the ruthless and warlike Zulu of Shaka fame. Whether the name comes from their ferocious and deadly attacks or is a reference to the flanking advances and pincer movements used when overpowering their enemies, I can't be sure – either way, both are much feared.

The Flying Ace – the Dragonfly

- Dragonflies were around before the dinosaurs! In fact, a fossilized dragonfly with a wingspan of 28 inches (70cms) has been dated at 250 million years. Other than being smaller, modern-day dragonflies do not look very different from their ancestors. They are often brightly coloured and have a long slender abdomen, with two pairs of long, slender wings. A significant distinction from other flying insects is that they do not fold their wings over their bodies but instead they are held outstretched when at rest. They are a predatory insect active during the day, hunting gnats, flies and mosquitoes - definitely on our side!

- The dragonflies' speed (up to 48kms/hr) and ability to manoeuvre makes them able to out-fly their prey. Dragonflies also have the advantage of excellent eyesight. Each of their two large compound eyes is made up of thousands of six-sided units each containing a single lens making approximately 30,000 lenses per eye. Together, these smaller eyes enable a dragonfly to detect even the slightest movement. If you were to try sneaking up to catch a dragonfly, you would almost certainly come up empty-handed.

- Unlike most insects, which either flap both pairs of wings in unison (bees and butterflies), or flap the hind pair only (beetles), or have only one pair (flies), dragonflies can flap or beat their wings independently. This means the front wings can be going down while the back ones are coming up. They can loop-the-loop, hover and fly backwards with ease. They flap their wings relatively slowly though, at less than 30 beats per second (bps), compared to 300 bps for a honey bee. Perhaps it is more than a co-incidence that the helicopter and the dragonfly share a similar shape?

- Dragonflies are often mistaken for damselflies, which are similar in body structure though lighter in build; however, the wings of most dragonflies are held flat and away from the body, while damselflies hold the wings folded at rest, along or above the abdomen, and have a weaker, fluttery flight.

The Stately 5 (kudu, sable, oryx, eland, roan)

The members of this prestigious group are all large, stately antelope with a certain aristocratic bearing. They tend to have well developed false hooves, have hoof glands in the feet and, with the exception of the kudu, boast horns in both males and females.

Greater kudu (*Tragelaphus strepsiceros*)

- One of the most strikingly beautiful of the antelopes, the Greater kudu is best distinguished by the spectacular spiral horns found in the males. These can reach lengths of up to 2.4m (8 ft) and are highly prized as hunting trophies.

- Males are grey in colouring with a distinctive fringe along the underside of the neck, starting beneath the chin. The females are a light chestnut colour. Both males and females have a distinctive crest of hair along the spine. Also noteworthy is the pink colouring inside the large ears and a chevron of white hair running between the eyes.

- Kudu boast between 6 and 12 prominent white stripes that run vertically down the body and act as camouflage by breaking up its shape and colouring. If alarmed they stand still and are very difficult to see.

- Kudu are browsers and inhabit woodland areas.

- Young male kudu will usually form small bachelor groups. Adult males only join the females, who form small groups of six to 10 with their offspring, during the mating season.

Sable (*Hippotragus niger*)

- Perhaps the most regal of this group, the sable antelope boasts a magnificent set of horns that sweep back in an arc over its back, enabling them to be used very effectively against predators such as lion. Horns are found in both sexes but are much longer in males, being up to 1.2m (3.75ft) in length.

- Males are almost jet-black whereas the females are chestnut to dark brown. Both sexes have a distinctive and contrasting white under-belly and tan-coloured ears. Calves are born with a camouflaging, sandy brown coat that darkens as it gets older.

- Like the oryx and roan, sables have a black face-mask with a pronounced black stripe along the bridge of the nose. The reason, or explanation, for this 'mask' is not known.

- Sable are water dependent and never very far from the nearest river or watering hole, going down to drink at around the same time each day.

- Some of the best locations for finding sable are Hwange, Chobe and Kafue National Parks and areas north of the Okavango Delta and Moremi GR in Botswana as well as Ruaha and Katavi in Tanzania.

- The so-called giant sable of north-western Angola is endangered, and was actually feared extinct until a population was discovered a few years ago in that war-ravaged country. The giant sable is a particularly impressive animal, with males having horns up to 1.6m (5.2ft) in length!

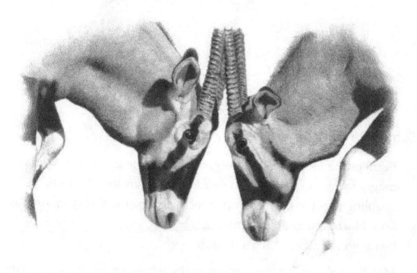

Oryx (*Oryx gazella*)

- There are four sub-species of oryx: the fringe-eared oryx of southern Kenya and Tanzania, the beisa oryx, found only in the more arid regions of Kenya, the gemsbok, found throughout Namibia and the Kalahari in southern Africa, and lastly, the scimitar-horned oryx, once common in North Africa but now extinct in the wild.

- The oryx is a large antelope with long, spear-like horns, a distinctive black face-mask and fawn-coloured body. This is a true desert-adapted animal, able to survive intense heat, dispersed food and little or no water.

- Its entire lifestyle is geared towards the conservation of energy and fluids – seeking out shade during the heat of the day and if no shade can be found, aligning its body to the sun so as to present the smallest surface area to the sun.

- The oryx survives the absence of surface water by feeding at night or in the early morning after the dried grasses and herbs have absorbed the dew. It also picks up moisture from the leaves of thorny shrubs and succulents, and from the roots, bulbs and tubers it digs up. It thrives on Tsama melons when in season, and can get up to four litres of water a day in this way.

- A number of unique adaptations allow this desert-dwelling animal to survive the rigours of the most arid regions in Africa. One tactic it employs is to raise its own body temperature. It can plod steadily through the unrelenting heat despite a body temperature of 45°C (11°C above normal). The key to the oryx's survival, however, is its ability to reduce the temperature of the brain-bound blood by about 3°C – read more about this under *Anatomical specializations and adaptation in the Animal Physiology section.*

- Dehydration is a major problem and the oryx combats this in two ways. Firstly, it drops its metabolic rate, thus reducing respiratory evaporation and urinary and faecal water loss. Secondly, where possible, it will lie up in shade during the day or, when exposed, will orientate itself east-west to present the minimum amount of body surface to the blazing sun.

Eland (*Taurotragus oryx*)

- This is the largest antelope in the world, weighing in at up to 680kgs (1500lbs). The males have dense fur on their foreheads and a prominent dewlap - a loose fold of skin that hangs down from the neck. Both sexes have slightly curved horns. The horns of the female are longer but thinner than those of the male. Usually fawn or tawny-coloured, elands turn grey as they get older, especially the adult males.

- Despite its size, the eland can jump surprisingly well – clearing a 2.5m (8ft) fence from a standing start.

- Although eland are often considered plains-dwelling animals, they browse more than graze, seeking out areas where shrubs and bushes form part of the landscape. They are also not water dependent.

- You may hear a distinctive, and clearly audible, clicking sound when an eland bull walks past that appears to emanate from the ankle. The closest explanation I have come up with relates to caribou in Alaska, whose hooves click like Spanish castanets. The sound is caused by tendons slipping over joints inside the caribou's hooves!

- The eland's size and docility as well as its rich milk, tasty meat and useful skin have encouraged research on its use in game ranching.

- The Giant, or Lord Derby's eland, are found in the open forest and stony bush country of the Sudan and parts of West Africa. With more prominent white stripes down its body length and a deep chestnut colouring, the Giant eland can weigh over 750kgs (340lbs). Its dewlap starts at its chin, as opposed to the throat, and it sports a dark collar around its massive neck. The species is mainly nocturnal (a likely adaptation to hunting).

Roan (*Hippotragus equinus*)

- They are roan-coloured (meaning a dark base coat with a mixture of white hairs) with a white underbelly and a short erect mane. Like the oryx, the face has a distinct black face-mask whereas the horns, although shorter, sweep back like the sable. They have large, donkey-like ears.

- The roan antelope inhabits lightly wooded country and grasslands, being a niche grazer of medium high grasses. Unlike other grazers they are not attracted by freshly sprouted grass.

- They are also very territorial and anti-social, preferring not to be in the presence of other animals.

- Weighing up to 270kgs (590lbs) these are the second largest antelope in Africa after the eland.

In addition to this grouping, and no less impressive, are a) the very attractive **nyala** (*Tragelaphus angasii*) the males of which are described as "the most handsome animal" and the females as "a rich red sienna that positively glows in the sunlight"; b) the furtive **bushbuck** (*Tragelaphus scriptus*) and c) the forest-dwelling **bongo** (*Tregalaphus euryceros*) who both sport unique and lovely colouring.

The smaller in stature, but no less stately, lesser kudu (*Tragelaphus imberbis*) is found in the more arid areas of Ethiopia, Somalia, Kenya and Tanzania below 1200m. With less spectacular spiral horns, the species is distinctive in having more closely aligned vertical white stripes down the body and two prominent white markings on the underside of the neck. A beautiful antelope and a much prized sighting on safari.

The Wet & The Swift

The Wet Ones (Tribe *Reduncini*)

In this category I have placed those antelope that live surrounded by water, or always in proximity to water:

Waterbuck (*Kobus ellipsiprymnus*)

- The waterbuck is easily distinguished by its forward-facing arched horns which sweep backwards and upwards, with the tips pointing forwards.

- Even more distinctive is the tell-tale white ring around the rump (except in the case of the defassa waterbuck, found in parts of East Africa, where the rump is completely white).

- The shaggy, coarse coat is reddish brown to grizzled grey in colour, darkening with age. It has an oily coat from the waterproofing secretions of its sweat glands and its flesh can have an unpleasant odour. It is considered low down on a lion's menu choice.

- Not often seen in water, it will however flee into water if pursued as it has limited speed and endurance.

- When disturbed waterbuck have a unique gait as they trot away – look out for it.

- Mainly grazers, they will eat types of coarse grass seldom eaten by other grazing animals, but will also browse leaves from certain trees and bushes.

- Waterbuck have a quite formalized courtship routine that see the male approach the female with raised foreleg

Sitatunga (*Tragelaphus spekeii*)

- Sitatungas are Africa's only true amphibious antelope, living exclusively in papyrus swamps and marshes. They are the only bovid able to stay in water permanently.

- They are good swimmers with hooves that are long, thin and splayed to prevent them sinking into the swamplands.

- The sitatunga's shaggy, oily coat is another adaptation to an aquatic habitat. The males' coats are greyish-brown, whereas the females' are a reddish-chocolate brown, with six to eight vertical white stripes on the body.

- These elusive antelope are extremely shy and unfortunately extremely difficult to locate on safari.

- Males are considerably larger than females and have long, twisting horns.

- They eat bulrushes, sedges and the leaves of bushes in the swamps, as well as grass and fallen fruit in adjacent riverine forests.

Ugandan kob (*Kobus kob thomasi*)

- Ugandan kob are found in wetland areas, such as floodplains, where they feed on grass and live together in small groups of up to 40 individuals, either females and calves or just males.

- The Ugandan kob is known for their unusual mating behaviour. Unlike most other antelope, the kob has permanent breeding grounds, called leks, where almost all mating takes place. Many such mating grounds have been in continuous use for at least 50 years. Lekking grounds, usually located on a knoll or an elevated area near water, are roughly circular in shape and are 20 to 100 yards in diameter. Within the lek the males establish small territories, fighting off rivals and marking their territorial boundaries by whistling! Competition for the innermost territories is fierce, and males hold their place for only a day or two before being ousted. When female kob come into oestrous, they are attracted by the concentrated deposits of hormone-rich urine that accumulates in the leks (and perhaps by the incessant whistling?).

- The white-eared kob (*kobus kob leucotis*), found in Sudan and Ethiopia, participate in a large-scale migration that takes place between Boma National Park in Southern Sudan and an area the Sudd, a vast wetland the size of Belgium. Each year hundreds upon thousands (estimates claim upwards of 1 million) white-eared kob, tiang antelope and mongalla gazelle take part in a 1500km migration to rival that of the great herds of the Serengeti.

Lechwe (*Kobus leche*)

- Lechwe are a semi-aquatic antelope found in floodplains bordering swamps, rivers and marshes where they eat fresh shoots and leaves and aquatic plants. Their legs are covered with a water repelling substance that assists them to flee quickly from predators through knee-deep water. Extremely at ease in the water, and good swimmers, lechwe can be seen grazing in water up to their shoulders.

- The long, rough, greasy coat varies in colour from bright chestnut to red-brown. Males generally darken with age. The under parts, neck, chin, mouth and lips are white. The black-tipped tail has a bushy white 'flag' on the underside. The foreleg has a black stripe. The body is long, with the hindquarters higher than the shoulders. The hooves are long, splayed, and relatively narrow, as an adaptation to the marshy environment. The elegantly swept back horns are found only in males.

- Due to the constant fluctuations in their habitat, male lechwe do not hold extended territories. Instead, 'lekking' is observed, with males staking out and defending small patches of a few square metres within a common 'arena' or lek. See the explanation on leks under the Ugandan kob above.

- Lechwe are highly dependent on the specialised wetland habitats for which they are adapted, and have been eliminated from much of their former ranges as wetlands have been drained, regulated or otherwise influenced by man's activities.

- There are two species of lechwe: the common lechwe (*Kobus leche*) and the Nile lechwe (*Kobus megaceros*). The latter can be found only in a region of South Sudan called the Sudd together with Gambella NP in western Ethiopia. Of the former you may encounter three sub species on safari: the red lechwe *(Kobus leche leche)*, found along

the Caprivi Strip in Namibia,the Linyanti and Chobe Rivers, Okavango Delta in Botswana, and Luiwa Plains in Zambia, and two subspecies endemic to Zambia: the Kafue lechwe (*Kobus leche kafuensis*) found on the floodplains of the
Kafue River and distinguished by the increased amount of black on the front legs, and the black lechwe *(Kobus leche smithemani)* found in the Bangweulu Swamps, which are noticeably darker in colour.

Reedbuck (*Redunca arundinum*)

• Living in vlei (seasonal wetland) areas in close proximity to water, the common reedbuck is in fact fairly uncommon, but widely distributed throughout southern and central Africa. It is a somewhat nondescript antelope, with its most distinguishing feature being the horns, which in males, grow backwards and then curve forwards similar to a waterbuck (but somewhat less substantial).

• Reedbuck are most active at night but will drink several times a day.

• Two other reedbuck species, the mountain reedbuck and bohor reedbuck, are much less common, with the latter's range extending north into East Africa.

The Swift Ones (Tribe *Antilopini*)

This grouping includes smaller, fleeter antelope who claim the unfortunate distinction of forming the dominant food source for the multitude of predators that roam the plains...

Thomson's gazelle (*Gazella thomsonii*)

- Named after the explorer Joseph Thomson, and colloquially known as the 'tommy'.

- Although perhaps not as widely distributed as the Grant's gazelle, Thomson's gazelles are still the most common gazelle in East Africa. Easily distinguished from the similarly coloured Grant's gazelle by their smaller size and a dark stripe that runs horizontally along its body.

- The Thomson gazelle is exceptionally alert to sounds and movements, and its fine senses of hearing, sight and smell balance its vulnerability on the open plains.

- They also have an unusual characteristic of stamping their front feet as a signal when disturbed! Like the impala and springbok they too like to display their fitness in stiff-legged dance movements!

Grant's gazelle (*Gazella granti*)

- The Grant's gazelle, although similarly coloured to the 'tommy', can be further distinguished by the broad white patch on the rump that extends upward onto the back whereas the white patch on the Tommie stops at the tail.

- Like the tommy, the scentless newborn Grant's fawn is carefully hidden in good grass cover for the early part of its life. After giving birth the mother licks the fawn clean and finally suckles the fawn before moving away to graze nearby. She then returns three to four times during the day to suckle it. This lying-out period can be two weeks or more.

- Grant's gazelle males have developed several ritualised postures. For example, the territorial male stretches and squats in an exaggerated manner while urinating and dropping dung. This apparently warns other males to stay away and reduces the number of confrontations. Younger males will fight, but as they grow older the ritualised displays often take the place of fights. When fighting does occur, it also is ritualised. It starts with 'pretend' grooming, repeated scratching of the neck and forehead with a hind foot and presenting side views of the body. If neither combatant is intimidated, they may confront one another and clash horns, trying to throw the other off balance.

- Neither the Thomson's nor Grant's gazelle is to be found outside East Africa.

Springbok (*Antidorcas marsupialis*)

- The springbok is the only gazelle-like antelope found in southern Africa, inhabiting the more arid regions of South Africa, Botswana and Namibia.

- Up until the early 1800s, and during times of extreme drought, massive herds numbering over a million would move outside their normal range in search of grazing. This was known then as the 'trekbokken'.

- The Latin name *marsupialis* derives from the existence of a pocket-like skin flap which extends along the middle of the back to the rump. The springbok can lift this flap, which makes the white hairs underneath stand up in a conspicuous 'fan' or crest, and at the same time secreting an odour to attract females.

- Springbok often perform bouts of repeated high leaps known as 'pronking' or 'stotting' (Afrikaans: pronk = to show off). When pronking, the springbok performs a series of vertical leaps into the air with its back bowed, legs stiff, and on occasion, with the white fan/crest lifted. It is recognised that springbok pronk to demonstrate their agility and strength to impress females and ward of predators, but at times in seems that they are merely in high spirits!

- Springboks are fast sprinters and can reach a speed of up to 80 km/hr (50 miles/hr) - a good match for any cheetah on the open grass plains.

- They have adapted to survive extreme heat and drought, feeding off both grass and bush vegetation, depending on what is available; grazing at night when the grass retains more moisture than during the heat of the day; mating in the dry season so that their vulnerable lambs are born to coincide with the summer rains. It is thought that, in extreme cases, springbok can go a lifetime (roughly 10 years) without ever having to drink water.

Impala (*Aepyceros melampus*)

- The impala is perhaps the most underrated antelope in Africa. Due to its widespread distribution and abundance in most wildlife reserves it is practically ignored by safari-goers after a few days. But this is a beautiful animal – both graceful and with attractive colouring - any safari would be poorer without them.

- One of the reasons that impala are so numerous is that they are extremely hardy and adaptable - being able to feed on both grasses (grazer) and leaves (browse) although proximity to water is usual.

- Impala are extremely agile and capable of spectacular leaps, with jumps as long as 10 metres or more. When alarmed the herd will explode into a mad scatter, with individuals leaping above and across one another, confusing their pursuers and showing off their fitness and speed.

- Like other antlered ungulates, impala have a defined mating season referred to as the 'rutt'. During this period, adult males enter into a contest for dominance and the right to secure a harem of females with which to mate. Physical changes occur during this time; their necks thicken, their coats become darker and they acquire a musky scent. They vocalize loudly, day and night, making barking sounds somewhere between a leopard's rasp and a dog's bark. Exhausted by such intense competition males can seldom hold their territories for more than a few months, sometimes only weeks, at a time.

- You may hear comments that infer that impala are able to withhold giving birth until the first rains have arrived - it seems more likely that the nutrients found in the first flush of new grass trigger hormonal changes that induce birth – but whatever the explanation, it is uncanny how the majority of calves in any year are born immediately after the first rains have fallen.

- The majority of African antelope belong to tribes or groups of related species, but the impala is one of a kind. One of the more obvious anatomical features that distinguish the species is the distinctive tuft of black hair on the hind legs. These cover scent glands and are thought to release a pheromone (chemical) into the air when being pursued. Such signals, it is deduced, are more easily picked up in the air than on the ground and may help the animals to regroup, or stay together, when panicked by a predator.

- Sometimes referred to as the "McDonald's of Africa" – firstly, because it is such an important prey species for most predators (a

popular take-out), and secondly because the markings on its rear-
end are not unlike the ubiquitous 'golden arches'!

Gerenuk (*Litocranius walleri*)

* The word 'gerenuk' comes from the Somali language, meaning
  "giraffe-necked" and aptly describes its most distinguishing feature
  – its remarkably long neck. Combined with long legs and powerful
  hindquarters, the gerenuk is purpose-built for browsing tender
  leaves and shoots standing on its back legs – its most characteristic
  pose. With colouring very similar to the impala, gerenuks also have
  a small head for their body size, with disproportionately large eyes
  and ears.

* Being a specialised, niche browser, with the ability to reach up
  higher than other gazelles and antelope, gerenuks are able to
  survive in dry thorn-bush country, gleaning sufficient water from
  the leaves of shrubs and bushes, and not having to rely on grass.

* Like many other gazelles, gerenuks have pre-orbital glands in front
  of the eyes that emit a tar-like, scent-bearing substance that they
  deposit on twigs and bushes to mark their territory. They also have
  scent glands on their knees that are covered by tufts of hair, and
  have yet another set of glands between their split hooves!

* Gerenuks use several vocalizations, including a buzzing sound
  when alarmed, a whistle when annoyed, and a loud bleat when in
  extreme danger.

* In their courtship ritual, the male gerenuk approaches a female in
  heat and repeatedly taps her with one of his front legs under the
  belly or on the flanks. He may even rub her with his pre-orbital
  glands to deposit his scent before mating.

Primates (gorilla, chimpanzee & baboon)

As well as boasting three of the great apes (gorilla, chimpanzee & bonobo) Africa is host to a range of baboon and monkey species that can be found across the open savannah to the tropical forests of West Africa:

Mountain Gorilla (*Gorilla beringei*)

- Named after the German, Captain Robert von Beringe, who in 1902 was the first European to record, and kill, two mountain gorillas in what was then known as German East Africa (now Burundi, Rwanda and Tanzania).

- It is thought that little more than 700 of these animals remain in the wild. Today they are found only in Rwanda, Uganda and the Democratic Republic of Congo (DRC) at altitudes ranging between 2800 and 3400m (8000 and 10,000ft).

- They differ from their more common cousins, the western lowland gorilla, only in size (being larger), colour (black rather than black and brown) and having a longer, silky coat as opposed to the shorter and sparser coats of the lowland variety.

- Mountain gorillas are shy, retiring animals that live in small social groups of between 4 and 35 individuals comprising a mature male, females and their offspring, and are considered to be clever and gentle creatures.

- In a 40-50 year lifespan, a female gorilla might have only 2-6 living offspring. Females give birth for the first time at about age 10 and will have offspring every 4 to 6 years. They are able to conceive for only about three days each month. The female produces a single young, and in rare cases, twins.

- Gorillas are totally vegetarian, eating leaves, roots, vines, bark, shoots, wild berries, thistles, bamboo and nettles. They rarely need to drink since their diet is so rich in succulent herbs, from which they get their liquids.

- When gorillas walk, they put their feet flat on the ground, and use the knuckles of their hands. Their arms are so long, they can swing their whole body forward between them!

- The dominant males are recognisable both by their enormous size (nearly 6ft (1.8m) tall and over 200kgs (450lbs)) and also by a distinctive 'saddle' of grey or silver hair. These large lads are referred to as 'Silverbacks'. They are also known for their chest-beating displays and frightening charges!

- When attacked by humans, leopards, or other gorillas, the Silverback will protect the group even at the cost of his own life.

- Like other non-ruminating mammals, Gorillas do not produce the enzymes necessary to completely breakdown the cellulose contained in the plants they eat, and are known to practice coprophagy, an interesting phenomenon where an animal ingests its own faeces. To combat this lack of enzymes the Gorillas produce two types of faeces, the normal hard pellet produced during the day and often seen on the ground, and a second type, known as caecotropic faeces, which are soft and gelatinous and excreted at night. The gorillas re-ingest these faeces to extract more nutrition and to assist their digestive process. Another African mammal that practices coprophagy is the scrub hare.

- Gorillas have been known to live for over 50 years in captivity but seldom live past 40 years in the wild.

- They spend approximately 30% of their time feeding, 30% travelling or moving and 40% resting.

- The gorillas which inhabit the shrinking habitat of equatorial Africa – both the mountain gorilla which lives in the mountain ranges between Rwanda, the Democratic Republic of the Congo, and Uganda together with the western and eastern lowland gorilla which live further west - have become endangered through hunting and logging throughout their ranges. Scientists warn that less than 10% of their remaining habitat could be left undisturbed by the year 2030.

Chimpanzee (*Pan troglodytes*)

- Noisy and curious, intelligent and social, the chimpanzee is the mammal most like a human, and reputed to be a 98% genetic match with man *. So close a relative are we that a blood transfusion from a chimpanzee would be accepted by the human body.

- The chimpanzee has a thickset body with long arms, short legs and no tail. Much of its body is covered with long black hair, but the face, ears, fingers and toes are bare. Their hands are very much like those of humans, with four long fingers and an opposable thumb that allows them to grip firmly and to pick up objects. Their feet have five toes, also including an opposable big toe, and can thus grasp objects with both their hands and their feet! They even have the same number and type of teeth as us.

- Each night, chimpanzees fashion a nest of leaves and branches in which to sleep. After descending from their night nests in the morning they hungrily feed on fruits, their principal diet, and on leaves, buds and blossoms. After a while their feeding becomes more selective, and they will choose only the ripest fruit. They usually pick fruit with their hands, but they eat berries and seeds directly off the stem with their lips. Their diet consists of up to 80 different plant foods.

- Chimpanzees supplement their diet with meat, such as young antelope or goats. Their most frequent victims, however, are other primates such as young baboons, colobus and blue monkeys.

- Chimpanzees are individualistic and do not live in cohesive groups like gorillas and monkeys, but rather live in communities that share a common home range.

- The discovery, by Jane Goodall, that chimpanzees used 'tools' for certain purposes surprised the world. With the ability to pick up small objects between thumb and index finger they can prepare and use grass stems or sticks to fish for insects.

- They are still to be found in the wild in the forests of East and West Africa. Gombe Stream National Park in Tanzania, formed in 1968 after years of research by Jane Goodall, was the first park in Africa specifically created for the protection of chimpanzees. It is also

Tanzania's smallest at 52sq. kms.

- The number of chimpanzees in the wild is steadily decreasing. The wilderness areas, necessary for their survival, are disappearing at an alarming rate as more forests are cut down for farming and logging.

- As our closest relative, the chimpanzee is vulnerable to many of the same diseases, and their capture for medical research contributes to their decline, especially in West Africa. In addition, recent outbreaks of the incurable disease Ebola hemorrhagic fever, threatens to decimate important chimpanzee populations in the Republic of Congo and Gabon. They are also a casualty of the bush meat and pet trade.

- The bonobo (*Pan paniscus*), until recently called the pygmy chimpanzee, is also endangered and is found in the wild only in the Democratic Republic of Congo (DRC).

* Although this might seem an alarmingly close match (98%) it is probably worth pointing out, in order to gain some perspective, that we also share nearly 20% of our DNA with chickens! It is now thought that equally as important as DNA in determining what and who we are, is ribonucleic acid or RNA (described as the main regulator of what goes on in a cell - its operating system if you like). Whilst the DNA of humans and chimpanzees might be very similar their RNA is noticeably different.

If you are interested to learn more about primates (monkeys, chimps, gorillas, marmosets, lemurs' et al) I can highly recommend taking a look at the Primate Info Net website of the University of Wisconsin (pin.primate.wisc.edu/).

Baboons (Genus *Papio*)

- Three types of savannah baboon are found in Africa – the chacma (southern region), olive (central and East Africa) and the yellow baboon (East Africa north of the equator). They are also closely related to the gelada of the Ethiopian Highlands as well as the forest baboons of West Africa (the drill and mandrill).

- The gelada (*Theropithecus gelada*), or bleeding-heart monkey, erroneously called the gelada baboon, is in fact a species of Old World monkey, once widespread across the continent with only remnants now remaining in the Ethiopian Highlands.

- The baboon-like mandrill (*Mandrillus sphinx*) of the West Africa rainforests are in fact the world's largest monkey.

- Baboons are intelligent and crafty, extremely adaptable and numerous, and found in surprisingly varied habitats across the continent.

- Adult males are formidable in size and strength with canines longer and sharper than those of a lion!

- Baboons are omnivorous, feeding on wild fruits, roots, leaves, seeds, grass, flowers, insects, lizards, birds and their eggs, and other mammals if the opportunity presents itself. On occasion, they will kill and eat a newborn antelope or snatch an unwary guinea fowl.

- They live in highly structured hierarchical societies of up to 100 individuals. Their internal politics is complicated and vigorously contested – as anyone who watches them for even a short time will attest. Dominance over competing individuals together with alliances is prominent in their behaviour.

- A female baboon inherits its status in the hierarchy from its mother. Young males, who must leave their natal troop at about 4 years of age, need to find acceptance elsewhere. Unable to challenge the dominant males, young males work their way into favour by befriending females. They do this by grooming them, bringing food and even babysitting!

- Facial gestures and body posture are used extensively to denote status and confidence. Interaction between members is continuous and not without squabbles.

- Baboons use over 30 vocalizations ranging from grunts to barks and screams. Non-vocal gestures include yawns, lip smacking and shoulder shrugging!

- In the early mornings and before retiring each evening they spend time in mutual grooming, a key means of forming bonds among individuals as well as keeping themselves clean and free of external parasites.

- Baboons are largely terrestrial although they spend the evenings in the relative safety of the trees and climb freely for fruit and other food during the day.

- Young juvenile baboons ride on the backs of their mothers like jockeys, while the younger babies cling to their underside and held with one hand.

- The angle of the baboon's tail is thought to indicate its status within the troop – the more erect, the higher the status.

- Baboons in captivity have been known to live up to 45 years, whilst in the wild their life expectancy is around 25 to 30 years.

Birding..

Birds are probably the most conspicuous, numerous and widely distributed of all animals. Many are spectacularly colourful, breathtakingly agile, serenading us with their songs and fascinating us with the many amazing facets of their lives. They have mastered not only the air, but the land and waterways too. They come in a multitude of shapes and sizes, undergo remarkable migratory journeys and offer the enthusiastic safari-goer an endless bounty of discovery and pleasure.

Africa boasts over 2,000 bird species, about 25% of the world total. Of the 108 families of birds to be found in Africa, 17 are unique to the continent – including the secretary bird, hammerkop, turacos, wood hoopoes, whydahs, guinea fowl and mousebirds.

Around 400 species migrate to different parts of Africa from Europe and Asia - referred to as Palearctic migrants. Many other species also migrate within Africa each year in order to reach their favoured breeding grounds (intra-Africa migrants). Interestingly, none of the Palearctic migrants breed when they come to Africa.

So what is 'birding' all about?

First of all, and most obvious, you need to be able to tell one bird from another – at least if you want to begin to get to know their individual traits, bird calls, distribution, habitat and nesting habits. Start by being clear in your own mind the differences between the major groupings - raptors (birds of prey), water birds like storks, cranes and ducks, ground-dwelling birds like quail, francolin and lapwings and those that make up the bulk – woodpeckers, kingfishers, shrikes, hornbills and so on. Being observant is the key. Shape, size, colouring and flight patterns are all clues to recognition. Each of the bird groups has their own distinctive body and bill shape. Combine this with size, colouring, wing shape or leg length (by way of example) and you can start to narrow down the options still further. Perhaps you might also have picked up on a particular characteristic – a distinctive flight pattern or posture. I think you're getting it – yes?

Having your own bird identification (guide) book (or ebook on your phone or tablet) is certainly an advantage, although not necessary in order to begin your appreciation of birds (and birding). Your guide will certainly assist by pointing out the more colourful and interesting species that you encounter.

As well as pictures and illustrations of the birds themselves, a bird book also provides information on species distribution and preferred habitat. This information is often necessary to help you to narrow down the choices or to confirm that the bird you think you have seen actually occurs in the area. There are descriptions of their calls, breeding habits and individual characteristics, all of which can help in making a positive identification.

A good pair of binoculars is also a must – at least 8 x 40 although I prefer a 10 x magnification (10 x 50 or 10 x 42) – see the Read this before you go chapter for a full explanation.

But even with a good bird book and an excellent pair of binoculars it will take time for you to become a proficient 'birder' – be patient. You will soon find yourself captivated by the sheer diversity and colour on display, looking out for 'specials' and marking each sighting on your bird check list at each of your safari destinations. Acquiring the knowledge to become an expert 'birder' takes time and perseverance, but as they say, the journey is half the fun!

Some interesting facts about birds

- Today's birds are survivors of the last mass extinction at the end of the Cretaceous period, 66 million years ago. Birds are in fact dinosaurs, evolving from the fierce predatory dinosaurs of that time into the spectrum of flapping, feathery fowl that we see today.

- Despite only having a single lung, birds have an extremely efficient respiratory system to feed the muscles necessary for flight - this includes air sacks that ensure air breathed in does not mix with air being expelled, and in this way ensuring a supply of oxygen rich air to the lungs even at higher altitudes (when soaring or migrating).

- Birds have large eyes in relation to their body size with densely packed photo-receptors ensuring excellent colour vision (up to 5 x that of humans).

- Whilst the frequency range heard by birds is not much better than humans (they can hear down to 1 Hz vs 60 Hz for humans), their hearing is more acute allowing them to distinguish different sounds more readily.

- Not having teeth, birds utilise a second stomach, called a gizzard, to break down their food by means of powerful contractions and ridged stomach walls (often assisted by ingesting grit or small stones to aid the process).

- Many birds have a protective membrane (transparent for birds that go underwater, or otherwise milky) to protect the eye. This membrane acts like an eyelid, moving from the inside to the outside of the eye, and back.

- On safari, you may see birds 'dust bathing' on the road – this is their way of reducing parasites (fleas and mites) on the skin and plumage by lying in the warm soft sand, wriggling and fluffing out their feathers to get as 'dirty' as possible, and then standing up and shaking their whole body in the hope of choking and dislodging any unwanted visitors!

- Birds preen themselves (a type grooming) by combing through their feathers with their beak using an oil from a gland at the top of their tail. They also like to bathe in water.

- Birds' eggs are generally oval or egg-shaped as this makes it easier to pass through the oviduct. Interestingly, many are more pointed at one end, thus ensuring that the egg will spin in a circle if kicked/knocked. This also ensures that 3 or 4 eggs will 'fit' neatly together in the nest, pointy-ends facing inwards, for ease of incubation.

- Birds, like reptiles, expel/void their solid waste and urine together and this is why most bird droppings appear white (the urine having evaporated).

- Interestingly, nearly all birds have only 10 primary feathers (those at the end of the wing) and 12 tail feathers irrespective of size. The primary feathers of 'soaring' birds spread out like the fingers of the hand, and in this way act to release the pressure along the edge of the wing in flight.

- Birds are fascinating in so many ways – varying beak shapes and sizes, tail shapes, a plethora of nesting possibilities, egg markings, size and shape, different bird calls, along with differing foot designs…an endless source and study and amazement!

Some other aspects of birding...

The summer breeding season in Africa (September through March) is a great time for courting displays and the magnificent breeding plumage of individual bird species – look out for carmine bee-eaters, paradise fly-catchers, red-headed weavers, golden orioles, pin-tailed whydahs, and red bishops among others.

Birds' nests too, vary greatly in size, shape and design and can be rather interesting. Ask your guide to show you a weaver bird's nest, or that of a sunbird or a hammerkop. Some are built of grass (like the sociable weaver who build entire apartment blocks out of grass), others with sticks, whereas many use holes in trees or tunnel into river banks. Nest sites also make good locations for photographing birds as it is one place where you know the bird will return. There is always activity around the nest site; building, sitting on eggs or feeding chicks.

Another positive aspect of becoming a 'birder' is that it leads you into the realm of bird calls. This can be extremely rewarding, and will undoubtedly enhance your appreciation of the African bush. If you can begin to identify even a half dozen bird calls while on safari this will definitely bring you some small reward. The morning that you wake up and recognize for yourself the distant "five bob, two and six" call of the ground hornbill or the descending "glug, glug, glug.." of the white-browed coucal will be momentous and will have you waking each morning with the expectation of being greeted into the new day by these magical sounds. During the day you will begin to realise that the bush is filled with bird calls of all styles, from the resonating call of the purple-crested turaco (lourie) to the monotonous tones of the turtle dove – and at night listen out for the fiery-necked nightjar and pearl-spotted owlet amongst others. Keep an ear open for some amazing duets too (tropical bou bou, black-collared barbet, and white-browed robin).

Many people become 'avid' bird watchers and are known as 'twitchers' or 'birders'. Unless you are like-minded I recommend avoiding long term exposure (more than an hour) with extreme 'twitchers' – they are nice people all, but do have a tendency to be overwhelming in their desire to identify absolutely every bird that roams within 2 kms of the vehicle (seen and unseen!).

You should also be aware of the term 'specials' in birding parlance. A 'special' is obviously a bird sighting that is rare or limited to a very select location. This may sound a tad droll but the fun part is seeing how 'excited' true birders get when discussing such 'specials'! Some folk will plan their entire safari in order that they may have the opportunity to locate just a single 'special'. On my first safari to Uganda I was fortunate enough to be taken to an area inhabited by the amazing Shoebill. This is a most unusual, and extremely rare, stork-like bird with a bill not unlike a Dutch clog. Equally amazing is its colouring – almost gun-blue – quite fabulous! Beware… it's catching!

You may want to master a sampling of jargon for non-birders: 'LBJ' refers to a "little brown job" and covers a host of small brown(ish) coloured birds of equally indistinguishable features! 'BBJ' is then the bigger relative and an 'ABT' indicates a sighting of yet "another bloody toppie (bulbul)"!

Joking aside, here are a few of the more easily recognizable, mostly colourful, and commonly seen birds that you should look out for on safari:

- Flamingos - both lesser and greater.

- Lilac-breasted roller – ubiquitous and absolutely beautiful.

- Pied kingfisher – wherever you have water you will see these small black and white kingfishers – easy to identify and the only kingfisher that hovers (lots of other kingfishers too!).

- Bishops & whydahs – with their stunning breeding plumage in the summer months.

- Bee eaters – there are always bee-eaters around and they are all lovely, but possibly the most stunning is the carmine (look for their breeding colonies from Sept/Oct along the river banks).

- Goliath heron – by far the largest of the egrets and herons with lovely colouring.

- Hornbills – whether it's the red-billed, yellow-billed or grey -

they're everywhere! Note the distinct looping flight pattern and their melodious but repetitive call.

- Fish eagle – a large eagle with a pure white head and iconic call.
- Saddle-billed stork – the most colourful of all the storks with its long black and red bill and bright yellow saddle.
- Owls – in all shapes and sizes, from the tiny owlets to the giant eagle owl.
- Glossy starlings – catch them in the sunlight and they just gleam – stunning!
- African hoopoe – common and distinctive with its golden brown colouring and crest of head feathers.
- Crowned crane – perhaps the most colourful of the larger water birds.
- Lapwings (plovers) – found throughout in various disguises.
- Sunbirds – the hummingbirds of Africa!
- Bateleur eagle – often to be seen souring overhead.
- Secretary bird – along with korhaans and bustards they dominate the savannah.

As always, there is much to learn – do you know what distinguishes a duck from a goose? No? Well, for a start, geese are predominantly grazers (vegetarian) whereas ducks will also eat insects, amphibians (frogs) and (small) fish. Ducks generally feed in shallow water, geese more on land (or islands). Geese have longer necks and honk, whereas ducks quack. Male and female geese have the same colouration, but in ducks the sexes are quite distinct. Nearly all geese are migratory (the Egyptian goose being a notable exception), but only a few ducks migrate. Interesting, don't you think?

So, what gives birds their fabulous colouring?

Colouration in birds

Birds display an astonishing variety of colours, and this is one of the main reasons why we find them so attractive to look at. But how do birds create such beautiful colours?

There are two main elements that play a role in defining a bird's colouration - pigment and keratin layers.

The two main pigments that give feathers their colour are melanin and carotenoids. The combination of these different pigments results in a specific feather colour. Melanin produces black or dark brown colours, while carotenoids produce red, orange and yellow feathers.

In addition, a number of bird species, including glossy starlings, wood hoopoes, ibises, and geese have what is described as 'iridescent' feathers that seem to literally 'shine' in direct sunlight. These iridescent colours are created by the reflection of certain wavelengths of light, rather than from pigmentation.

Let me explain.

Feathers are essentially modified scales and made from keratin (the same stuff found in human hair and skin). If, in the construction of the feather, the keratin is layered or dotted with air spaces, the green and blue 'iridescent' colours are reflected back to our eyes (a process called 'scattering'), with all other colour wavelengths passing through. Thus it appears that the bird's colouration switches between green and blue depending on the angle of the light that falls on it. Fascinating, don't you think?

Grasses, flowers & trees

With all the living, breathing bounty in store for you on safari you could be forgiven for not paying as much attention to some of the less glamorous species – the grasses, wild flowers and trees that are all around you...but they are certainly worth a mention.

Grasses

Grass is grass, right? Well yes, but grasses are quite possibly the most useful of all plants. The cereal grasses, rice, wheat, maize, barley, oats, sorghum, and millet supply three-quarters of Man's energy and over half of his protein. They provide the grain and forage that animals need to produce the meat, milk, and eggs that supplement our cereal diet. Grasses feed the world.

Grasses also protect the soil from erosion, are used in construction, and beautify our surroundings. It is believed that grasses and herbivores evolved at about the same time, and in fact, without the ability of grasses to continue to grow again after being eaten almost down to the roots, a large number of animal species could not have evolved at all. Don't take grasses lightly!

Of course you didn't come all the way to Africa to study the grass! But they are important to the wildlife, and the amount of available grass (or lack thereof) will often determine what you see (or don't see) on safari.

Wild flowers

The wild flowers of Africa tend to be subtle in their display, both in the woodlands and open savannah. But if you are on safari through spring and summer you will certainly be rewarded by some extremely lovely and delicate sightings (and scents). None more so than the amazing, but brief, wild flower display each spring (Aug & Sept) in the Namaqualand region of South Africa, where a carpet of flowers cover the landscape in a plethora of colour. The profusion of flowers that you can see in the Ngorongoro crater, and the adjoining Serengeti, in April/May makes for a stunning scenic feast too, and would be one reason why I would choose this time of year and avoid the brown, drab, dry and dusty months that follow!

Another unique area for flora is the Cape province of South Africa, where fynbos (from Dutch 'fijn bosch' = fine bush) is the major vegetation type of the Cape Floral Kingdom. Although the smallest, it is reputed to be the richest of the world's six floral kingdoms, its closest rival being the South American rainforest! Fynbos plants include the King Protea, South Africa's national flower, the beautiful Red Disa, symbol of the Cape Province and the popular garden pelargoniums, commonly known as geraniums.

A few of my favourite wild flowers when on safari are those of the sicklebush (*Dichrostachys cinerea*) or Chinese-lantern tree (or Kalahari Christmas tree!), the velvet-looking flowers of the Sausage Tree (*Kigelia Africana*), the white flowers of the baobab (Adansonia digitata), the golden-yellow balls of the many acacia species along with the beautifully delicate Sabi star (*Adenium obesum*), and the fried-egg flower (*Oncoba spinosa*).

Look out also for the flame lily (*Gloriosa superba*), fire-ball lily (*Scadoxus multiflorus*), and the many flowering aloes to be found in the more arid regions...plus the host of local varieties wherever you go on safari.

Africa's Trees

Although Africa is often perceived as a land of endless open grass plains (Serengeti and Masai Mara) and sandy deserts (Sahara and Kalahari), perhaps more significant are its trees. We tend not to really notice trees. They're just there. What can possibly be of interest? Let's take a look...

Plants, including trees, are the only living organisms on our planet that can extract and fix (or absorb) carbon – the principal building block of life. As a by-product of that process, oxygen, essential to all mammals including mankind, is produced. By feeding on grasses and the leaves of trees animals are able to convert the carbohydrates they contain into energy for their survival.

Trees are the lifeblood of any wilderness ecosystem and are responsible, at least in part, for the great diversity of life we see on safari. Virtually all animals, birds and insects are dependent on, or benefit from, the presence of trees. The types of trees that are found in a particular area will determine, to a large extent, what animals and birds you will find in that area. Getting to know the more dominant trees and shrubs will inevitably lead you to a better understanding of where to look for the very animals and birds you wish to find. In what is referred to as the bushveld in southern and central Africa, trees dominate the landscape - yet another source of interest and fascination on safari.

The tree itself is an amazing feat of design. Like other members of the plant community it uses the sun's rays to turn carbon dioxide into its component parts of oxygen and carbon through the remarkable process of photosynthesis. Through localised growth at the meristems (plant tissue consisting of actively dividing cells), trees produce leaves, while a layer known as the vascular cambium, just beneath the bark of the tree, divides to produce bark on the outside and wood on the inside. Growth also occurs in its root system, enabling it to both absorb nutrients from the soil and anchor itself - while additionally preventing erosion by holding the soils together. Some root systems are shallow but others can be extremely deep – the Zambezi Teak, for example, has two times more biomass under the ground than above it!

Growing from a single small seed, a tree continues to grow throughout its life, and often that can be a long life. The leadwood (*Combretum imberbe*) takes centuries to reach maturity, and the larger baobabs (*Adonsonia digitata*) that you might see on safari, can be well over a thousand years old. But it is often a tough life, for it must withstand the effects of wind, storms and drought. A tree is trapped by its fixed location and must learn to deal with whatever life throws at it – its survival dependent on its hardiness. The life of a tree is also a cyclical battle with grass, fire, floods and drought. Some species of trees are the undisputed record holders as the largest, tallest and oldest of all living organisms.

As you listen to your guide, you will undoubtedly come to realise that almost every tree has some significant use for man too – be it medicinal, food from fruit, wood for fire (heat) or shelter, or just simple shade on a hot, windless day - the humble tree.

Getting to know (a little) about trees on safari

You are sure to find that getting to know the various trees you encounter on safari will not be easy! The different mammals and bird species are a 'walk in the park' by comparison. But don't be disheartened – the rewards are worth the perseverance. Once again, it comes down to the art of observing. Even a small appreciation of trees will greatly enhance your safari experience – I promise!

From a safari vehicle the best you can hope to do is begin to memorise the different tree shapes and sizes – and texture (whether they are say spindly, thick and luxuriant or dull in colour). Unfortunately, trees change their appearance according to the seasons. They may have no leaves at certain times of the year, or may be covered in flowers or fruit at other times. A mature tree is also likely to look quite unlike its younger self. This does add to the confusion but do not be daunted by the challenge – with practice you will soon be able to pick out a range of the larger, and more common, tree species. Do not give up. Enlist the help of your guide.

On foot you are able to get up close and it is a good idea to concentrate on the finer details - those characteristics that remain constant – the size, shape and formation of the leaves or the texture of the bark, shape and colour of the fruit or pods etc. These finer details provide more definitive clues to a tree's identity, for example: the mopane has a distinctive butterfly-shaped leaf and rough textured bark, the sausage tree (*Kigelia Africana*) is distinguished by its dark velvet flowers, huge sausage fruit and smooth, grey bark, the camel thorn (*Acacia erioloba*) by its ear-shaped pods and small pinnate (on each side of the midrib) leaves, and so on.

Some advice – try to get to know only ten of the more dominant species in any one area you visit – such as the baobab, African ebony, raintree, sausage tree, mahogany, acacia family, mopane and leadwood. Study their various shapes and sizes and take note of any distinguishing features – rough or smooth bark, depth of colour, flowers or pods and so on. Get your guide to tell you about their uses to Man or their significance for the wildlife, each has a story to tell – a myth or a legend, a distinguishing feature or an explicit smell. Read more on the subject below under Medicinal uses of trees.

If nothing else, you should try to notice which trees are in flower or fruit – both attract birds and animals in abundance. Elephant love the fruits of fig trees (Ficus family) and the pods of different acacia trees, and will go from tree to tree on their daily rounds, making these good places to look out for them.

Whilst some trees, like the mopane and miombo woodland varieties, dominate vast tracts of the continent it is the more iconic symbols of Africa that you are likely to notice first on safari – the many acacia species, the baobab, and the palm. These are among the best known silhouettes and feature prominently in the imagery of Africa.

Medicinal uses of trees

Trees are also a source of traditional medicine, from cures for stomach ulcers to the treatment of dysentery and diarrhoea. The bark, roots, seeds or leaves of specific trees when boiled, burnt or applied as a paste can treat a range of ailments – here is a sample:

- For abscesses and skin disorders (including burns): a cream made from the sausage shaped fruits of the Sausage Tree (*Kigelia africana*) are used.

- If you need an enema – use the bark of the Natal Mahogany

(*Trichilia emetica*)!

- An infusion of the roots of the Russet Bushwillow (*Combretum hereroense*) is used as a remedy for stomach complaints.

- For the relief of common colds – inhale the smoke from burning the roots of the Raintree (*Lonchocarpus capassa*).

- Stomach ulcers – try a concoction of the roots of the Tamboti tree (*Spirostachys Africana*), while the sap of the same tree is good for the treatment of boils.

- Treat thrombosis with the blood-clotting properties of the seeds from the common Coral Tree (*Erythrina lysistemon*).

- As a cure for bilharzia and blackwater fever, an extract from the root of the Long-tailed Cassia (*Cassia abbreviate*) is considered extremely effective.

- As a treatment for dysentery and diarrhoea, the bark of the Marula tree (*Sclero-carya birrea*) is used in traditional medicine.

"For humankind the inherent and practical value of plants, and especially of trees, is as old as man himself" - Malcolm Funston, Bushveld Trees.

Did you know...and it's just not true!

It is often fun to run through a series of interesting facts - did you know:

- That only four cats are able to "roar"? These are lion, tiger, leopard and jaguar? Roaring is made possible by a special two-piece hyoid bone in the throat. The lion's roar can be heard up to 8 km away and is used to proclaim territory and to rally any straying members of the pride.

- That the African wild dog is thought to have evolved separately from other canines as much as 2 million years ago. They are a separate species and cannot interbreed with close relatives such as wolves and jackals, or any other species for that matter?

- That snakes, having evolved to no longer require limbs, have a greatly reduced left lung and their kidneys do not sit side by side but follow one another along the length of their bodies?

- That ground squirrels use their bushy tails as parasols! This enables them to forage during the hottest part of the day.

- That only the female mosquito feeds on blood, whilst the male feeds on nectar?

- That geckos are able to 'stick' to seemingly smooth surfaces by means of minute hairs on their toes which catch in small cracks?

- That monitor lizards lay their eggs in termite mounds, the termites then seal the hole dug by the mother resulting in a living incubator of constant temperature and humidity?

- That each turn in a set of a male kudu's horns represents roughly 2 years of life?

- That a chameleon's tongue is twice as long as its body?

- That malaria carrying mosquitoes are silent? So all those mosquitoes that you can hear outside your net might bite, but they don't carry the virus!

- That in some snakes there can be as many as 24 muscles linked to each pair of ribs that run the length of their body! In fact tree snakes, like the boomslang and vine snake, have locking vertebrae that reinforce the spine thus allowing one third of the body to be suspended in mid-air.

- That although looking rather slow-motioned, the giraffe can actually reach speeds of between 50-60kph?

- That baby giraffe are born with their horns flat on their head and they stand erect within a few days. They finally fuse fully with the skull after about 4 years.

- That the elephant shrew has the same toe configuration as the elephant? They both have 4 toes on the front feet and 5 toes on the back feet!

- That within a spotted hyena clan, all females are dominant over all males? The females are generally larger and more aggressive than the males.

- That crocodiles swallow stones that then facilitate the grinding of food inside their stomachs, and also act as ballast?

- That some lizards, such as skinks and geckos, have a 3rd eye called the pineal eye? They use this to detect shadows of birds of prey from above.

- That the first thing a baby zebra does after being born is ingest its mothers excrement! This is to obtain bacteria which helps digest their food.

- That oxpeckers are removing not only ticks but as importantly, tick larvae, from their hosts? Interestingly, oxpeckers are not tolerated by elephants.

- That the skin of a hippo can crack and even become infected due to sun damage. Fortunately, to counteract this, hippos have special subcutaneous glands which secrete an oily substance which acts as a natural sun-block, moisturiser and antibacterial agent. This secretion turns a reddish-orange colour when exposed to the sun.

- That the queen termite can live for 50 years, producing 30,000 children every day!

- That pythons are the only African snake to have sensory glands on their lips? This enables them to sense the presence of warm blooded prey in the dark, when they are most active.

- That chameleons also use their ability to change colour to communicate with each other? e.g. during mating, the male chameleons will change to extra-bright colours such as reds, yellow and blues, in order to attract a mate. If that mate wants to reject him, then she will change into a drab colour such as black or brown, but if she wants to accept, then she will also change into bright colours.

- That frogs, like chameleons, can change their colour to blend in with their background?

- That a crocodile can lunge out of water at a speed of 70km/hour?

- That the fastest snake is probably the black mamba, which can achieve 15mph (25kms/hr) on level ground and 20mph (35kms/hr) when 'sprinting'?

- That the black mamba doesn't get its name from the colour of its skin, which is actually a greyish colour, but from the pitch black colour on the inside of its mouth?

- That a giraffe can get by on only 5 minutes sleep a day?

- That when walking, buffaloes move only one leg at a time so that three feet are always on the ground.

- That the strongest fibre in the world is a spider's web?

- That leopards pluck the fur from monkeys and genets that they have caught before eating them? This is probably due to the fact that they have relatively dense fur, which might result in digestive problems for the leopard.

- That an elephants tusks continue to grow throughout its life but are constantly being worn down as the elephant is always using them to feed?

- That around eighty percent of hippo communication takes place under water? As well as the familiar "wheeze-honk", a combination of squeals, grunts and clicks are made below the surface, very similar to whales and dolphins!

- That herons can usually be distinguished from storks by the way they fly? Herons fly with their necks tucked in, whilst most storks fly with necks outstretched.

- That due to the prehistoric arrangement of a crocodile's teeth it is unable to chew its food? Instead it tears off meaty chunks and swallows them whole.

- That lions have extremely rough tongues, with backward curving horny papillae covering the upper surface? This helps the lion to literally lick meat from bones, and to remove parasites during grooming.

- That spotted hyena cubs are born with their eyes open and their teeth fully developed, lacking only their adult markings?

- That the ground hornbill, which nests in holes in a trees, is a co-operative breeder whereby an alpha couple will breed and the others in the family group will help raise the chick.

- That most birds will preen several times a day to remove dust, dirt and parasites from their feathers and to align each feather in the correct position? The uropygial gland is found near the base of the tail and produces an oily substance that helps to waterproof feathers and keep them flexible.

- That the female crocodile guards her nest of as many as 70 eggs for 3 months before the eggs hatch, urinating regularly on the nest to keep the eggs moist. Once hatched, the young hatchlings are carried down to the safety of the water in their mother's 'gular pouch'.

- That male birds tend to outlive their mates? Male birds have matched chromosomes in the same way as female mammals have two X-chromosomes (including women) whereas men have both an X and a Y chromosome (the Y-chromosome having only a small complement of genes). The females' 'spare' X chromosome protects them from any genetic mutation on the other X-chromosome. Males have no such protection. Women are thus carriers of, but rarely suffer from, diseases like haemophilia which are caused by the mutation of X-chromosome genes. In birds this is reversed.

- That black rhinos only have hair on their ears, tail tips and eyelashes?

- That warthogs retreat into burrows when threatened and to sleep at night. In these burrows the adult warthog makes a special upper ledge or chamber where the piglets sleep, and are therefore protected in the event of heavy rain or flash flood.

(Courtesy: The Bushcamp Company, Zambia)

It's just not true!

But sometimes the things we hear told are just not true - here are a selection of common misconceptions:

That giraffe perform romantic 'necking' displays!

In fact, these are young males mock fighting – by striking each other using their 'horns' in a sequence of blows countered by an exaggerated jump. They appear to take turns, as a giraffe cannot strike and jump at the same time! You will notice that one of the distinguishing features of giraffe males is that their horns are bare from such fights, whereas in the females the horns are tufted. In older males the fighting gets more serious and you will hear resounding body blows!

That hyenas are purely scavengers!

In many areas hyena are solitary scavengers, relying on misappropriating the kills of smaller predators including leopard, cheetah and even lion on occasion. But where game is more numerous hyenas will regularly band together and engage in co-operative hunting and are a genuine hunting force.

That the hippo kills more people in Africa each year than any other animal!

This gets a lot of air time, and I assume it is because they are such big and fearsome looking animals. But in reality, besides being vegetarian, hippos are remarkably tolerant of human encroachment on their domain (apart from the fiercely territorial bulls who can get nasty). But if a villager is taken by a crocodile, it is more likely that they will report this as a hippo attack as the authorities will often appease the village by shooting the offending hippo and in this way provide a lot of much sought-after meat. #justsaying

That male lions do not hunt!

Sure, if they can they will leave the hunting to the females who are leaner and faster but when some extra muscle is needed it is the big males that step in to get the job done. Male lions, before becoming pride males, may spend a number of years hunting for themselves or with their brothers. They are extremely capable hunters – no question.

That elephants get drunk from overindulging in the fruit of the marula tree!

It may make for a good story and a durable myth but science, and logic, suggest otherwise. It is estimated that it would take two litres of ethanol (fermented biomass) to make an adult elephant tipsy...meaning that they would have to eat about 1,400 ripe and fermented marula fruits, in a very short space of time, to get even close to being drunk.

That hippos kill more people than any other animal in Africa!

This is a statement of 'fact' so generally accepted that you will find it quoted in many prominent reference books on Africa. But it has little basis in (actual) fact. Whilst it is true that the humble hippopotamus is an extremely large beast with a formidable array of weaponry, it is a surprisingly tolerant animal that, given due respect, is more than happy to let one pass. Yes, the males can be territorial and they can react aggressively when surprised or pressured, but a regular killer of people – I think not. After all, hippos are vegetarian and ask only to be left in peace to snooze the day away on the banks of the river! Now a crocodile – that's another matter?

That hyenas are hermaphrodites!

Female hyenas have essentially the same outward-looking genitalia as males. They urinate, mate and give birth through a fully erectile clitoris that is the same size and shape as a penis. Internally, the female is a perfectly normal female, with ovaries and a uterus.

So how then can you tell them apart?

Firstly, female hyenas are much larger than their male counterparts. A mature female will also have prominent nipples and the genitalia will be partly pink. She may also be noticeably fat. Perhaps more noticeable is that the belly profile of males curves upward at the hind legs, whereas the female's belly is flat due to the presence of a small udder at the rear of her abdomen.

That porcupines shoot their quills at their attackers!

A porcupine's quills usually lie flat against its body, but if danger threatens, the porcupine raises and spreads them, reversing towards the danger. lions and other attackers risk getting quills embedded in their faces as they attempt to flip the rodent over to bite its soft underbelly. The porcupine's reversing strategy often works and after each encounter new quills grow to replace lost ones.

That the Kalahari is a desert

The Kalahari is not strictly speaking a true desert and can more accurately be described as a large semi-arid sandy savannah, or semi-desert. Being mostly covered in grass, and scattered trees, the Kalahari offers excellent grazing after good rains and supports more animals and plants than a true desert, such as the Namib in Namibia. A desert is generally defined as 'a dry, barren region, usually having sandy or rocky soil and little or no vegetation.'

The name Kalahari is derived from the Tswana word *Kgala*, meaning "the great thirst", or *Kgalagadi*, meaning "a waterless place".

That crocodiles store their prey under water until it rots!

This is merely a fanciful tale to send shivers down your spine! In reality, other crocodiles and fish would soon steal any 'food' stashed under water.

That a cheetah's claws are more like a dog than a cat

Contrary to popular belief, cheetahs retain the same physical apparatus to retract their claws as other cats. They have precisely the same elegant arrangement of muscles and ligaments in each toe that extends and withdraws the claws as do all other cats, but they are only considered to be weakly retractable (or semi-retractable) with the rear claws fairly blunted and almost permanently extended. However, the large and strongly curved dewclaw on the front legs is remarkably sharp and is used to 'hook' their prey in a chase .

That the source of the Nile is at Jinja on Lake Victoria

Quite incorrect! The true source of the Nile is in fact to be found in Nyungwe Forest in Rwanda.

That ostriches bury their heads in the sand

Not true! They do however habitually ingest small stones and pieces of gravel. These particles, known as gastroliths, lie in the bird's gizzard where they help grind down its food

That supporting 'lion petting' or 'walking with lions' helps research and bolsters lion numbers

Lion breeding centres (or farms) are nothing more than money-making enterprises. They do not promote conservation in any form. Your desire to pet a lion cub will lead to a life of habituation for which there is no return to the wild - despite claims to the contrary. In most cases these lion cubs will end up being hunted in what has been dubbed the 'canned hunting' industry. Be warned.

In an interesting development, the Botswana government has now banned elephant-back riding, following a total ban on hunting! TripAdvisor has also announced that it will not be showcasing any suppliers who run unsustainable animal activities. Elephant rides, swim-with-dolphin experiences, and attractions that allow visitors to pet lions and other exotic animals are no longer going to feature on the website. Take that.

That Rhino horn is considered to be an aphrodisiac

The truth is that rhino horn was never considered to be an aphrodisiac in Asian medicine. This myth has been falsely propagated by western media for so many years that it is now considered fact. But rhino horn has been used in Chinese medicine for a variety of ailments for more than 2,000 years; ranging from poisoning to hallucinations, typhoid to carbuncles and boils - but never as an aphrodisiac. More of a concern is that the richest Asians (including government officials) give rhino horns for bribes and gifts due to its high value, with only the wealthiest people able to afford it, thus increasing its allure.

That China is the biggest importer of rhino horn, creating and continuing to drive the demand for poaching

The final destination for the majority of rhino horn poached in Africa currently is Vietnam and Indonesia (although China and Japan remain the largest markets for elephant ivory).

"It is only in the solitude of nature we may finally understand that this earth is the only paradise we will ever know or need." - Russel Gammon, private guide and historian.

The night sky..

Scorpius

Not to be outdone by the sightings on land by day, each night the African sky puts on a dazzling display of stars, clusters, nebula, constellations and planets in arguably one of the most amazing sights in nature. How often have you stopped long enough to truly appreciate its beauty?

The night sky is best viewed where there is little or no artificial light. That means far away from civilization (and especially big cities). Where better than a game reserve in Africa?

Many factors can affect your star-gazing though. Weather is an obvious factor – both a cloudy sky and haze in the atmosphere can hinder good viewing. A full moon is not good for star gazing, and in truth the week before full moon is not the best either as the sky is still too bright. Worth noting though is that each evening *after* the full moon, the moon will rise almost an hour later. This means that until the moon rises you will be in pitch darkness – absolutely perfect for looking at the stars (as long as there are no clouds!). Otherwise, the best time for stargazing is when there is a New Moon, approximately two weeks after the full moon.

The seasons too can affect the quality and clarity of the atmosphere itself – the air after a good rain is crisp and clear, but the hazy smoke-thickened skies of late winter can make the night sky less than ideal, although on balance, the winter months (dry season) provide more clear skies than the rainy summer months and coincides nicely with the high season for safari-goers.

Some star gazing tips…

Dark adapted eyes

The retina's in our eyes are made up of rods and cones. The cone receptors are sensitive to colour and are concentrated in the centre of the eye where they are able to provide sharp detail. The rod receptors are not as numerous and are absent from the centre of the eye – they are however, more sensitive to light and allow us to see in the dark (albeit only in black and white). In order for the rods to become effective our eyes need to become 'dark adapted'; whereby a biological pigment, rhodopsin, regenerates in the rods to enable them to become more light sensitive. The cone cells adapt within 10 minutes but then are overtaken in performance by the rod cells. But the rod cells can take 30 to 45 minutes to reach peak sensitivity, so be sure to allow sufficient time for this to take effect.

Averted vision

Another trick to learn is what is called 'averted vision'. When looking at a constellation or star, and once your eyes have become 'dark adapted', you should practice looking a little to the side of the object you are looking for so that its image falls outside the central part of your eye - where there are more rods (the more colour-sensitive cones are at the centre of the eye). By using the rods instead of the cones in your eyes, you will have better light sensitivity and will thus be able to view the star, planet or constellation with greater clarity. It feels a little awkward at first but is effective.

Using binoculars

When on safari, although you may not have made the connection, you already have the perfect instrument for viewing the heavens – your binoculars. The human eye is not adapted to seeing at night. This is because the eye, or more specifically the pupil, is just not large enough to let in sufficient light for night viewing. By using binoculars, with their larger 'openings' (e.g. 10 x 50mm) the amount of light falling on each of the 50mm diameter lenses, being much larger than the pupil of an eye, greatly increases the amount of light reaching your eyes. The 10x magnification of the binoculars is of no consequence (in star gazing) as 10 x something so small - is still extremely small! Similarly, a telescope may make a star appear brighter but not bigger! In fact, I would go so far as to say that binoculars are more practical than a telescope when on safari. They are far easier to use in locating a star or planet than an unwieldy telescope, and have the added advantage of not needing to be set up on a tripod. To be fair though, telescopes do come into their own when looking at the moon and the planets, as the extra light and clarity can provide better detail than you will see through binoculars. Using binoculars you can potentially see between 20-25,000 stars in the night sky.

Star-gazing apps

There are a number of excellent star gazing apps that use the GPS technology on your mobile (cell) phone or iPad/tablet to graphically illustrate the many constellations in the sky or pinpoint the location of the stars and planets wherever you might be on safari – well worth downloading before you leave home.

What to look for...

Stars

A star is an enormous spherical ball of incandescent gas produced as a result of continuous nuclear reactions at its core. These reactions generate heat and light, and it is this light that we see shining in the night sky. Stars are so distant that they appear only as points of light in the night sky; they appear to twinkle (or scintillate) because of turbulence in the Earth's atmosphere.

There are an estimated 200,000 stars in our galaxy, with the naked eye being able to distinguish, at most, around 2,000 individual stars from a single location.

Shooting stars are tiny pebbles from interplanetary space on a collision course with Earth, and are incinerated about 100 kms above the earth as they enter our atmosphere.

The Sun

The Sun is the nearest star to earth and is at the centre of our Solar System. The Earth and other matter (including other planets, asteroids, meteoroids, and comets) orbit the Sun. Energy from the Sun, in the form of sunlight, support almost all life on Earth via photosynthesis, and drives the earth's climate and weather.

In the distant past the energy stored in petroleum and other fossil fuels (like coal) was originally converted from sunlight by photosynthesis. Ultraviolet light from the Sun has antiseptic properties and facilitates the production of vitamin D, but also causes sunburn and skin cancers. Ultraviolet light varies greatly with latitude because of the longer passage of sunlight through the atmosphere at high latitudes - this variation is responsible for many biological adaptations, including variations in human skin colour in different regions of the globe.

Anthony Fairall, in his book Stargazing from Game Reserves,

compares the Earth's relationship with the Sun to that of the position of your chair beside a campfire on a winter's night – we (the earth) are not so close as to get too hot, and not so far as to be too cold. This is an interesting analogy that underpins the very basis for life on earth.

Planets

The name Planet means "wanderer". The planets occupy no fixed place in the sky as do stars and hence are not shown on star charts. Their place in the night sky is different from week to week, month to month, and year to year – this is because each has its own orbit relative to the Sun (and to us on Earth).

Planets do not twinkle as stars do, but if you see a bright star not shown on a star chart, then you may be sure it is a planet. Planets do not produce any light of their own; instead, they shine by reflecting a proportion of the sunlight they receive back out into space. The proportion of sunlight they reflect (known as the albedo) depends upon the planet's size, the amount of cloud cover it has and - where there is little or no cloud cover - the reflectivity of the features on its surface.

The five brightest planets - Mercury, Venus, Mars, Jupiter and Saturn can easily be seen with the naked eye if one knows when and where to look. They are visible for much of the year, except for short periods of time when they are too close to the Sun to observe. All of the planets will not normally be visible on a single night, however.

When looking to identify the planets follow these clues:

- **Venus** shines with a brilliant white light and is the brightest planet in the night sky- brighter even than all the stars in the night sky. It is often the first 'star' that we can see as dusk descends at the end of the day. Look for it in the west in the evening and in the east before sunrise, but never late at night.

- If it is very bright (brighter than the brightest star but fainter than Venus) with a white light, it's probably **Jupiter**.

- If it is a pale orange-yellow or orange-red, it's most likely to be **Mars**.

- If it is pale yellow and as bright as the stars, but not as bright as the other visible planets, it's likely to be **Saturn**.

- If it resembles a reasonably bright star (i.e. it appears to 'twinkle' but is relatively small) and is seen low in the west in the early evening, or low in the east before sunrise, it's probably **Mercury**.

The Moon

The Moon revolves around the Earth approximately every 27.3 days. The gravitational attraction that the Moon exerts on Earth causes the changing tides in the sea. The light of the moon that we see from Earth is actually a reflection of the light from the Sun. So on a full moonlit night, we are actually being illuminated by sunlight that is bouncing off the Moon. We see more of the Moon (waxing) or less of it (waning) as the Moon's orbit changes the angle relative to the Sun. We experience a Full Moon each month, with the expression "once in a Blue Moon" being derived from the uncommon occurrence of a Full Moon occurring twice in one month (which only happens once every 2 to 3 years).

When the Moon passes between the Sun and Earth it is called a Solar Eclipse. When the Moon passes through the Earth's shadow (the Earth is then between the Sun and the Moon), this is called a Lunar Eclipse. Total Solar Eclipses (where the Moon exactly covers the Sun as it passes between the Earth and the Sun) are rare events and limited to a very narrow band across a specific location. This is considered by many as one of the most spectacular natural phenomenon and entices many people to travel to remote locations around the world in order to observe it.

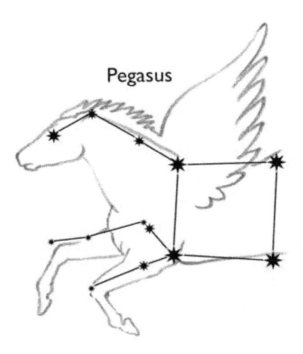

Pegasus

Constellations

Early civilizations named distinctive clusters of stars after animals, objects, heroes, gods, and beasts from their stories and myths. We call these star groupings - constellations. Many of these myths were created to explain changes in the sky through the seasons, for example: the ancient Greeks told the story of Orion, the hunter, who leaped into the sea to escape a scorpion's bite – this was used to explain why the constellation Orion disappears from the sky when the constellation Scorpius rises.

All in all there are 88 constellations in the night sky. By joining the individual stars in a constellation by imaginary lines, unmistakable outlines or figures can be seen, although their resemblance to their given name is not always so obvious! The Southern Cross (Crux), although the smallest constellation, is one of the most prominent and easy to find. Orion's belt, which is part of the constellation Orion, is another easily recognized object, as is the long tail of Scorpius.

The constellations move across the night sky, gradually shifting their position each evening as the seasons change. We are able to see different constellations in different parts of the world. In the past, people used the constellations as guides or markers. Some used the constellations to navigate their boats across the sea, to mark seasons of the year, or to locate special stars. Identifying constellations on safari can be both fun and frustrating – good luck!

The Celestial "Big 5"

The 5 constellations considered to be the most significant to an amateur 'safari' astronomer, or casual observer, would be:- Crux (commonly known as the Southern Cross), Orion, Leo, Scorpius, and Pegasus. Not all of these constellations are visible at all times of the year. Some of the imaginary figures are in fact upside down when viewed from southern Africa – for example, both Orion and Leo are upside down whereas Scorpio and Pegasus are right-side-up. Some of these figures take some imagination too, I hasten to add! Study the illustrations on the preceding pages to make identifying the Celestial Big5 a little easier.

Leo

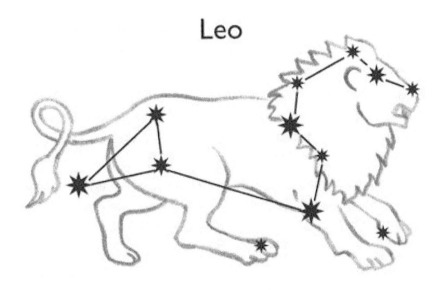

Some Star gazing trivia

1. Not all **constellations** are visible at all times of the year.

2. Many of the planets in our solar system have their own **moons** – Jupiter has 63 and Saturn 56!

3. A **light year** is the distance that light can travel in one year – equivalent to approximately 10 trillion kms or 6.2 trillion miles.

4. Our **Galaxy** is about 100,000 light years across.

5. We live about 25,000 light years from the centre of our Galaxy. As a means of comparison, a ray of light takes little more than a second to reach the moon from earth.

6. The nearest of all the stars to earth is the **Sun**.

7. The stars in the sky are all suns and only look small because they are so much further away. Most are, in fact, far larger than our Sun.

8. Much as city lights appear to glow from afar at night, so too do the millions of stars in our galaxy – this forms a luminous band that encircles us and is what we call the **Milky Way**. The glow of the Milky Way comes from stars outside our galaxy, thousands of light years away!

9. Some of the **planets** that we see are only light 'hours' away from Earth, and appear as very bright stars (e.g. Mercury, Venus, Mars, Jupiter and Saturn). One of them – Venus, is sometimes bright enough to be visible in the daytime.

10. These planets (mentioned in 9. above) meander through that band of sky known as the **Zodiac**, which includes the sun signs of Aries, Taurus, Gemini, Cancer, Leo, Scorpio, Sagittarius, Capricorn and Pisces - best known from Greek Mythology.

11. A **shooting star** is a meteor (bits of dust or rocks from space that get sucked into the Earth's gravitational pull) that is passing through the earth's atmosphere. The combination of the incredible speed at which it strikes the air particles means it is effectively burning up as it passes across our vision. If it makes it to earth, and doesn't disintegrate, we call it a meteorite.

"The descent of the African night is never forgotten. There is nothing more complete than to rest by a fire on a canvas seat, with tobacco and a drink, as the sky grows blue dark and the stars sharpen with the clarity peculiar to Africa, until the rim of the firelight seems surrounded by a second, outer world alive with the night sounds of contesting animals, and then to lie awake learning the language of the bush, the low, panting grunt of a lion, the sudden rush of hooves as zebra or antelope flee, the menacing cough of a leopard defending its kill from a hyena." Bartle Bull, Safari – A Chronicle of Adventure

Africa - its people

More than a billion people live in Africa, currently making up less than 15% of the world's population despite being the second largest continent and representing 20% of the total land mass. But it is estimated that Africa's population will double by 2050 - a somewhat sobering statistic.

Here are some interesting statistics about Africa (estimates):

- Population growth rate = 3.5% per annum
- Percentage of population under age 25 = over 70%
- Most populous city = Lagos, Nigeria (17.5m)
- Most populous nation = Nigeria (170m)
- Number of languages spoken = over 2,000
- Number of Muslims = 420m (mostly North Africa)
- Number of Christians = 480m
- Percentage of population dependent on agriculture = 66%
- Number of democratic governments = 19 out of 54 nations
- Average life expectancy in sub-Sahara = 46 years
- Number of spoken languages - around 2,000

The Peoples of Africa

Despite the fact that over a third of the population now live in cities and have adopted western ways of dress, materialism and technology, Africans still retain a rich cultural heritage. You might find it interesting to explore some of the influences that have shaped the African people of today…and their origins.

Bantu, Khoisan & Pygmy peoples

The vast majority of the tribal groups that make up east, central and southern Africa are of Bantu origin, a term first used in 1862 by Dr Wilhelm Bleek. The Bantu originated in south-eastern Nigeria and spread first eastward and later southwards, all the way to South Africa. All the Bantu languages of today are very closely related considering the vast territory they cover, leading historians to believe the Bantu came to dominate sub-equatorial Africa relatively recently and quickly. By about 1,000 AD they had reached modern day Zimbabwe and South Africa. In Zimbabwe, the first major southern hemisphere empire was established with its capital at Great Zimbabwe near present day Masvingo. It controlled trading routes from South Africa to north of the Zambezi river, trading gold, copper, precious stones, animal hides, ivory and metal goods with the Arab traders of the Swahili coast. By the 15th century the Empire of Monomotapa, as it was known, had surpassed its resources and had collapsed, with the city of Great Zimbabwe being abandoned. By this time the Bantu peoples had completed their colonization of southern Africa, with the exception of the western and northern areas of the Cape.

In present day South Africa, two main Bantu groups have developed - the Nguni (Xhosa, Zulu, Swazi) who occupy the eastern coastal plains, and the Sotho-Tswana who live on the interior plateau. It was the Xhosa, who had been gradually migrating south-west in the late 18th and early 19th centuries, who made the first tentative contact with the Dutch Trekboers trekking north from the Cape colony.

Before the Bantu, the southern half of Africa is believed to have been populated by Khoisan speaking people, today relegated largely to the arid regions around the Kalahari. Khoisan is the name for two major ethnic groups - the hunter gatherer San, formerly known as Bushmen, and the pastoral Khoi, formerly known as Hottentots. The Khoisan languages are noted for their 'click' sounding consonants.

Over the centuries the many branches of the Khoisan peoples have been absorbed or displaced by Bantu peoples migrating south in search of new lands, most notably the Xhosa and Zulu, both of whom have adopted the Khoisan clicks and other borrowed words. The Khoisan survived in the desert or in areas with winter rains which were not suitable for Bantu crops. During the colonial era they lived in South Africa, Namibia and Botswana, and were massacred to genocidal proportions by Dutch and English settlers. They contributed greatly to the ancestry of South Africa's 'coloured' population.

Today, it is only in parts of the Kalahari that the San people continue to live as their nomadic hunter-gatherer ancestors once did, although social changes (and government persuasion) is rapidly bringing their simple lifestyle to a close.

According to neutral gene analysis, the Khoisan are similar to other sub-Saharan African populations. Physically, however, the Khoisan, with their short frames, yellow-brown skin, 'peppercorn' hair, epicanthic eye folds, and small arms and feet, are quite distinct from the darker-skinned peoples who constitute the majority of Africa's population. A distinguishing feature of Khoisan women, and men to a lesser degree, is a tendency to carry a high degree of fat accumulation in and around the buttocks. This is called steatopygia. This tendency has also been noted among the Pygmies of Central Africa and in many Brazilian women.

What seems certain is that steatopygia, in both sexes, was fairly widespread among the early races of man. Steatopygia would seem to have been a characteristic of a race which once extended from Somalia to the Cape of Good Hope, and from which stock the Khoisan and Pygmies are the survivors.

The Khoisan show the largest genetic diversity in mitochondrial DNA of all human populations. Y chromosome data also indicates that they were among the first lineages to branch from the main human family tree. The San people themselves say that they were the first of all human beings. Not only genetic, but archaeological evidence bears them out. The distinct characteristics of all human varieties, from those of Eastern Asia to those of Northern Europe and the American continents, all have beginnings in the physiology of the Khoisan people.

The 'Pygmy' people are the indigenous inhabitants of central Africa. The term Pygmy (plural: Pygmies) refers to people of short stature from several ethnic groups of central Africa whose adults have an average height of only 1.5m (4 feet 11 inches) or shorter. Also known as Forest People, they are hunter-gatherers who live partially, but not exclusively, on the wild products of their environment and trade with neighbouring farmers to acquire cultivated foods and other material items.

Interestingly, the Hadzabe people of Lake Eyasi in northern Tanzania, share a similar use of click consonants in their language to the San (Bushmen). But modern genetic research has shown that the Hadzabe are actually more closely related to the Pygmies of central Africa than to the Khoisan peoples of southern Africa.

"...San culture: entirely without malice or hostility, these gentle, remarkable people had (and still have) a profound belief in sharing: in co-operation within the family, between group and group, between humankind and the environment. Custom and conviction excluded personal hostility; nature, both animate and inanimate, was sanctified, hallowed in the mystic rituals of the hunt and the entranced dance, and in the lively rock paintings and engravings that grace some thousands of sites throughout the subcontinent." Peter Joyce – This is Botswana

Nilotic peoples

Alongside the Bantu speaking peoples of central and southern Africa are another language group known as Nilo-Saharan. Primarily a language family of the African interior, including the greater Nile basin and its tributaries, as well as the central Sahara desert, they include the Fur and Dinka of the Sudan, the Maasai, Samburu and Turkana of Kenya and Tanzania, and the Luo and Longo of Uganda.

Arab, European & Asian influences

The influence of Arab, European and Asian populations over the centuries has left an indelible mark on the continent of Africa. In North Africa the impact of the Arab world has been marked, in both religion and culture. In east, central and southern Africa, the migration of Asians, predominantly from the Indian subcontinent, brought over to labour in the growing sugar cane industry, has also played a role, especially in business. European colonialists, and their descendants who have remained in Africa, also shaped the history of this land. In South Africa, the Afrikaners (simply meaning *African*) are considered the only 'white' African tribe - descendants from the Dutch, German, Portuguese and French Huguenot settlers.

The Africans of today

"What I generally get from being in Africa is a sense of warmth and openness. As a stranger, you are always welcomed." Naomie Harris

A trip to any country would not be complete without meeting the people. I have watched in fascination at visitors' enchantment with the peoples of Africa – and there is a good reason – they are hospitable, pleasant company and genuinely friendly and welcoming. Africans are by nature warm and open and will go out of their way to assist you. Take time out on your safari to spend some time with them.

Like most third world countries, Africa's traditional lifestyles hold much fascination for westerners. Their traditional homes, dress and customs are often both rudimentary and simplistic, yet colourful – especially the different forms of dress and body decoration – from body paint to scarification (cutting or branding patterns on the skin), to lip plates, masks and headdresses.

A number of indigenous groups still hold fast to their traditional way of life despite the pressures of a modern society currently blossoming in their country. The Samburu, Himba, Maasai and San (and others) live simple lifestyles close to nature, without the temptations of western society. Spurning the modern technological world and the pursuit of material well-being, their way of life is rich in other ways and without the stresses and strains of modern living.

The following is a list of some of the more fascinating tribes that you may encounter when on safari -:

- Himba of Namibia
- San (Bushmen) of the Kalahari
- Zulu and Xhosa of South Africa
- Maasai – Kenya and Tanzania
- Samburu and Turkana - Kenya
- Omo River tribes (Karo & Hamar, Geleb, Mursi & Bodi) of Ethiopia
- Taureg and Wodaabe of Niger
- Pygmy or Forest People of central Africa

Beliefs and practices

Although it is difficult to generalise, especially about the people who inhabit an entire continent, there are some common beliefs and practices that you might find interesting:

Greetings

The rituals surrounding greetings in African culture are many and varied, but in all cases, greetings between individuals form an extremely important part of how a person conducts themselves. It is important to go through the pleasantries - saying hello, asking after family, making general conversation before you move on to more serious matters. You should not launch directly into the desired subject, no matter the urgency (almost), as we tend to do in the west.

Try to keep this in mind.

Be aware

Because of their friendly nature, and willingness to please, Africans tend to tell you what they think you want to hear - especially a visitor to their country. But they do not always know what the right answer might be, and often their reply can be misleading. If someone appears to delay their answer, it is likely only to give themselves more time to decide what answer would make you happiest. They do not like to be harbingers of bad news (nor admit that they do not know the answer). I once overheard a guest ask her driver how far it was to the next lodge. Caught between admitting that it was likley longer than the guest might find comfortable, the driver merely stated "a little bit long way, but not so much". Be aware.

Keep calm (at all times)

In your dealings with the locals, do not raise your voice or lose your temper (or swear in even the mildest way) – patience really is the key. Even though Africans know that westerners can be pushy and demanding, this is the one thing that really annoys them about western culture (our impatience) and they will react accordingly – especially an official. Such behaviour is seen, quite rightly from their perspective, merely as a lack of respect for local custom.

Land Ownership

The right to own land is perhaps one of the most fundamental differences between western cultures and the people of Africa. Before the advent of European colonisation it would no more have occurred to an African that he owned the land he lived on than that he owned the sky above his head (land was tribal property, with families allotted plots by the headmen of the village). In this sense, it is not difficult to see the affiliation that Africa may once have had with communism and socialism in its heyday (with land mostly state owned, and granted to farmers on 99 year leases). Having said that – the modern African is very much oriented towards free-enterprise, is often extremely entrepreneurial and ever more materialistic! But this historic legacy lives on with vast tracts of land still held by communities without individual title. This adds an element of complexity, and sometimes conflict, in balancing the needs of modern day Africa and the traditions of indigenous groups who cling to their traditional way of life.

Time

Africans have a somewhat loose relationship with time, and this can become unnervingly frustrating on occasion. But perhaps it is just that we have grown more impatient in the west (and east); it has been said that "westerners have watches, Africans have time!"

"Hurry, hurry has no blessing" (Haraka, haraka haina baraka) - Swahili proverb.

Political Authority & Tribalism

With notable exceptions (the Zulu of South Africa being one) many of the African tribes historically had a fluid political organisational structure with no recognized political authority. Although both large and small 'states' developed, decision-making was at the village level. The elders of each village, or collection of villages, were entrusted with the weighty decisions or pronouncements affecting the community. This is a situation which remains in many African villages today and which can often lead to tribal conflict.

African politics is one subject I mean to stay clear of – the seemingly endless cycle of corruption, greed, economic collapse and military coups speaks for itself.

One should be aware however, that tribal tensions can and do exist at different times and in different parts of the continent. Tribal heritage is an important part of their everyday fabric and often dictates (or clouds) their thinking.

Language

It is an interesting fact that the early African languages had no written form (or script). African writing systems were virtually non existent prior to the arrival of Europeans and Arab traders. Two points of interest arise from this fact – firstly, that the written form of the individual local languages, especially in sub-Saharan Africa, became heavily influenced by European and Arabic scripts (although other parts of Africa had made use of symbols and writing in various ways for some time) and secondly, that little or no written history exists prior to the arrival of the Arabs and Europeans.

Religion

African people practice many religions, including Islam, Christianity, Judaism and Hinduism, although Christianity is possibly the most firmly established of the non-indigenous religions. This rich cultural pluralism allows alternative beliefs and practices to coexist, with major religions being practised alongside indigenous religions and traditional beliefs and practices.

Marriage

An African marriage is symbolized, and made legal, by the transfer of bride wealth (bride price) from the groom's family to the bride's. This is sometimes referred to as Lebola or Lobola. Such a bride price differs from the historical European equivalent where a suitable marriage attracted the provision of a dowry, with the groom's family benefiting rather than the bride's.

Most African cultures permit polygamy – the marriage of a man to more than one wife, although this is becoming less common.

Marriage formalities are very important to Africans, with marriage rites according to tribal tradition being followed very strictly, although in modern day Africa, many couples now prefer a "white wedding" with a flowing white wedding dress, veil and corsage!

Family

Africans are deeply family orientated. They are gentle and generous to their children and have an inherent love of all children. But it is their obligation to the extended family that is most marked. In times of hardship, and unemployment, those family members who are able, are required to support those experiencing hardship. A brother will automatically take on the responsibility of a sibling's wife and family upon his death. Respect for the older members of the family is also very marked and quite humbling. Even today, African children are still taught the African values of sharing, respect for authority, good neighbourliness and a sense of belonging to the larger community.

Names

Like most cultures, Africans and their naming conventions can be complex. A Setswana proverb, *ina lebe seromo*, means: you are your name; your name is your destiny; it is who you become, and it is you. The Tswana of Botswana, like most if not all Africans, understand that your name defines your fate, it shapes your life. Thus for most Africans, names bear deep meanings. There are also many tribes whose families are defined by their 'totem name': Ndlovu (elephant), Dube (zebra) etc. But more recently naming conventions been leaned toward the more colourful of English names like Beauty, Lucky, Honest, Godsent and Gladness - and it is these more 'modern' names that you will often encounter on safari!

Work

In traditional African society the concept of 'paid' work did not exist. A man's role was to hunt, defend the home and watch over the cattle (and perhaps raid the neighbouring tribes!). He was the head of the household and later, as an elder, he would take part in local village politics. As these communities became more settled, with central government and the rule of law taking hold, so the man's role diminished *. Women on the other hand, have traditionally been burdened with not only raising the children, but also with tending the fields, preparing the food, gathering roots, berries and firewood, trapping fish, brewing the beer and attending the markets. In fact, woman tend to be the 'bread-winners' in this respect. As the population has gradually moved to the cities so they (both men and women) are engaging more and more in paid employment – what we refer to as 'work'. Many urban dwellers still maintain their traditional roots and return to their 'rural' home regularly where, quite often, their extended family continues to live.

* Besides the true hunter-gatherers – the San and Efe (Pygmies) - many rural Africans to this day are either pastoralists, tending their cattle, or subsistence farmers, growing only enough to feed themselves. Some communities rely more heavily on fishing, but generally crops like maize (corn) and sorghum or millet, along with a selection of vegetable crops, form the basis of their livelihood with little being traded or sold for profit.

Cattle

Cattle are the cornerstone of African society. In the minds of many Africans, their whole lives revolve around their cattle. The cattle provide food and act as beasts of burden in the practical sense, but are far more important as; above all, they represent an individual's wealth and social status in the eyes of others.

Traditional healers

Even today, in times of trouble and illness, Africans will turn to their ancestors and traditional diviners/healers to assist them. Diviners or witchdoctors are still considered to be a powerful influence in African society. Easily recognizable by their ornate headdresses, wildebeest-tail fly whisks and other symbols of authority, they throw bones and interpret them to divine the truth or to assist in finding a cure for their patients. Traditional healers, or *nyangas* or *wagangas,* have a vast knowledge of plants and roots which they blend to form natural remedies for the treatment of illnesses. From various barks, fruits and roots they make medicinal potions, or *muthi,* which is often mixed with dried snakes, bones or animal innards for good measure!

Cultural exchange (and the borrowing of beliefs and rituals)

The different tribal groups found throughout Africa today have had extensive contact with one another over many years. This has resulted in significant cultural exchange between them, with neighbouring societies borrowing elements of each other's rituals over the years. So much so that the existing cultures are themselves made up of many threads, and continue to evolve even today. This rich cultural pluralism allows alternative beliefs and practices to coexist. Here, major religions are practised alongside each other, and medical treatments have their origins in both indigenous and modern medicine. Architecture and language have been heavily influenced by outside cultures with European languages, such as English, French and Portuguese now spoken as the working language in many African countries.

There are numerous examples where Africans have 'borrowed' aspects of other cultures to affect and enhance their own. One that comes to mind is the unusual 'traditional' dress of the Herero woman of Namibia who proudly wear very colourful, flowing Victorian-era dresses, together with a shawl and an elaborate headpiece in the shape of a cow's horns. This style of dress derives from the German missionaries who lived among the Herero during the 1800s!

Body decoration (& traditional attire)

Various forms of body decoration are common throughout Africa including body paint, ochre, clay, feathers, masks and headdresses. Some of the more exotic include lip plates worn by the Mursi of Ethiopia and beaded corsets worn by Dinka herdsmen!

When you first encounter traditionally attired people - such as the Maasai, Samburu, and Xhosa - you could be forgiven for thinking that they have dressed up for some special occasion. This is not the case. Although some body decoration and jewellery is made to be worn at particular events - such as for marriage or circumcision ceremonies - most pieces are worn throughout an individual's entire 'stage of life'. For example, a married woman might amass beaded necklaces as she grows older, an indicator of her increasing wealth and her place in life. Young Maasai boys, before embarking on the rituals that surround their coming of age and symbolized with a circumcision ceremony, will spend the months prior dressed in traditional black and white face paint to indicate their coming status or 'stage of life'.

Scarification and piercing, which denotes bravery in men and body beautification for women, are common. Using a knife, razor blade, sharp stone or hook, ornate patterns are created on the face and body. Ash is then rubbed into the wound to promote infection and scar tissue growth. The wound will then heal to reveal the desired raised scarring.

The Mursi of the Omo River region of Ethiopia, to this day, still practise one of the most remarkable traditions that you can witness – here, the women wear a 12 cm (five-inch) clay plate in the lower lip - usually when in the presence of men.

Masks and headdresses are worn in ceremonies and are often used to hide the faces of lawmakers involved in settling disputes.

Beaded jewellery too has a rich tradition in African culture. With the introduction of colourful glass beads from Europe around a hundred years ago, trinkets brought to Africa as objects of trade, beads have become a powerful element in African life. These tiny, colourful pieces of glass, varying in shape and size and pre-drilled with precise center holes, could easily be strung on threads or sewn onto leather.

Their variety meant they could be arranged in contrasting colours, as single strands or a variety of geometric patterns. This revolutionized the art of 'dressing up' across many parts of Africa. Each piece of jewellery or article of clothing, by way of its shape, patterns, and colours, would speak of the wearer's culture and tribe. A person's status or 'stage of life' would be declared by wearing a specific pattern or colour combination. The Zulu of South Africa once used the different colours to convey a specific meaning, with beads being used as part of messages and 'love notes' between suitors. In East Africa the Maasai, Samburu and Turkana use beadwork for status and adornment, and in southern Africa the Zulu, Ndebele, and Xhosa are much admired for their attractive beadwork patterns.

All of these forms of beautification, and symbolism, offer the visitor a fascinating insight to the lives of the different cultures across the continent. Ask your guide to explain some of their meanings…

African dance & music

Africans love to sing…and to dance *. Both feature prominently at gatherings and celebrations – to express joy or sorrow. While the dancing is spontaneous and voluntary, the drumbeat provides the rhythm that holds the dancers together. In villages throughout the continent, the sound and the rhythm of the drum expresses the mood of the people. The drum is the sign of life. Its beat is the heartbeat of the community - such is the power of the drum to evoke emotions and touch the souls of those who hear its rhythms. In an African community, coming together in response to the beating of the drum is an opportunity to give one another a sense of belonging and of solidarity, a sense of community. It is a time to connect with each other, to be part of that collective rhythm of life in which young and old, rich and poor, men and women are all invited to contribute to the occasion.

* In Africa, music and dance are not thought of as separate art forms and generally there is only one word to describe both. For example, in

Swahili the word "ngoma" may be translated as "drum", "dance", "dance event", "dance celebration" or "music", depending on the context.

African Superstitions & Folklore

Africans are a superstitious people – they won't go near a praying mantis and will throw a complete fit if you approach them with a chameleon in hand! Much folklore and reverence is attached to the hyena, and even the plain hammerkop is viewed by most Africans with trepidation*. Whether considered harbingers of ill fortune, agents of evil, or associated with witchcraft, many animals and birds have a profound effect on Africans.

African folklore however is more fun to relate – like the story of how the hippo came to live in the river:

The hippo, which was originally placed on this earth to live on the open grasslands, was a greedy beast and soon grew enormously fat and uncomfortable. In the heat of the day the hippo would suffer greatly and would plead to God to allow him to live in the river to stay cool. But God had seen the appetite of this hippo and said no – for he feared that the hippo would eat all his fish! After much thought, the hippo again pleaded with God to live in the river, this time promising that he would not touch the bountiful fish that lived there, and to prove this, he would spread his dung with his tail when defecating each day so that God could see for himself that there were no fish bones there! So to this day, the hippo lives in the river by day and goes out to eat grass at night when it is cool, and always remembers to spray its dung with its tail so that God can see that no fish had been eaten!

"(Mma Ramotswe thought......) Then there was Mr. Mandela. Everybody knew about Mr. Mandela and how he had forgiven those who had imprisoned him. They had taken away years and years of his life simply because he wanted justice. They had set him to work in a quarry and his eyes had been permanently damaged by the rock dust. But at last, when he had walked out of the prison on that breathless, luminous day, he had said nothing about revenge

or even retribution. He had said that there were more important things to do than to complain about the past, and in time he had shown that he meant this by hundreds of acts of kindness towards those who had treated him so badly. That was the real African way, the tradition that was closest to the heart of Africa. We are all children of Africa, and none of us is better or more important than the other. That is what Africa could say to the world: it could remind it what it is to be human." - Alexander McCall Smith, Tears of the Giraffe

* African folklore tells us that the shape a hammerkop's head (or its 'hammer') contains a third eye that it uses to look into your soul. If a hammerkop flies off before you can get near it, that is a sign that it does not like what it sees (in your soul). But if you are able to approach the bird your soul is 'clean and good'! Hence they are much feared (and avoided).

Digital photography

"If someone gets that very special shot – that once-in-a-lifetime photograph – we are far too quick to label him or her as lucky. I believe that luck only really strikes when preparation meets opportunity" - Michael Poliza, Professional Wildlife Photographer

What to take on safari

Photography, like any endeavour, will always benefit from a little planning and preparation. If you are serious about your photography, take the time before you leave home to think about not only what equipment you will need to take on safari, but also what type of images you are hoping to capture.

Here are some pointers to help you decide:

- **Cameras**: buy a good digital camera (DSLR if the budget will allow). Even the latest 'point and shoot' digital cameras, that have 8 mega pixels or more, do a surprisingly competent job. Many digital SLR, and compact cameras, also have video capability and each year the array of features gets bigger and better – 3D, HDR, time-lapse, panorama, dual recording (capturing still images whilst 'filming') – the list goes on.

  For the more serious photographer a second camera body is always a good idea. Not only does it serve as a backup in case one body should fail (and this happens), but also because it will allow you to have different focal length lenses on each giving you more flexibility in dealing with whatever situation arises on safari.

- **Lenses**: for the more serious photographers amongst you, the old adage "spend 80% of your budget on good glass (lenses)" still applies - perhaps slightly less so in the digital era with the higher cost of SLR digital camera bodies (and the availability of better quality zoom lenses) – but none-the-less a useful adage to keep in mind.

You will need at least a 300mm lens for wildlife photography (and preferably a 400mm and upwards) – either as a prime lens (fixed focal length) or as a zoom (100-400mm as an example). Bird photography with anything less than a 500mm lens is very challenging (unless the bird is large and you are very close!). Get a mix of the fantastic new zoom lenses and whatever you think you can afford in (fixed focal-length) telephoto lenses (f2.8 to f4). A mid-range 70-200mm and a wide angle (22 – 28mm) should complete the kit.

Note that many digital cameras use a smaller sensor size (rather than a full frame sensor) that effectively multiplies the focal length of your lenses by a factor of 1.5 (Nikon) and 1.6 (Canon). This means that a 200mm becomes a 300mm and a 300mm becomes a 450mm and so on! Whilst it is certainly true that full-frame sensors (as opposed to the smaller sensors with the 1.5x factor) produce a better quality image at the same resolution, the digital SLR's with the smaller sensor are generally cheaper and require less expensive lenses (plus of course the benefit of the 1.5 multiplying factor).

- **Filters**: protect your lenses with a UV (ultraviolet light) filter and always use a lens hood to cut down on lens flare (these will often need to be purchased separately). Polarizing filters can also come in very handy - they help to increase colour contrast, saturation and cut down haze, remove the reflection from water and darken blue skies through the middle of the day. Most auto focus cameras require a circular polarizer (learn to use it before you leave home). Neutral density graduated filters are also useful for reducing the intensity in bright skies without losing detail in the foreground; by helping to even out the exposure values in scenes with contrasting bright and dark areas such as landscapes on bright early mornings and overcast days (to tone down the bright white sky). Speak to your local camera shop about the options. A warning – both polarizing and graduated filters require a level of preparedness, and time, that wildlife photography does not always offer - sightings are often fleeting!

- **Macro**: consider taking a macro lens (or extension tubes) to capture the smaller wildlife and plants in close-up. Macro photography is a whole new challenge though and will require even more equipment if it is to be done right - including a tripod, one or more TTL flash units, a collapsible reflector (to deflect light onto your subject)...together with patience and a fondness for experimentation. Whilst most wildlife photography is centred on big telephoto lenses (and larger subjects) there is a host of other 'smaller stuff' – flowers, insects, reptiles that are often just ignored. Any macro photography on safari is likely to be limited to the immediate locale of your safari camp and will need to be undertaken between game drives, and when not imposing on other guests. That said, don't let any of these challenges put you off the opportunity to satisfy your macro ambitions.

- **Tele-converters**: 1.4, 1.7 and 2x tele-converters are definitely worth considering as a less expensive way of boosting focal length (be aware that this does reduce the amount of light hitting your sensor and as such you will lose an f-stop or more and so are more suited to 'faster' lenses (f2.8 & f4). They may also result in slower focusing in low light and low contrast conditions.

- **Tripod/Monopod/Clamps**: take a tripod and/or bean-bag (and use these wherever possible). If you are not planning on doing any serious landscape, low-light or macro photography - or do not use large lenses (400 to 600mm), then a tripod is debatable – they are awkward to carry and add weight. If you are only planning to take wildlife images from vehicles, you will find that there is little opportunity to use a tripod at all and a beanbag will be more practical (although a monopod can come in handy from the back of an open 4x4 vehicle where the resting options can be limited).

Closed 4x4 vehicles (common in East Africa) have both a pop-top and side windows to rest your beanbag, but for those with larger telephoto lenses, a clamp in conjunction with a ball-head or gimbal bracket is more ideal. A cable release (or remote) for landscape work is also advisable.

- **Drones:** With the advent of this new technology, unmanned aerial vehicles (UAV's) equipped with a camera/video, there has been a rise in the number of people wishing to use such equipment on safari. It is important to note that, apart from the obvious disturbance to other guests and wildlife (in some cases considerable), this type of drone/quadcopter has now been prohibited in a growing number of national parks and game reserves across the continent, and in some countries it is illegal to fly UAVs without a licence. Without prior permission it is *not* advisable to operate a drone whilst on safari.

- **Flash**: in my opinion, a flash has limited use on safari (apart from macro/close-up and indoor use) and you may not find use for one at all - but when it is needed there is no substitute! Fill-in flash can be the difference between a nice shot and a great one! In this case, an external mounted flash (using an extension arm and cable) is the best option to avoid flat, front-on lighting. On safari your subject will often be out of 'reach' for a standard flash and here a Flash X-Tender (or Better Beamer), designed to work with a long telephoto lens and a TTL flash unit, will certainly help (but for best results take the flash off the horse-shoe if possible). This amazing accessory can give you an extra 3 stops in flash 'reach'. Great for late evening or backlit subjects (leopard in a tree) and night drives (although using the light from the spotlight is often sufficient).

- **Batteries & Storage**: take ample spare batteries and flash (storage) cards - these may be difficult (or impossible) to obtain in remoter parts of Africa. Digital cameras are voraciously power-hungry, and you will be surprised at how quickly those cards fill up! Buy quality flash cards and make it a practice to always format the card each time you transfer images to your storage device – it ensures a 'clean' card (without any bad sectors) and will prolong the life of the card.

Get the correct adaptors and check what plug configuration is standard for that country (two vs. three prongs, square vs. round etc) so you can get the correct adaptor(s). If you have multiple devices requiring charging (phone, iPod, tablet, camera, and video) it might be an idea to take along a double adaptor too. Refer to *Safari travel tips: Electric current* earlier in this book.

Look to download your flash cards onto a portable photo storage device or laptop/tablet. The latest digital storage devices (with or without a viewing screen) are inexpensive and are all you need to store your image files quickly and efficiently. They are also small and weigh a lot less than a laptop computer! Where possible, be sure to keep more than one copy of your digital image files (burn an extra copy to CD if you get the chance). Cloud storage whilst on safari is going to be a challenge due to poor speeds (even with WiFi becoming more common in camps and lodges).

- **Other Equipment**: a battery grip is a good option – it serves both to extend the battery life (as it takes 2 batteries) and also gives you useful controls for vertical shooting. Some will even give you the option to use AA batteries as an alternative to your re-chargeable batteries (in an emergency).

- **Cleaning kit:** dust can be a real problem with digital cameras on safari – especially when it gets onto the sensor. Be sure to take a good blower brush and cleaning materials and always be extremely careful when changing lenses – this is the time when dust gets into your camera through the front door! Always store your camera in your camera bag when not in use. Do not attempt to clean your sensor and be extremely careful not to touch the sensor (should you be tempted to use your blower).

- **Camera bag:** take a good camera bag (or better still – a camera backpack if you have multiple lenses, bodies etc). On safari your camera bag is where you will also keep your sun block, sunglasses, binoculars, bottle of water and book - be sure it is of adequate size and comfortable to carry. A central handle and a shoulder strap will make carrying a lot easier.

Other suggestions

- For those digital SLR users: taking along a pocket-sized point-and-shoot camera is also worth considering for the round-the-fire scenes, fun shots in the vehicle and other less formal picture opportunities.

- A small LED torch or head torch, a heavy duty blower – for cleaning the sensor, a compass (to check sunrise and sunset directions), a small microfibre cloth (to clean dusty equipment), and a rain-proof bag in case of a sudden shower.

- Invest in the best equipment you can afford. Generally speaking, you do get what you pay for. There is a good reason that the best prime lenses are super expensive – it is because they give the best results!

Please note:

Charter flights: be aware that you may need to comply with weight restrictions on safari, especially if you are making use of small charter planes between camps (as little as 15kgs (30lbs) for your entire luggage). Try to pack accordingly.

If you are planning to put your valuable camera equipment into the hold on the flight to Africa I would strongly advise 3 things: pack them carefully into a Pelican (hard) case, place 3 or 4 FRAGILE stickers on the outside, and secure the case with at least two external combination locks!

"If you're not using what you already have, you won't use what you think you need. Many people think you need a really good camera to take good photos

and – sure – it's nice to have a great camera. But the way to get great photos, is to use the camera you've got." - Ken Duncan, Professional Landscape Photographer (Australia)

Photographic tips

Before getting into the tips and traps of photographing on safari, I would like to preach some restraint; try not to get so caught up in the photography that you forget to enjoy the experience itself. It does happen, I know, I've been there! If all you wanted was to take home a portfolio of animal pictures you could just as easily have gone down to your nearest zoo (and saved yourself a lot of bother). Be sure to take in everything you see, hear, and smell and get the most out of every aspect of being on safari.

Taking good photographs on safari

- The first thing you need to be able to do is master your camera. This is especially true of today's digital cameras which now allow you access to a mind-boggling array of settings and options. Keep your instruction manual handy and practice getting to know your camera – both so that you understand it's potential and also so that you can efficiently make those setting changes on the move (and under pressure).

- Your camera's LCD screen is often difficult to see properly in daylight, and it is often difficult to check anything more than the composition on the LCD. Setting your LCD to display both the image and associated histogram(s) is an option worth considering. By checking the histograms regularly (as you shoot), and using exposure compensation (+/-) to correct where necessary, you will ensure that your photographs are correctly exposed from the start. Getting it right in-camera is always the aim, even if you're shooting RAW.

- By setting the 'display highlights' feature to be ON will make the over-exposed parts of your image 'blink' repeatedly in your LCD screen and act as a visual warning signal during shooting. Think about setting your exposure compensation to -1/3 to -1/2 so that you are consistently under-exposing your images to avoid any over-exposed areas in your images (you can always recover under-exposed (dark) areas but over-exposed areas are lost forever).

- The essence of good photography is learning to read the light. In Africa the best light for wildlife photography is early morning, up to around 10:30am, and late afternoon, after 3:00pm, when the light offers warmth and softness (with pre-dawn and post-dusk before/after the sun has risen/gone down giving sensational colour on longer exposures for landscape shots). Be aware that the midday sun leaves images flat and without contrast, lacking in detail (and colour). This can be deceptive when looking through your viewfinder – but the results are nearly always disappointing. Make use of polarizing and neutral density filters to reduce contrast or correct washed-out skies.

- Don't give up because the weather is somewhat inclement (overcast/raining) – days like these can offer their own rewards - gathering storm clouds for example, with overcast conditions providing less contrast and more consistent lighting (especially for close-ups).

- Always use a beanbag or tripod even if your lenses have image stabilizers - especially with longer focal lengths. You need to be as steady as possible to get crisp, clear images. Shooting from a safari vehicle can be a challenge (see more on this in the section below). You should note however, that many professional photographers recommend turning off the image stabilizer on your lenses when using a tripod (despite the manufacturer's recommendations to the contrary).

- For the enthusiast, the options provided with TTL metering, auto-bracketing, shutter and aperture priority all offer the opportunity to experiment – don't just leave your camera on AUTO!

- Consider setting your camera to 'P' for program. Many

photographers say that "'P' is for professional!" Program mode allows you to concentrate on composition, rather than fiddling with controls, but allows you to use program override (P*) when necessary to increase/decrease shutter speed or adjust the aperture as required using the command dials - all without even taking your eye from the viewfinder – the best of all worlds?

- While 'centre-weighted' metering will often give you the most accurate (or true) exposure readings of your subject for most wildlife photography, especially with close up portrait style shots, both spot and matrix metering have their place. What is important is that you use the metering system in your camera as a tool. Get to know the best situations in which to use each and how switching between them can affect your image.

- Set your shutter to continuous. With wildlife photography you never know when you will need to shoot off a continuous sequence to capture a fast-moving scene. Out of a burst of 4 or 5 shots it is likely that only one will capture the exact moment you were looking for.

- Take advantage of your camera's ability to store pre-set shutter/aperture combinations that you can select quickly when needed e.g. motion blur (slow shutter), portrait (shallow depth-of-field), flight (super-fast shutter speed) etc.

- Don't forget the basics – light, composition, subject matter. And remember, photography is about capturing the spirit of the moment. Some people just seem to have an 'eye' for what is interesting in a scene, or knowing what the best angle is, or lighting option. For the rest of us, it takes a level of conscious thought and dedication!

- Remember the rule of thirds. This is one rule that has stayed the test of time. By way of explanation: imagine a set of grid lines over the image (3 rows, 3 columns); always try to place your key subject on one of the points where the lines intersect. In landscapes, position your horizon on either the upper or lower horizontal line on the grid with your main subject on one of the vertical lines. A common mistake is placing the horizon across the middle of the frame. This leaves your image with 50% sky, and unless the sky is to be the main feature (cloud formations, sunsets) you have wasted half the image! The interesting stuff is in the foreground! A strong foreground interest will add a whole new dimension to your image.

- Talking of rules – there is another rule of thumb worth mentioning: that is the shutter speed rule which states that your shutter speed setting should be at least the reciprocal of the focal length of the lens. In other words, if you are using a 300mm telephoto, the shutter speed should be 1/300th of a second or faster if you want sharp images. If you are using a beanbag or a tripod this guideline does not strictly apply. Even with modern image stabilization, I still feel that this is a guideline worth following.

- And since we are talking about large telephoto lenses, be sure to be aware of the compression and depth of field characteristics of such long focal length lenses. There are two ways in which long lenses alter a subject or scene. First, they compress the elements that make up the composition. This means that they make the foreground seem like it is closer to the background than it really is. The longer the lens, the more compressed the image is. In this way the subjects in a scene can be made to look much closer together than in reality – a handy trick in wildlife photography. Second, telephoto lenses have such shallow depth of field that foreground and background elements in front of and behind the subject are often out of focus. This too can be used to dramatic effect and is sometimes your friend, but sometimes your foe. Be aware of both characteristics when planning your shot.

- Take every opportunity to recharge your batteries! This may sound simple and logical but will be more of a challenge than you imagine on safari. You will virtually always be on the move, on game drives, having meals or participating on various activity options. It is up to you to work out when is the best time to get your batteries charged. In some locations limited re-charging resources may be in high demand – work with the camp manager to get the desired result.

- Make full use of the range of ISO (light sensitivity) settings available on your camera. Do not only increase your ISO when the light is poor (low light conditions) – increasing your ISO in good/bright light is a way to achieve faster shutter speeds, for example: when shooting with longer telephoto lenses. With the latest digital sensors increasing the ISO in good light will not result in reduced image quality (as can be the case in low light at higher ISO settings).

- White Balance (WB) settings too can be notched up/down to good effect if you are shooting in JPEG (in RAW the WB can be adjusted in post processing). The same sunset will look quite different at different WB settings – have a 'play'.

- Exposure compensation is another invaluable tool for the DSLR user (usually located on a separate button near the shutter release button) - whilst you will generally rely on your camera's metering system, as discussed above, there are situations in which it will be necessary to override the exposure meter, either to increase or reduce the amount of light, in order to get the best results.

- RAW images are infinitely superior to JPEG – but only if you are technically in tune with the added requirements of storage and image processing. Learn about post-production in RAW – you will never look back!

- Be 'at the ready' at ALL times – you never know when the perfect shot will present itself. Quite often this will be when you least expect it – relaxing around the camp, when you have stopped for a picnic lunch, or at that African border post. Always be on the lookout for that interesting, or unusual, photograph that will capture your safari experience!

- Learn to be patient if you want to get that special shot – sit, watch and observe. When you get the urge to rush on to the next sighting – stop – and remember where you are – who cares about time? And when the game viewing is slow, focus more on the smaller things –

flowers, spore prints or colourful insects; and when the light is not quite right – wait – it is bound to change.

- Try different lighting scenarios - backlit subjects and animals in silhouette are just one example of how to make your images more dramatic or evocative. Of course, sunrise and sunset are a must as are longer-exposure pre-dawn and post-sunset scenes.

- Use roads, tracks or rivers to draw the viewer's eye into the picture's main subject – or use clouds, shadows or branches to frame your image or to give your images more punch and character. Subjects reflected in water can be very evocative.

- Look for patterns in the scene – waving grass, lines of flamingos - or colour combinations that catch the eye.

- If you have mastered the art of HDR (merging multiple exposures), stitching (panoramas), and time-lapse photography be sure to include these in your everyday safari photography - when you stop for a tea break, back at camp, or at sunset drinks!

- Include people too! It would be easy to come home with only wildlife portraits and stunning landscapes but no people – get your photo taken with that silverback (making sure he is at a safe distance!), or have a friend stand at the base of that enormous sand dune to give your photograph a sense of scale, or use a wide-angle lens to capture the scene including everyone in the game drive vehicle looking out - always fun.

- If shooting a wildlife portrait – it is the 'eye' that is crucial (or wet nose!).

- Where possible, try to take pictures of the same subject from different angles (and depth-of-fields) - and look out for those unusual angles that will give your image a certain WOW factor - from above for an overall perspective - out the roof hatch - or from down low to make your subject look more imposing.

- Also, don't forget to shoot verticals to change the composition layout (and to capture subjects like giraffe).

- For real impact – get in close! Use your telephoto lens to capture the coat pattern on a giraffe, the long eye-lashes of an elephant or the flicking tail of a lion – fill the viewfinder! With people, move in closer to your subject, change the angles and reduce empty space – add that WOW factor!

- Although close-up portraits give the subject impact it is often those shots that include the distinctive features of that region that are the most meaningful, and give your image context. A picture of a zebra is a picture of a zebra – but a picture of a zebra looking out over the desolate and dusty Etosha pan has real meaning.

- Be careful to 'fill the viewfinder'. A common mistake is to have the sky fill half the frame. This makes for very dull and uninteresting images! Not only does half your image have nothing of interest it makes the cameras job of reading the light that much harder as the sky will almost always be brighter than the subject – so you will either have a dull subject and a perfect sky or an overexposed sky (too bright) and a backlit subject. Rather, place the horizon at the top of the viewfinder and incorporate more of the foreground. This does add an element of difficulty to good photography – finding enough interesting material to fill the viewfinder!

- Try capturing movement in your images. By 'panning' or using slower shutter speeds (1/15 and 1/30 sec) you will get some interesting (blurred) images – be it a waterfall, animal walking/running or bird flying…try it out.

- When photographing people and how they live please be aware of the apprehension they may feel towards having their photograph taken by a stranger. This may even be taken as an act of disrespect. Permission should always be sought. Be warned that a simple apology (western style) will not suffice. Negotiating permission can also be a rather unpleasant experience and is best left to your guide.

- Getting to know your subject is always a benefit to photography – being able to predict an animal's behaviour will help you be ready for that perfect shot. Listen to your guide - he/she is likely to be able to predict what will happen next and be able to position the vehicle accordingly.

- Select only one main subject and compose the image to bring that subject out. There can be secondary subjects in the frame but they shouldn't detract from the chosen subject.

- Use the weather to your advantage – just because it is raining doesn't mean you should put your cameras away. A springbok huddled in the rain makes a stunning photo! Haze, dust, clouds all make for dramatic images. As the weather changes you will often find that the light gets more interesting and offers more opportunity to create something a little different.

- If the opportunity arises to take photographs from a plane or helicopter – a) don't miss out on the opportunity, and b) be sure to set your shutter speed to at least 1/500 (or higher) and increase your ISO if necessary. Also, if flying during the middle of the day or over water, a polarizing filter can often give more clarity to your images.

- One other thing – to every rule there's the exception. Breaking the rules sometimes creates the exceptional.

- If there is one negative aspect of the new digital age, it is that you will likely end up with so many images that the post-processing process will be daunting – develop an efficient system for handling your files, starting with a meaningful file naming structure and using folders to keep track of all those image files.

- But be sure to be selective about the images you share with others. You will be judged on the pictures you show not the ones you don't – so don't include any of the less than perfect images and try not to show too many (less is more!).

- Lastly, now that you have all these wonderful wildlife photos, be sure to share them with friends and family – sign up to one of the many photo gallery websites and/or print your own photo books, calendars and cards – it's so easy.

What makes a good image?

"I feel the most memorable images, the images we go back to again and again, the images we hang on our walls, the images that resonate deeply within us, are the images that move us emotionally...the key is how to make someone else who wasn't standing next to you when you took that image of the elephant in the middle of the Serengeti, feel the same way about it that you do. You have your emotions already tied up in that image because you were there when you took it. You remember the long flight, the sound of the elephant's legs swishing through the grass, the heat of the African sun, the smells. How do you create an image, so impactful, that it communicates the emotion of how you felt when you shot it, to someone who wasn't there?" Lorne Resnick, professional photographer.

Another well-known photographer, Frans Lanting from National Geographic, talks more about how your image needs to 'tell a story' and how it is less about the technical aspects and more about deciding what story you are wanting your image to portray and working to capture that moment. In his line of work, only a handful of images will be selected for a story, and each one needs to tell a story of its own.

Photography is an art, it is about capturing an emotion, about telling a story...but it is subjective and so what appeals to one person may not appeal to everyone. So get out there, be bold, be daring...but mostly, enjoy the experience.

More advanced topics

For those of you who are more technically inclined, and sufficiently perfectionist, here are a few select topics that you may want to pursue to improve your photography (many of these 'tricks' were not even possible before the advent of digital photography and add significantly to the creativity of the art):

- Lens focus sweet spot - when attempting to achieve a landscape image with maximum depth-of-field (sharp focus), from infinity to just a few metres from your camera, you need to aware that each of your lenses has its own focusing sweet-spot and this will not simply be infinity (∞) but more likely, just off infinity; and can be very simply established by shooting a suitable scene using manual focus (and with the image stabilizer off) and comparing the results.

- Ideal aperture for each lens – similarly, each of your lenses will have an f-stop that offers the best compromise between depth-of-field and sharpness. Surprisingly, this will often be at an f-stop of between 5.6 and 8 (and not 11 or 16 as you might expect). Do your own tests.

- Stitching – with advances in computer software the art of stitching a sequence of images together to produce one continuous image is no longer a particularly specialist task. But it should be noted that merely shooting a sequence of overlapping, hand-held images will not produce the technically exact results you are looking for unless a number of further steps are adopted. Firstly, for best results, use a tripod. Secondly, each lens has a defined 'nodal point' – the point at which the lens+camera combination should be attached to the tripod in order that each consecutive image is shot along the same horizontal plane (and thus avoiding curved horizons or mismatched sequences). Thirdly, you should be careful to set your camera to manual – both focus and exposure, so as to ensure consistency across the multiple images (and overlap your images by between 40 and 60 percent). Shooting in portrait (camera held vertically), rather than in landscape, will also ensure more foreground and allow more leeway for cropping the final 'stitched' image.

- High Dynamic Range (HDR) – is a digital photography technique whereby multiple f-stop exposures (-2, 0, +2) of the same scene are layered and merged using image editing software to create a more realistic, or dramatic, effect. The combined exposures enable a wider range of tonal values (dynamic range) than is capable of being recorded in a single image. Whilst our eyes, in conjunction with our brain, are capable of 'seeing' into shadows and at the same time toning-down areas of brightness, a digital camera does not have this capability without some help from post processing. This is a powerful technique that can be very rewarding and can now be found in some digital SLR's and smartphone apps.

- Multiple exposure - if you are looking to be more 'arty' you might try using the multiple exposure setting on your DSLR. This will allow you to take two or more exposures on a single frame (with a set 'fade') with the first 'press of the shutter release' being overlaid with successive 'shots' of lower intensity. Give it a go and let your creative side take over!

- Star Trails and Time-lapse photography - both of these 'techniques' require you to set up your camera to take a series of pre-defined exposures that can either be combined to create a dramatic 'star trail' or be used to generate a short video (moving clouds, sunrise, animals coming down to a water hole for example). These are both significant topics in their own right and I would suggest some pre-reading and practice *prior* to going on safari.

- Image processing – there are many tricks to be learn in terms of processing/manipulating your images to get the best results (or the desired effects). Most RAW images are flat (lack contrast) and soft (lack sharpness) and will require some tweaking – why not learn the tricks at a photo workshop and get the most out of your photographs? Important to understand are WB (colour and tint), contrast (levels/curves), saturation and sharpening. Be careful not to over saturate or over sharpen your images as this leads to an unnatural 'look' – there is a fine balance between 'just enough' and 'too much' and this takes a good eye (and practice) to get right.

Taking photographs from a safari vehicle

Here are a few pieces of advice specifically to address taking photographs from a safari vehicle.
- Be careful to get set and steady. You do not have the luxury of a tripod when in a safari vehicle. A bean bag, monopod or clamp (with ball-head and/or gimbal bracket) is essential. Vehicle

movement and awkward angles are a constant challenge. Be sure to request that the engine be turned off – the vibration of the engine will cause imperceptible camera shake and can ruin a great photograph.

- Be aware that when taking pictures from a safari vehicle you will most likely be at a height above the animal you are shooting – this is not ideal. Some of the best wildlife portraits are taken from a position at or below the eye level of the subject. The closer the animal to the vehicle the more pronounced the problem. A picture of the top of a lion's head is not a prize winner, but again, this is not immediately apparent when looking through the viewfinder. Ideally, you should be at least at eye-level with the animal you are photographing – and that can be tricky with a ground squirrel! There is not a lot you can do about this, unfortunately, as your driver/guide is going to be unwilling to allow you to exit the vehicle so that you can lie in the grass! But do be aware of the problem and try to minimise it where possible. With closed 4x4's (or mini-buses) with pop-tops, rather shoot out of the side window if your subject is close. If you are on foot, and it is safe to do so, get down on your stomach – you will love the results. In areas where you are allowed to go 'off-road' the temptation is to get as close as you can – this is not always good for photography – discuss this with your guide, if you have bigger lenses it would be better to back-off to achieve a more flattering angle.

- You may find, especially in open 4x4 vehicles, that there are not many places to 'rest' your long lens to get steady. This can be a challenge and you will need to be a little creative – use the frame, roll-bars, the seat in front of you, your own seat or arm rest (with yourself squatting in the foot well), your knee (with your foot resting on the edge of the vehicle) or perhaps consider a monopod which allows you to swivel with ease.

- Also, be aware that there will likely be other people in the vehicle – any movement they make will affect your shot, and vice versa. Work out a system between you so that you do not ruin each other's photo opportunities. Set up some basic ground rules/protocols/signals that let everyone know you are taking pictures and need the vehicle to be absolutely still.

- The vehicle will often stop with the subject to be photographed on the 'other' side! The guide will be conscious of providing the best angles to each of the people on the vehicle – not necessarily in turns but certainly in an equal manner. You may need to request that he/she move to a better position for yourself once the others have had the opportunity to take some pictures themselves. Try not to be selfish in this regard and work with the guide to maximize your results.

Isak Dinesen, in her book Shadows in the Grass, said about 'hunting with cameras' – *"It is a more refined sport than shooting, and provided you can make the lion join into the spirit of it you may, at the end of a pleasant, platonic affair, without bloodshed on either side, blow one another a kiss and part like civilized beings."*

A last word..

I trust that you have enjoyed your trip to Africa, whether it be your first or one of many, and that this travel companion has in some small way helped you to get the most out of your safari.

Tell your friends, tell your family, tell your colleagues. If one place in this world needs a good rap, its Africa.

I will leave you with this interesting insight:

"Although we seem to be retreating from the world in which we evolved to seek solace in artificial trivia, maybe more of us will discover the simple truth that the novelist, Jostein Gaarder, sums up so succinctly: 'people would have gone absolutely wild if the astronomers had discovered another living planet – they just don't let themselves be amazed by their own" Wild Africa, BBC series

Come again soon....until then.

AFRICAN BLESSING
May the African sun always shine on you;
May the rhythm of its drum beat deeply in your heart:
May the vision of its glory fill you with joy:
And may the memory of Africa be with you, always.

About the author

I was born and raised on a farm in Zimbabwe, but currently live in Australia where this book was written. Until 2004, while still living in Zimbabwe, I owned and operated a safari business in Mana Pools National Park, taking overseas visitors on canoeing trips down the Zambezi or hosting them at our mobile tented camp. I now work with my wife in our travel consultancy business, African Encounter, where we are both able to indulge our passion for Africa while providing a travel advisory service to the many people who want to travel to Africa each year. Whenever the opportunity arises I accompany tours to Africa to get my own Africa 'fix' and to keep in touch with a continent close to my heart.

You can contact me on patrickb@africanencounter.com.au

About the artist

William Sykes was born, and still lives, in Zimbabwe. From an early age he had a unique drawing ability, later attending Art College in Cape Town, South Africa where he studied Graphic Design and Photography. While working in advertising, he continued to practice fine art in his spare time and now pursues this as a full time career. William has received great acclaim for his fine pencil sketches although he also enjoys working in oils.

William can be contacted on williamsykes@zol.co.zw

Glossary

Adaptation: the adjustment or changes in behavior, physiology, and structure of an organism to improve its survival rate by becoming more suited to its environment.

Alpha (male or female): (first letter in Greek alphabet). Refers to the top-ranking member(s) of a group of animals that forms part of a complex social system based on a dominance hierarchy. For example: within Wild dog pack dynamics only the alpha female will have pups. In hyena clans, the alpha (or dominant) female passes on her status to her daughter and may also enforce her breeding rights.

Altruism: behaviour that benefits another while inflicting a cost on itself.

Aquatic: applies to animals that live predominantly in fresh water but can, and do, move readily on land (unlike most marine mammals).

Arboreal: refers to animals that live in trees.

Averted vision: refers to the practice of looking slightly to the side of a distant object (a star or constellation) in order to improve the eye's ability to detect detail - useful in star-gazing.

Bachelor herd: an all-male social group.

Banda: a basic shelter or hut constructed of local materials.

Biome: an ecological community type, such as savannah or desert.

Browser: a herbivore that feeds on plants *other than* grass, particularly foliage (leaves). To browse: meaning to feed on leaves.

Boma: an enclosure for keeping livestock at night.

Bovid: a species of cloven-hoofed mammals belonging to the family *Bovidae*

Boss: a term used to describe the massive base of horn that bridges across the forehead of the Cape buffalo.

Bushveld: a term used in southern Africa to describe thick woodland.

Canines: describes the carnivorous members of the Canidae family that include dogs, wolves, foxes, coyotes and dingoes.

Canopy: the uppermost layer of a tree.

Carnivore (and carnivorous): a meat eating mammal.

Carrion: the remains of dead animals.

Constellation: refers to a region of the night sky that contains a distinctive grouping of stars that have been named for some imaginary creature or object.

Crepuscular: active at dusk and dawn.

Crop: a thin-walled expanded portion of the alimentary tract used for the storage of food prior to digestion that is found in many animals, including gastropods, earthworms, leeches, insects, and birds.

Cud: refers to the partly digested grass and/or leaves that a ruminant regurgitates, chews and swallows again while ruminating.

Culture: behaviour transmitted from one animal to another by (usually imitative) learning (e.g. young animals learning from older ones).

Deciduous: a term used in reference to trees or shrubs that lose their leaves seasonally.

Dewclaw: a sharp, curved claw (actually a toe) found at the back of the front legs above the feet of many carnivores.

Dewlap: a fleshy fold of skin at the throat and lower neck of some large ungulates e.g. eland.

Dimorphism: literally means having two body types; sexual dimorphism is where males and females have physical differences.

Diurnal: refers to species that are primarily active during the day.

Donga: a gully or ravine/dry river bed, often thick with bush.

Ecology: the scientific study of the interaction of organisms with their environment (including other organisms within that environment).

Ecosystem: a community of organisms together with the physical environment in which they live.

Endangered: an animal that is threatened with extinction.

Endemic: exclusively native to that region ("native to").

Flatdog: (or flattie): slang for crocodile.

Fly camp: a minimalist camp, generally without tents but may feature mosquito nets hung under a tree.

Flehmen: the grimace associated with testing for chemical signals produced by sexually receptive females, which is used by some carnivores and nearly all ungulates to test for oestrus. By pulling back the lips and flaring the nostrils the vomeronasal organ (or Jacobsen's organ), located between the roof of the mouth and the nasal passages, is able to detect whether or not a female is receptive to mating.

Galaxy: the gigantic disc-shaped stellar system in which our Sun is situated, one of billions in the Universe.

Genus (plural genera): the next taxonomic level above species in the Latin binomial system, e.g. *Equus zebra* (Genus species) = Mountain zebra

Grazer: an animal that eats grass.

Gestation period: refers to the duration of pregnancy in animals.

Habitat: an animal or plant's surroundings that offers everything it needs to live.

Habituated: an animal that has been introduced to, and has accepted the presence of, human beings.

Harem: refers to a group of females guarded by a male who maintains mating rights over them by driving off other males.

Herbivore: an animal whose diet consists of plant food.

Hide: a camouflaged structure from which one can view wildlife without being seen.

Hierarchy: used to describe a linear or pyramid social structure in which an animal is dominated by those above it in the hierarchy and in turn is dominant over those below it.

Home range: the area occupied by an individual or group over a period of time but not marked or defended as a territory.

Induced ovulation: where repeated copulation's are necessary before the female releases an egg - the ovary does not release eggs spontaneously.

Infanticide: describes the killing of young (babies to juveniles) by adults of the same species.

Infrasound: sound with a frequency below the lower limit of human hearing (below 20 Hz).

Innate: inborn features that an animal shows at birth or develops later independently of environmental influences. Innate features are likely to be genetically programmed – although 'innate' and 'genetic' are not synonymous. No mammal behaviour is fully innate.

Instinct: instinctive behaviours are those that are driven from within the animal. Often used as a synonym for innate.

Insectivore (insectivorous): specialising in eating insects.

Juvenile: the stage between infancy and adolescence.

Keratin: the tough, fibrous substance of which horns, claws, hooves, scales and nails are composed.

Kopje: (kop = Afrikaans for head) a small hill, typically a rocky outcrop. Pronounced kop-ee.

Kraal: refers to a local village or enclosure for cattle.

Latrine: the site used for accumulation of excrement or droppings in carnivorous/insectivorous species.

Learned behaviour: the modification (or learning) of behaviour from experience.

Lek: a designated breeding ground or arena where males gather, staking out adjacent territories (within the breeding ground) into which females in estrous come to mate with the fittest and most centrally located males (a mating system employed by kob, lechwe and topi).

Leucism: the near absence of melanin (dark pigmentation) in the cells of hair and skin - a partial albinism. *See also melanism.*

Mammal: a warm-blooded animal that produces milk for its young.

Melanism: a condition where the skin and fur cells have more of the dark pigment melanin than usual making the animal appear almost black (or dark brown) and body markings/patterns are harder to detect.

Metatarsal gland: found only in impala within the black, furry blotches above the hind hooves. Thought to release a scent used by the rank as a 'follow me' signal.

Midden (dung): pile of droppings from regular use of the same location by grazers/browsers – acts as a territorial and scent-marking signal.

Migratory: a species or population that moves from one region to another, usually in response to seasonal changes (better food/grazing or water).

Milky Way: the visible portion of our Galaxy that forms an encircling band.

Montane: African mountain habitat, including forest, grassland, bamboo zone, moorland, etc.

Musth: an Urdu word meaning 'intoxicated' – musth is a term used to describe an elephant bull in a heightened sexual state as a result of an increased level of testosterone. A bull in musth is identifiable by a noticeable discharge from the temporal gland behind the eye, a continuous discharge from the penis and an extremely aggressive and irritable manner!

Natural selection: a process whereby animals that are less able to face the challenges presented by their environment produce less offspring than those better equipped.

Ngoma: a tribal feast with dancing.

Nocturnal: refers to species that are primarily active at night.

Nomadic: refers to species that have no defined home range or territory.

Oestrus: the behaviour associated with ovulation ('in heat') and the only time that females become sexually receptive (in most but not all mammals).

Omnivorous: a mixed diet including both animal and vegetable foods.

Pachyderm: a large, thick-skinned mammal.

Palearctic migrant: refers to birds which migrate to Africa from Europe and Asia (north of the Himalaya foothills) during the northern winter.

Pan (calcrete): refers to a location where the soils are permeated with calcium salts which facilitate the formation of a hard surface which in turn holds rain water.

Panga: an African machete.

Piloerection: erection of the hair on the neck and back to make an animal look bigger and more intimidating.

Planet: a body, in orbit around our Sun or other stars, that shines by reflected light.

Predator: any animal that subsists mainly by eating live animals.

Prehensile: (tongue, tail, fingers) adapted for seizing or grasping especially by wrapping around.

Preorbital: in front of the eye, where a gland occurs in many ungulates.

Prey: an animal hunted by a predator for food.

Pronking: a distinctive arched back, bounding gait performed by springbok as a form of display. *See also stotting.*

Refection: the habit of re-ingesting its own faeces to maximise the absorption of nutrients - common among rodents and hares.

Rete mirabile: describes the network of capillaries in the head that act as a heat-exchanger to effectively reduce the temperature of blood flowing to the brain, fooling the brain into thinking the body temperature is normal and thus reducing water loss through cooling - found in desert-adapted antelope.

Ruminant: an ungulate with a four-chambered stomach, which chews the cud as part of the ruminating process.

Rut: refers to the loud barks or roars from the dominant male in the mating period or breeding season – especially applies to the larger herbivores e.g. impala.

Rodent: refers to mammal species belonging to the Order *Rodentia*. Most rodents are small and characterized by having two incisors in the upper, as well as in the lower jaw which grow continuously and must be kept worn down by gnawing.

Savannah: vegetation characteristic of tropical regions which experience extended wet and dry seasons comprising grassland, deciduous and leguminous trees – an open grassy landscape with widely scattered trees.

Scavenger: an animal that lives off of carrion or the remains of animals killed by predators or from natural causes.

Scat: refers to animal faeces.

Scent gland: an area of skin packed with specialized cells that secrete complex chemical compounds which communicate information about the identity and the social and reproductive status of the animal.

Scent marking: the use of urine, faeces or glandular secretions to anoint an object with a chemical signal.

Shadow stripes: refers to the paler brownish-coloured stripes between the black stripes on zebra - mostly occurring south of the Zambezi River.

Shamba: a cultivated plot of ground or native farm.

Species: population(s) of closely related and similar organisms which are capable of interbreeding freely with one another.

Spoor: a track (footprint) or trail made by an animal.

Star: a large incandescent spherical body, like our Sun, powered by nuclear fusion.

Stotting: a straight-legged, bounding gait together with a rocking motion and lifting of the rear legs - used by some antelope when alarmed e.g impala.

Symbiosis: an association of two different organisms in a relationship that benefits one or both partners.

Subspecies: population(s) that have been isolated from other populations long enough to develop genetic differences sufficiently distinctive to be considered a separate grouping.

Symbiotic: a mutually dependent relationship between unrelated organisms.

Termitarium: a mound constructed by a termite colony.

Terrestrial: living on land or ground dwelling (as opposed to arboreal or aquatic).

Territorial: animals that defend a particular area against (same sex) rivals of their own species.

Tribe: a group of people united by traditional ties.

Ungulate: a mammal with hooves.

Veld: an Afrikaans term for savannah or grasslands.

Vertebrate: an animal with a spinal column and skeleton of bone, including amphibians, reptiles, birds and mammals.

Wallowing: utilizing muddy pools of water to keep cool.

Zodiac: the encircling band of constellations, against which the Sun and planets appear to move.